The Catholic
Lifetime Reading Plan

The Catholic
Lifetime Reading Plan

John A. Hardon, S.J.

DOUBLEDAY

New York • London • Toronto • Sydney • Auckland

Published by Doubleday, a division of Bantam Doubleday Dell Publishing Group, Inc.
666 Fifth Avenue, New York, New York 10103

Doubleday and the portrayal of an anchor with a dolphin are trademarks of Doubleday,
a division of Bantam Doubleday Dell Publishing Group, Inc.

Library of Congress Cataloging-in-Publication Data

Hardon, John A.
The Catholic lifetime reading plan/by John A. Hardon.—1st ed.
p.   cm.
Bibliography: p.
Includes index.
ISBN 0-385-23080-X
1. Catholic Church—Bio-bibliography. 2. Catholic authors—
Biography. 3. Bibliography—Best books—Catholic Church.
I. Title.
Z7837.H37   1989
[BX891]
016.282—dc19   88-17037

PUBLISHERS' ACKNOWLEDGMENTS

My sincere gratitude to the following publishers for the use of quotations from authors
cited in *The Catholic Lifetime Reading Plan:*

The Catholic University of America Press: St. Justin Martyr, *The First Apology;* Lactantius,
The Divine Institutes; St. Vincent of Lérins, *Commonitorium.*
University of California Press: Eusebius, *In Praise of Constantine.*
Franciscan Herald Press: St. Francis of Assisi, *Rule of St. Francis.*
Burns and Oates: St. Catherine of Siena, *The Dialogue;* Prosper Guéranger, *The Liturgical
Year;* William Bernard Ullathorne, *The Groundwork of the Christian Virtues;* Alice Meynell,
Essays; G. K. Chesterton, *The Catholic Church and Conversion;* Fernand Cabrol, *Liturgical
Prayer: Its History and Spirit;* Ferdinand Prat, *Theology of St. Paul;* Marie Joseph Lagrange, *The
Gospel of Jesus Christ;* Bl. Edith Stein, *The Science of the Cross;* Pierre Pourrat, *Christian Spiritual-
ity;* Francis Trochu, *The Curé d'Ars.*
Clarendon Press, Oxford: Coventry Patmore, "The Toys," from *The Oxford Book of English
Verse;* Ronald A. Knox, *Enthusiasm.*
Sheed and Ward: Ottokár Prohászka, *Meditations on the Gospels;* Edward Leen, *In the Likeness
of Christ;* William Thomas Walsh, *Isabella of Spain;* Paul Claudel, *The Satin Slipper;* John
Peter Arendzen, *What Becomes of the Dead?,* Gerald Vann, *The Divine Pity;* Romano
Guardini, *The End of the Modern World;* Arnold Lunn, *Now I See;* Charles Journet, *The Church
of the Word Incarnate;* Frank Sheed, *Theology and Sanity;* Hubert van Zeller, *We Die Standing
Up;* John C. H. Wu, *The Interior Carmel: The Threefold Way of Love.*
Muller: Henri Ghéon, *Christmas in the Market Place.*
Longman: Owen Francis Dudley, *The Tremaynes and the Masterful Monk;* Katherine Burton,
The Great Mantle; François Mauriac, *Life of Jesus;* Dietrich von Hildebrand, *Transformation in
Christ.*
Routledge & Kegan Paul: Augustin Poulain, *The Graces of Interior Prayer.*
Macmillan Publishing Company: Jacques Maritain, excerpted from *The Degrees of Knowl-
edge.* Copyright © 1959 Jacques Maritain; copyright renewed. Reprinted with permis-
sion of Charles Scribner's Sons, an imprint of Macmillan Publishing Company.

Acknowledgments

The author owes special thanks to many people, without whom *The Catholic Lifetime Reading Plan* could not have been written:

To Robert Heller, Theresa D'Orsogna, and Patricia Humienik of Doubleday for their encouragement, editorial cooperation, and patience.

To Rev. Christopher M. Buckner for his research in getting this volume first under way.

To Robert Hickson for his indefatigable research in assembling the Bibliography. Without him this Bibliography would simply not have been composed.

To Gary Maloney for his untiring work in typing, as well as his help in editing, the text.

To Mrs. David Prokop for her selfless help in assembling the data and typing the Bibliography.

To the Handmaids of the Precious Blood for their research, typing, and coordination of the sources and authors.

To Geraldine Donovan for her research and counsel on the composition of the manuscript.

To Mrs. Carol Egan for her expert typing of the manuscript.

To Robert More for his many hours of research in the libraries of Washington, D.C.

To Rev. Eugene M. Rooney, S.J., and his associates at the Woodstock Library at Georgetown University for their indispensable cooperation in the use of the library resources and their assistance in the research.

To Clifton Fadiman, whose *Lifetime Reading Plan* provided the impetus to this volume and whose insights gave invaluable direction on how it should be written.

To many others who, by their encouragement, counsel, and active assistance, made this Reading Plan possible.

The best way I can express my gratitude is with my prayers, asking Our Lord to bless them with an abundance of His graces.

Contents

The Catholic
Lifetime Reading Plan

Conversation with the Reader

The purpose of this book is to open up the treasury of wisdom found in the great Catholic writers over the centuries. In one sense, therefore, it is an honest effort to offer a Great Catholic Books program to the public. Certainly the books chosen for this Catholic Lifetime Reading Plan are among the outstanding in the twenty centuries of the Roman Catholic Church's history.

But there was a deeper reason for preparing the present volume. Anyone familiar with the Catholic Church in the closing years of the twentieth century knows that there is a crisis of identity in millions of once totally dedicated minds. The term "Catholic" has been used by so many people with so many different meanings that even among the elect there is confusion. Yet, by her own claims, the Roman Catholic Church has remained substantially the same, since the first Pentecost Sunday to the present day. This is easier said than proved. So that a second and more-profound reason for assembling this Reading Plan was to provide factual evidence that Catholic continuity is reality and not rhetoric.

The closing words of Christ in Matthew's Gospel are a prophecy and a promise. "Know that I am with you always," He said to all future generations. "Yes, to the end of time." (Matthew 28:20) How do we know?

We can know this by tracing the sequence of official Church

teaching from apostolic times to our day. Practically speaking, this would mean going back to the earliest papal declarations outside the New Testament and then moving up to the latest pronouncement of the Bishop of Rome. It happens that we have a full-length letter of Pope Clement I to the Corinthians written somewhere between the years 88 and 97. Through no less than sixty-five chapters the Pontiff exercises his authority to heal the discord that had arisen in Corinth. A few agitators had driven the people to revolt against their ecclesiastical superiors. Driven by envy, says Clement, the conduct of these dissenters is disgraceful. Let them do penance and their sins will be pardoned. The whole epistle is an implied exercise of supreme papal authority. It threatens, "If there should be some who will not listen to the words that God has spoken to them through us, they may be assured that they are in grave sin and in great danger. We are innocent of this sin." The Pope concludes, "You will be a source of great joy and happiness for us if you are obedient to what we have written to you in the Holy Spirit."

Documents of this nature can be quoted at length in one generation after another, all revealing the existence of apostolic authority in bishops under the Bishop of Rome and all teaching essentially the same doctrine that was first entrusted by Christ to the twelve Apostles.

There are single- and multivolume collections of the most important of such documents in English. They are useful reference works, but until recently were available only in Latin. And they are useful, even indispensable tools for anyone doing research in Catholic doctrine on matters of faith, morals, and divine worship. But, by and large, they are not within the scope of the Catholic Reading Plan.

Scope of the Present Volume

The range of this book is the whole of Catholic literary history, with stress on the term "literary." Understood in its broadest meaning, literature is such writings as have excellence of form or expression, and express ideas of permanent and universal interest. The writings may be in prose or verse, but the key factors are their beauty of expression and enduring content, appealing to every culture.

This is not a mere anthology or collection of literary masterpieces. It is a consciously planned program of self-education through systematic reading of some of the leading Catholic writers since the close of apostolic times.

A fair example of what I had in mind is St. Jerome's *On Illustrious Men*, written at the end of the fourth century. This book is rightly credited with having founded the history of Christian literature. It has come in for more than its share of criticism for omissions, poor organization, mistakes, and partiality. Yet, after more than fifteen hundred years, it is still a valuable source of information about the hundred and thirty-five writers whom it treats, from St. Peter to the author himself!

Unlike Jerome's work, this volume is limited to one hundred and four writers, including both men and women. Also unlike Jerome's foundational book, which covered less than four centuries, the Reading Plan covers nineteen centuries.

What criteria did I apply in choosing one hundred and four writers out of thousands who have written beautifully and profoundly as witnesses of their Catholic heritage?

Let me begin by saying that many, and I hope most, of the writers chosen have already established a reputation as classics in their field. To assure myself of this fact, I consulted every available study of the masters of Catholic literature. In one collection after another, certain names kept recurring. Thus, there could be no reasonable doubt about including men like St. Augustine and Dante or women like Sts. Catherine of Siena and Teresa of Ávila.

With others it was not so simple. A second criterion was what might be called a writer's "relevance" for our age. There are issues being raised today, and ideas being challenged in and outside the Catholic Church, that have long since been raised or explored by some of the greatest minds of history. To read what these minds have to say about God, and man, and happiness, and the purpose of our life on earth is enlightening. For one thing, it will help us to endure the upheavals to which modern society is subject, and not be shaken by the winds that threaten us today. The Church has not only weathered similar storms in the past but has become stronger than would have been humanly possible if she had not been periodically tested by experience.

A third criterion for choosing an author for the Reading Plan was the availability of his or her writings. This presented a real problem because the publishing trade keeps books in print only for a limited time. Whenever possible, authors were chosen whose writings are actually in print and therefore on sale when this Reading Plan was published. But there is no infallible way of predicting this. This is one difference between this and other "great books" programs or reading plans. Every effort was made to ensure that the writers and their works here recommended are currently in print. But Catholic books, like any others, are at the mercy of a nation's economy. The best way to make sure that booksellers will print the works of a certain author is for potential readers to provide a ready market. It is hoped that this Reading Plan will help to stimulate the market.

The Sources

After much reflection, I decided to open the Reading Plan with what I call "sources." They are the Bible, the Roman Catechism, the documents of the Second Vatican Council, and L'Osservatore Romano. Why begin with these? Two reasons seemed conclusive. These enunciate the premises on which should be based—and in that sense are the sources for—all authentically Catholic writing. And they define the boundaries, and thus the resources, of sound Catholic literature. Both reasons imply not only that Catholic Christianity considers truth to already exist and be provable but that the Catholic Church honestly thinks she is in possession of the truth, indeed that her Founder, who called Himself the Truth, entrusted to her keeping the preservation and communication of the truth until the end of time.

When St. Justin the Martyr in the second century boldly said, "All truth wherever it is found belongs to us as Christians," he was not making a wild boast. He was voicing the common conviction of every believing and knowledgeable Catholic ever since. That is why it seemed only honest to open this Catholic Lifetime Reading Plan with the four sources just identified.

Why these four?

The Bible is the written repository of God's own revelation to the human family. Unlike Sacred Tradition, which the Catholic Church considers coequal with Sacred Scripture, the latter *is* scripture—that is, something written—and therefore to be read. The Bible, therefore, is normative for all other, merely human writings. And if there is any book that every Catholic should include in a lifetime of reading, it had better be the Bible.

The Roman Catechism, published in the sixteenth century, is a synthesis of what the Catholic Church believes. Its importance derives from the historic fact that it was published to meet the most serious challenge that Catholicism has had to face in all her centuries of existence. The challenge was faced by the Council of Trent, which spelled out in lapidarian definitions what those who call themselves Catholics must believe. But the teachings of Trent are very formal and expressed in technical terms. That is why the Roman Catechism was written: to synthesize all of Catholic belief and practice in language that everyone can understand.

What makes the Roman Catechism so useful for English-speaking readers is that the English language has been the principal vehicle for shaping the culture of the Anglo-Saxon world since the sixteenth century. Call it contrast or comparison, but the ideas formulated in the Roman Catechism are quite different from those of modern Anglo-Saxon society. The least that Catholics need to know is the fundamental principles of their own unchangeable heritage.

The Second Vatican Council documents have yet to become known, even to most Catholics. Some mistakenly saw the council as the end of what they call the "preconciliar age." With everything in the material sciences undergoing such rapid and drastic change, some people assumed that the Catholic Church must undergo a corresponding radical change. The very substance of the faith, the moral order, and the essence of Catholic worship, it was said, will go through the same process of evolution as the world of space and time was assumed to be going through.

What the twenty-first council of the Church brought home, however, was that Catholicism is not a merely human institution. It partakes of the immutability of the God who became Man and who founded a Church that He promised to guide and preserve in her integrity, even to the consummation of the world.

L'Osservatore Romano was a logical choice to include among the sources for this Catholic Reading Plan. Available in English since the sessions of the Second Vatican Council, it gives English-speaking people an ongoing contact with the teachings and doings of the Vicar of Christ. It further gives them the assurance that other Catholics in other parts of the world are reading the same ideas and about the same events at the same time.

Living as we are in the new age of communications, Catholics need today more than ever the sense of solidarity with their coreligionists throughout the world. A publication like the Vatican newspaper, *L'Osservatore Romano,* provides the ground for this solidarity and helps sustain the faithful, even as Peter told the Christians of his day to be "strong in faith and in the knowledge that your brothers all over the world are suffering the same things" (I Peter 5:9).

The Variety of Catholic Literature

What kind of writings are included in this Reading Plan? Every possible kind, dealing with every possible subject matter, whether prose or poetry, whether narrative or essay, whether theology or philosophy, history or biography, whether homily or treatise, meditation or personal letter.

As intimated above, the Popes are not included among the one hundred and five authors of the Reading Plan. They are in a class by themselves and correspond to what we have come to call the Church's magisterium, or teaching authority. Their role in shaping the mind and heart of Catholicism is unique and, as the faithful believe, indispensable.

Yet, not a few writings of bishops in communion with Rome

have been included. Why? Because they reflect Catholic truth as lived out in practice, not because they were official teachers of that truth. Thus, Augustine, Bede, and Cyprian spoke and wrote what we now consider literary classics. And they need to be read by anyone who wants to be nourished on their wisdom. They are therefore a necessary part of the Catholic Reading Plan.

A more serious question is why the Bible should not have been given more attention. Why give so much space to reflections on the Bible and explanations of the Bible, but limit ourselves to a few pages on reading the Sacred Scriptures and some recommendations on the Bible as instructive inspiration?

The reason is basically the same as that for the omission of formal ecclesiastical documents. Sacred Scripture is God's own revelation of Himself and His will to the human family. The very word "bible" means "book." Indeed, *the* Bible is *the* Book, the one divinely inspired and therefore divinely intended to be read until the end of time. There is a correct sense in which all Christian literature is about the Bible, Old and New Testament, and Catholic literature is no exception.

Some readers may be surprised, or even distressed, by what looks like inconsistency in the choice of authors. I make no apology for this, except to say it was quite deliberate. Someone might reasonably ask what St. Thomas Aquinas is doing in the same company with Anne Catherine Emmerich, or Butler's *Lives of the Saints* with Jacobus de Voragine's *Golden Legend,* or St. Athanasius' *Life of Anthony* with the *Little Flowers* of St. Francis of Assisi.

In my judgment, there was no choice if we are to be true to the genius of Catholicism. The Church is nothing if not a paradox—that is, an apparent contradiction that, in reality, is the whole truth. So, too, the Church's literature reflects many facets of human experience, ranging from sublime mysticism to simple religious thought, and from the heights of theological insight to the commonplace feeling of ordinary people in their relationship with God.

This is more than saying that any useful reading program should have something for everybody. It is more like saying that the Church founded by Christ is for everybody, the learned and the unlearned, the thinker and the dreamer, the young and the old in years and experience—and everyone in between. Providentially, the Church's literature reflects this breathtaking universality.

The Value of Sound Catholic Reading

We get some idea of the value of reading Catholic literature once we realize how much reading is done by people, even in our media-saturated age. There are thousands of newspapers throughout the world, some with a daily circulation of over a million readers. There are thousands of magazines, not a few with a monthly circulation of many millions. Tens of thousands of new books are published every year; some by now have achieved sales figures that are astronomical.

Everything we read stimulates our mind to think, and what we think determines what we desire, and desires are the seedbed of our actions. Given this iron law of human nature—from reading to thinking, to desiring, to acting—we are shaping our destiny by the ideas we choose to have enter our minds through print.

A thousand lifetimes would be too short to read everything readable. Nor is everything in print worth reading. Common sense, not to say enlightened prudence, tells us we must be selective. The secret is to know what to read.

Until not many years ago a book like *The Catholic Lifetime Reading Plan* would have been useful but hardly necessary. All this has changed dramatically in the last half of the present century. There is such an avalanche of printed matter demanding reader attention that someone somewhere should offer to provide guidance. Among the areas in which guidance is needed, the most important is the library of Catholic literature.

Behind that last sentence is an act of faith. I believe the Catholic Church was founded by Christ to be the Mother and Teacher of mankind. Her Founder entrusted to her the fullness of His revelation. It is literally true that His words to the Apostles, "He that hears you, hears me," apply to the Church He established. What she teaches and the norms she provides are not only for professed Catholics: they are for the human race.

Given these premises, the present volume is not so much a handy manual for direction in Catholic reading as the synthesis of a lifetime reading experience that I share with others. From the thousands of professedly Catholic books read over the years, I have carefully chosen the works of one hundred and four authors, works I consider "basic" to a balanced understanding of the Catholic faith as lived out for two millennia of Christian history. The insights expressed by these writers are just the nourishment for the mind that the world desperately needs as it enters the twenty-first century.

SOURCES

The Bible

No apologies are necessary to open The Lifetime Catholic Reading Plan with the Sacred Scriptures. The word "bible" derives from the Greek *biblion,* which means "book." It is the book on which Christianity crucially depends and from which believing Christians derive so much of their knowledge of God and Jesus Christ, and of the Church, which He founded as the universal sacrament of salvation.

But if the Bible is *the* book of the Christian religion, it is meant to be read. The Second Vatican Council could not have used stronger words when it declared that it forcefully and specifically "exhorts all the Christian faithful . . . to learn 'the surpassing knowledge of Jesus Christ' (Philippians 3:8) by frequent reading of the divine Scriptures." The faithful are told, in the words of St. Jerome, that "ignorance of the Scriptures is ignorance of Christ." They are, moreover, to enjoy reading the Holy Bible. But all the while, "let them remember that prayer should accompany the reading of Sacred Scriptures, so that a dialogue takes place between God and man. For 'we speak to Him when we pray, we listen to Him when we read the divine oracles.' "

Since the Second Vatican Council, there has been nothing less than a biblical renaissance in the Catholic Church. Translations of the Bible, commentaries on the Bible, and courses, institutes, and seminars on the Bible have multiplied in a way that was simply unknown in all the past history of Roman Catholicism.

Not a few of the authors treated in the Reading Plan are scholars or commentators on Sacred Scripture. And they are only a few of many that could be recommended. My purpose here is more refined. It is to see two things that I consider crucial for a balanced Catholic approach to the profitable reading of the Bible. We should know that the Old and New Testaments are not two Bibles, one archaic and the other current, but one revelation. We should also know that the Bible is not only, though certainly, a source of instruction. It is also a necessary fount of our religious inspiration.

One Revelation

As Christians, we naturally come to separate the Bible into two parts, one which we call new and the other we call old. This is legitimate in the sense that there was a period before which Christ was physically conceived and born, and there is, of course, the period since, corresponding to B.C. (before Christ) and A.D. (anno Domini, the year of the Lord), respectively. I don't know why we shifted languages!

But the better we understand the Bible, the clearer it becomes that the Scriptures are one single continuum. They are one revelation from the same Holy Spirit Who is, because He is God, timeless. He has insights into God's Being, His providence, and His expectations of man that cannot and should not be dated. We do not date God. When He speaks, He speaks as the Eternal One.

Thus, the calling of Abraham, the Exodus, the Decalogue, the Psalms, and the prophecies of Isaiah and Jeremiah are no less meaningful today than they were when the events took place or when the words were spoken or written. In fact, they should be more meaningful and pertinent now, provided we change our perspective. Although they were written then, they were meant for all times. Since the Exodus, the Decalogue, the Psalms, and the great prophets, there has been an unfolding in salvation history. As a consequence, we can now better understand what the psalmist meant or the prophets foretold than when they wrote or prophesied. After all, this is not merely the word of man, it is the Word of God.

The correct Catholic understanding of the Old and New Testaments is that they complement each other. If we more frequently think of the New as complementing the Old, it is equally true the other way around. For example, Matthew simply assumed that what we call the Old Testament was perfectly understood. Again, the two Testaments interpret one another, and together they form one great revelation of God to man, spelling out in written form what God wants the human race to know, respect, and respond to, until the end of time.

Instructive Inspiration

Besides being a unitary revelation, the Bible is intended to both instruct and inspire us. Instruction is mainly directed to the mind, whereas inspiration is principally directed to the will. Instruction seeks to enlighten; inspiration seeks to motivate. Instruction is concerned to inform; inspiration is concerned to form! Why do I bring this out? Precisely to point out that no matter what we use—here, the inspired Word of God—it is true that we find what we are looking for. And if our incentive in using the Scriptures is to find instruction for the mind, we shall. There is much to enlighten us. But if, beyond that, we look to be moved and inflamed, we will find that too.

How are the Scriptures a source of instructive inspiration? Mainly in three ways. In the Scriptures we learn why God put us into this world: He put us into this world that we might possess Him in the world to come. That is the end, or the purpose, of all biblical motivation. God made us for Himself.

In the Scriptures we learn what we are to do to reach this goal of our destiny. We must observe the Covenant. If there is one "biblical word" it is "covenant." What is the Covenant? It is a contract that God makes with His chosen ones: "I have made you for Myself and you will reach me, provided in this world you know, love, and serve me."

Finally, in the Scriptures we also learn, and therefore are motivated, how to use the world in which we live. We have received one great gift from God, our liberty. We can choose from among the creatures who envelop us like an atmosphere those who will lead us to our destiny. And we can sacrifice, or not use, other creatures who would not lead us to heaven, no matter how pleasant they may be. This is the biblical "how" from Genesis to the Apocalypse.

Given these premises, the Bible is not just another, even great, book to be read. It is the one written source on which all other books worth reading depend and the one written goal toward which all other writing should tend.

The Roman Catechism

There is a one-volume synthesis of Catholic faith and practice that deserves to be better known. Sometimes called the Catechism of the Council of Trent, it is better known as The Roman Catechism.

This is no ordinary catechism. Years in the making after being decreed by the Council of Trent, the Roman Catechism is an authoritative synthesis of what Catholics should believe, how they are to live, and how they are to worship God through the sacraments and prayer.

The Roman Catechism has for more than four centuries been the single most authoritative one-volume, carefully organized, easily readable, and clearly expressed synthesis of Roman Catholicism.

Immediately intended for "pastors and all who have the duty of catechetical teaching," it is an indispensable source of information for anyone who wants to know what the Catholic Church believes and how she expects her members to practice their religion.

Although The Roman Catechism was published only three years after the Council of Trent, as early as 1546, when the council first convened, the assembled bishops were told about the people's dismal ignorance of even the rudiments of their faith. "There are few authentic teachers," the report declared.

"As a result the children are growing up without instruction and without formation, either by their parents or their teachers, in the Christian way of life, which they began to have and to know when they were baptized."

It was to meet this grave need for sound instruction in the basics of the true faith that The Roman Catechism was finally issued. Pope St. Pius V promulgated the new book to all the hierarchy with instructions to have it translated and made available to all who are responsible for religious instruction in the Catholic Church.

One Pope after another repeated the completeness and authenticity of the Roman Catechism as a repository of the Church's doctrine. Pope Clement XIII said it contains "that teaching which is the common doctrine of the Church, from which all danger of doctrinal error is absent." Pope Leo XIII spoke of "that golden book, the Roman Catechism," which is a "precious summary of all theology, both dogmatic and moral." Pope John XXIII said it was "the *Summa* of pastoral theology." Pope John Paul II explained that "the Council of Trent . . . lies at the origin of the Roman Catechism, which . . . is a work of the first rank as a summary of Christian theology [and] gave rise to a remarkable organization of catechesis in the Church."

The four parts into which the Roman Catechism is divided correspond to the divisions followed by the Church since early Christian times:

1. The essentials of Catholic belief are treated in explaining the twelve articles of the Apostles' Creed.

2. The seven sacraments are explained at length as the means instituted by Christ for living up to the hard demands of the faith.

3. The Ten Commandments are put into their New Testament setting to show that Christ did not destroy the Old Law but brought it to perfection.

4. After a detailed analysis of the nature, necessity, and practice of prayer in general, the seven petitions of the Lord's Prayer are given a full-scale treatment. There is a short concluding

chapter on the meaning of the word "Amen," which closes the Pater Noster.

There have been several excellent English translations of The Roman Catechism, notably the one published at Maynooth in Ireland in 1829 and in New York in 1923 and 1958. The most recent and definitive translation, done by Rev. Robert I. Bradley, S.J., and Monsignor Eugene Kevane, and published by the St. Paul Editions, is thoroughly updated, with Second Vatican Council and postconciliar documents and the New Code of Canon Law.

The Second Vatican Council

The twenty-first ecumenical council of the Catholic Church was first announced by Pope John XXIII on January 25, 1959. He opened the council on October 11, 1962, and closed the first session on December 8 of the same year. After Pope John's death in 1963, his successor, Pope Paul VI, reconvened the council, which had three more sessions in the fall of each succeeding year. The closing session ended on December 8, 1965. A combined total of 2,865 bishops and prelates attended the council, which issued sixteen formal documents as follows:

1. Constitution on the Sacred Liturgy *(Sacrosanctum Concilium)* sought to adapt more closely to the needs of our age those institutions which are subject to change, to foster Christian reunion, and to strengthen the Church's evangelization.

2. Decree on the Media *(Inter Mirifica)* defined the modern means of communication as those which can reach not only single individuals but even the whole of human society. It declared that the content of the media must be true, and—within the limits of justice and charity—complete.

3. Dogmatic Constitution on the Church *(Lumen Gentium)* explained the Church's nature as a sign and instrument of communion with God and of unity among men. It also clarified the Church's mission as the universal sacrament of salvation.

4. Decree on the Catholic Eastern Churches *(Orientalium Eccle-*

siarum) encouraged Eastern Catholics to remain faithful to their ancient traditions, reassured them that their distinctive privileges would be respected, and urged closer ties with the separated Eastern churches, with a view to fostering Christian unity.

5. Decree on Ecumenism *(Unitatis Redintegratio)* made a careful distinction between spiritual ecumenism, mainly prayer and the practice of virtue, and practical ecumenism, which actively fosters Christian reunion.

6. Decree on the Pastoral Office of Bishops *(Christus Dominus)* urged bishops to cooperate with one another and with the Bishop of Rome and to decide on effective means for using the modern means of communication.

7. Decree on the Renewal of Religious Life *(Perfectae Caritatis)* set down norms for spiritual renewal and prudent adaptation, legislating community life under superiors, corporate prayer, poverty of sharing, distinctive religious habit, and continued spiritual and doctrinal education.

8. Decree on the Training of Priests *(Optatam Totius)* centered on fostering vocations, giving more attention to spiritual formation, preparing for pastoral work and developing priests with a filial attachment to the Vicar of Christ, and loyal cooperation with their bishops and fellow priests.

9. Declaration on Christian Education *(Gravissimum Educationis)* told all Christians that they have a right to a Christian education, reminded parents they have the primary right and duty to teach their children, and warned believers of the dangers of state monopoly in education.

10. Declaration on the Relation of the Church to Non-Christian Religions *(Nostra Aetate)* urged Catholics to enter, with prudence and charity, into discussion and collaboration with members of other religions.

11. Dogmatic Constitution on Divine Revelation *(Dei Verbum)* distinguished Sacred Scripture from Sacred Tradition, declared that the Bible must be interpreted under the Church's guidance, and explained how development of doctrine is the Church's ever-deeper understanding of what God has once and for all revealed to the human race.

12. Decree on the Apostolate of the Laity *(Apostolicam Actuosi-*

tatem) is a practical expression of the Church's mission, to which the laity are specially called in virtue of their Baptism and incorporation into Christ. It recognizes that the laity have the right to establish and direct their own associations, on the condition that they preserve the necessary link with ecclesiastical authority.

13. Declaration on Religious Liberty *(Dignitatis Humanae)* affirms each person's liberty to believe in God and worship Him according to one's conscience and reaffirms the Catholic Church's revealed freedom for herself and before every public authority.

14. Decree on the Church's Missionary Activity *(Ad Gentes Divinitus)* defines evangelization as the implanting of the Church among peoples in which she has not yet taken root. It urges even the young churches to engage in evangelization as soon as possible and stresses the importance of adequate training of missionaries and their sanctity of life.

15. Decree on the Ministry and Life of Priests *(Presbyterorum Ordinis)* defines priests as men who are ordained to offer the Eucharistic Sacrifice, forgive sins in Christ's name, and exercise the priestly office on behalf of others in the name of Christ. Priestly celibacy is reaffirmed, and priestly sanctity declared to be essential.

16. Pastoral Constitution on the Church in the Modern World *(Gaudium et Spes)* identifies atheism as one of the most serious problems of our times, gives the most extensive treatment of marriage and the family in conciliar history, and declares the Church's strong position on war and peace in the nuclear age.

The best English translation of the documents of the Second Vatican Council is the one edited by Austin Flannery, O.P. In his introductory preface, Cardinal John Wright stated, "It is *the* collection of Council documents and their authentic interpretation that is indispensable for the serious student."

L'Osservatore Romano

L'Osservatore Romano deserves to be included among the sources in the Lifetime Reading Plan. It is the daily newspaper owned by the Holy See and published in Vatican City.

In 1861, during the last decade of the papal states, Marcantonio Pacelli, the substitute minister of the interior under Pius IX, headed a group of three men who started *L'Osservatore* as a private enterprise; the other two partners were the lawyer Nicola Zanchini and the journalist Giuseppe Bastia. Marcantonio was the great-grandfather of the future Pope Pius XII.

In 1890, Pope Leo XIII bought the publication and, without changing the name, made it the "Pope's own newspaper." In the years since, *L'Osservatore* has done more than keep the world informed about the affairs of the Holy See. It has published papal encyclicals and addresses and featured articles reflecting the mind of the Bishop of Rome. Even while being published under the scrutiny of the Italian government, it consistently stressed its character as the editorial voice of the Vatican. During the pontificate of Pope Pius XI (1922–39), it featured the Holy Father's mind on what finally became the Lateran Treaties (1929) with the Italian government, and during the reign of Pope Pius XII it kept the world informed on his thinking about war and peace.

L'Osservatore is responsible to the Papal Secretariate of State. Its editors and subeditors are papal appointments. A corps of correspondents provides coverage of foreign countries. While Italian is the language of the daily edition, weekly editions are published in other languages, including French, German, Polish, Portuguese, Spanish, and, since 1968, English.

The weekly edition in English is a treasury of information about the Pontiff. Besides giving the full text of his principal documents and talks, it relates news items and data that appear for the first (and perhaps only) time in English print. Thus, in the issue following the attempted assassination of Pope John Paul II on May 13, 1981, *L'Osservatore* printed the full text of the address he was to give during the general audience at which he was shot. The same issue gives the short message of the Pope that was heard by the thousands who gathered in St. Peter's Square on Sunday, May 17. The message had been recorded at the Pope's bedside in the Gemelli Hospital in Rome:

Praised be Jesus Christ.
Beloved brothers and sisters, I know that during these days and especially in this hour of the *Regina Caeli* (Queen of Heaven) you are united with me.
With deep emotion I thank you for your prayers and I bless you all.
I am particularly close to the two persons wounded together with me. I pray for that brother of ours who shot me, and whom I have sincerely pardoned.
United with Christ, Priest and Victim, I offer my sufferings for the Church and for the world.
To you, Mary, I repeat: *Totus tuus ego sum* (I belong entirely to you).

L'Osservatore Romano is indispensable for anyone who wants to keep up to date on the mind of the Catholic Church, as centered in the See of Peter.

AUTHORS

The Age of Persecution

The Catholic Church has been persecuted in every period of her history. However, the first three centuries of the Christian era are commonly known as *the* Age of Persecution because they show how promptly and aggressively the Church's enemies came to fulfill Christ's prediction to His followers, "If they have persecuted me, they will also persecute you."

These centuries also give us directives, as we may call them, on how to cope with rejection by the world that rejected Christ.

The Acts of the Apostles and the letters of St. Paul provide the revealed foundation for living out the Eighth Beatitude. But the writings of Ignatius, Justin, Irenaeus, Tertullian, Cyprian, and Lactantius show us how the early Christians lived up to—and died for—the great truths that the Savior bequeathed to His faithful. Even a man like Tertullian, though he died estranged from the true faith, highlights the inner conflict that everyone must expect who wants to remain loyal to the Divine Master.

1. *St. Ignatius of Antioch*

There are many reasons for beginning The Catholic Lifetime Reading Plan with St. Ignatius of Antioch. He suffered martyrdom at Rome (most probably in the Colosseum), the death he had so ardently desired, to become "the wheat of Christ . . . ground by the teeth of beasts." The accepted date (107) for his death makes him a contemporary of St. John the Apostle.

The seven letters Ignatius wrote on his way to martyrdom are the earliest second-century witness to the faith and practice of the early Church. They reveal many things:

- That Christianity was no mere philosophy, but an organized way of life.
- That the Church was a highly structured institution, headed by bishops as successors of the Apostles.
- That among the churches, the Church of Rome exercised a true primacy in the Christian world.
- That Jesus Christ was recognized and loved as the living God in human flesh and blood.
- That the Holy Eucharist was worshipped and received as the Real Presence of Christ on earth.
- That the spiritual life of the faithful was centered on the person of Christ, so that Christians were literally "Christ-bearers" for whose lives the Savior was the guiding inspiration.
- That the beginning of this spiritual life was faith in Jesus Christ, and its end or consummation was charity, or the selfless love of others out of selfless love for God.
- That the Church founded by Christ is the Catholic Church. Ignatius was the first to use the expression "Catholic Church," a term that was to have such a glorious future. No one has improved on his statement that "where Jesus is, there is the Catholic [universal] Church."
- That the worst enemies of God are heretics, whom Ignatius

describes in words that sound strange to our ears. They are "ferocious beasts, ravenous wolves, mad dogs, cowardly bites, animals with human faces, tombs and the columns of sepulchres, weeds of the devil, parasitical plants that have not been sent by the Father, and ready for Eternal Fire." The false doctrines they teach are "the stench of the devil."

- That our life on earth is only a preparation and training time for life in heaven with God.
- That the secret of happiness, even in this life, is the total submission of self to the will of God revealed by Christ.

There is a remarkable similarity of style in the seven letters of St. Ignatius. The first three, to the faithful at Ephesus, Magnesia, and Tralles, center on two main themes: loyalty to the bishops and avoidance of heretics and their agents. In the next letter the Philadelphians are urged to resist the dissidents and to preserve peace and unity in the Church. The faithful at Smyrna are especially warned against the errors of those who would reduce Christ's humanity to an illusion and the Real Presence to mere symbolism. In his letter to Polycarp, Bishop of Smyrna, Ignatius told the young prelate to be a true shepherd to his flock. In a class by itself is the letter to the Romans. It breathes the spirit of the first Christians, whose deep love of Christ made them eager to proclaim the Master to their pagan contemporaries and positively hungry for the crown of martyrdom.

The letters of St. Ignatius of Antioch are the brightest jewels of primitive Christian literature. Ordained by the Apostles, and successor of St. Peter in the See of Antioch, Ignatius is one of our earliest links with the inspired authors of the New Testament.

SPECIALLY RECOMMENDED
   Letters

2. St. Justin Martyr

The most important Greek defender of the faith in the second century, St. Justin (100–65), was born in Palestine and died in Italy. Converted from paganism as a young man, he immediately opened a school of philosophy in Rome. There he began to debate with the learned Roman philosophers of his day. His zeal for the person and teaching of Christ was such that he would travel from place to place, proclaiming not only that Christianity is the true religion but that no other religion is truly rational.

His logic in presenting the faith was unimpeachable. The foundation of Christianity, he argued, is the fact that God made us out of nothing but has destined us for heaven. We shall reach our destiny only if we use our free will, based on reason, enlightened by faith, according to the will of God. In his *First Apology*, Justin wrote:

We have been taught that God, in the beginning, in His goodness and for the sake of men, created all things out of formless matter. And if men, by their works, show themselves worthy of His design, they are deemed worthy, so we are told, to make their abode with Him and to reign with Him, being freed of all corruption and passion. Just as in the beginning He created us when we were not, in the same way, we believe, He will regard all those who choose to please Him, because of their choice, as worthy of immortality in communion with Him. Our coming into being in the beginning was none of our doing. But now, to follow those things which are pleasing to Him, and to choose them by means of the rational faculties which he has bestowed upon us: to this He persuades us, and leads us to faith.

Although Justin was a prolific writer, of his many works known to Eusebius, only three have come down to us. They are his two *Apologies* against the pagans and his *Dialogue with Trypho*. What especially stands out in these works is the open and honest character he reveals in dealing with persons who were openly attacking the Christian faith. Justin was convinced that "everyone who can speak the truth and does not speak it shall be judged by God." Since, by God's grace, he possessed the truth, he felt bound in conscience to proclaim what he knew was the truth.

Justin did not hesitate to address himself openly to the highest pagans of his day. Thus, his first *Apology* was written to the Emperor Antoninus Pius and his second to the Roman Senate. Written in Rome, the *Apologies* are the first in-depth defense of the Christian faith and of the Catholic Church based on history, reason, and provable facts. So truly is Justin the first apologist of Christianity that the very science of apologetics may be traced to the principles and method he set down in the first century of the Christian era.

Justin also pioneered in defending the faith against the learned Jewish critics of Christianity. The *Dialogue with Trypho* builds on a different foundation than the *Apologies*. While still appealing to reason, Justin assumed that Trypho, a Jew, believed in the Old Testament and accepted the Mosaic law.

Consequently, Justin explained to Trypho why Christians consider the law of Moses to have been only temporary and that Christianity is the new and eternal Covenant for all mankind. Justin went on to justify the belief of Christians in Christ's divinity, and the conviction, born of experience, that those who follow the teachings of the Savior are the true Israel foretold by the prophets.

St. Justin's spirited defense of Christianity finally brought about his end. When he refused to sacrifice to the Roman gods, he was put to death with many other martyrs, notably Sts. Charita, Chariton, and Liberianus.

No one has improved on St. Justin's explanation of free will, immortality, and the need for the sacraments. He is one of our earliest witnesses to the Holy Eucharist, the Sacrifice of the Mass, and the Real Presence.

SPECIALLY RECOMMENDED

The First Apology
The Second Apology

3. St. Irenaeus

During the second century, there were many outstanding writers on the Catholic faith. But none has been more influential than St. Irenaeus, Bishop of Lyons, who died a martyr in 202–3. He founded Christian theology.

Two of his writings, *The Presentation of the Apostolic Preaching* and *Adversus Haereses* (Against Heresies), are complete books. Other writings are available only in part. His main claim to fame is his reasoned defense of the Roman Catholic Church as the Kingdom of God that Christ established during His visible stay on earth.

Irenaeus' logic in defending the Church may be expressed as follows: Christ's teaching can be summarized in a series of declarative statements called the Creed. The divinely conferred right to fix the exact wording of the Creed and explain its true meaning belongs only to the Church. Within the Church, only the bishops, as the successors of the Apostles, can determine the words of the Creed and its correct meaning. The reason that only the bishops are able to do this is because they have inherited from the Apostles, through episcopal ordination, the supernatural light that this requires. It would be difficult to inquire into the teaching of all the bishops throughout the world. Moreover, this is not necessary. No less than Peter was prince of the Apostles in his day, so the successor of Peter, the Bishop of Rome, is normative for the successors of the Apostles in their day.

Irenaeus placed Christ at the center of theology. He coined the term "recapitulation," which has helped to shape Christian thinking ever since. Jesus Christ is the God who became man to redeem us from sin. He became true man, like us in all things but sin. He experiences all the stages of our human life. In spite of His virgin conception and birth, Christ grew in age as we do; He suffered trials and sorrows; and He died and was buried. He rose from the grave, even as we are destined to rise from the dead.

The Blessed Virgin plays a prominent role in the writings of St. Irenaeus. Mary's obedience erases the harm caused by the disobedience of Eve. Mary was a virgin before and after she gave birth to Christ. Although Irenaeus did not use the words "Mother of God," he affirmed Mary's divine maternity. As a result, he had a clear understanding of the harmony that exists between this privilege of Christ's Mother and the mission of her Son. She was His companion in the Redemption, and she is now the world's most powerful intercessor in heaven.

St. Irenaeus laid the foundations for the theology of holiness on which the masters of spirituality have since built. He clearly distinguished between the indwelling, uncreated Holy Spirit and the consequences of this indwelling, which we now call sanctifying grace. Irenaeus constantly stressed the importance of our free will in cooperating with the grace of God. Like Adam, we can resist the inspirations of the Holy Spirit. But we can also respond to these graces and merit further graces on earth and eternal glory in the life to come.

For Irenaeus, the believing Christian has access to knowledge that pagans and heretics simply do not enjoy. Faith gives light to the mind; it confers the power to see and understand that nothing else on earth can provide.

The link between St. Ignatius of Antioch and Irenaeus is St. Polycarp. Even as Ignatius had counseled Polycarp to "beg for an increase in understanding," so Irenaeus admitted how much he had learned from listening to the sermons of Polycarp.

SPECIALLY RECOMMENDED

The Presentation of the Apostolic Preaching
Against the Heretics (Adversus Haereses)

4. Tertullian

One of the great literary geniuses of all times, Tertullian was also a mysterious personality. He is the only author in the Reading Plan whose works we must immediately classify according to the three stages of his career: as a strong Catholic, as a wavering Catholic, and as the leading anti-Catholic of his day.

Born of pagan parents in Carthage about 150, he was converted to Christianity about 195, and almost immediately wrote his first book, *To the Martyrs*. After becoming a firm Catholic, he averaged more than one volume a year, including such a classic as *Apologeticus*, perhaps the outstanding piece of controversial writing in the Church's history. In his early writings, Tertullian takes up St. Irenaeus' argument that only the Catholic Church's hierarchy has the right to interpret the meaning of Sacred Scripture.

The turning point in his life was his attraction to Montanism. This was a sect, founded by Montanus, famous for its moral rigorism, claims to mysticism, and appeal to special lights from the Holy Spirit. Montanists considered themselves prophets of Christ's second coming. The substance of their doctrine was that the Holy Spirit was now replacing the revelation of Christ. Those who received the "new outpouring of the Spirit" would displace the hierarchy of bishops and the Pope as teachers and guides of the faithful.

For ten years, Tertullian's writings were orthodox beyond reproach. For the next seven years, his publications leaned heavily on the side of Montanism. And in the last years of his life, he was openly heterodox.

The Church has carefully distinguished these stages. She regards Tertullian as the first Christian theologian to write in Latin. She quotes him in her documents, including the Second Vatican Council. And she places him beside St. Augustine in most of his dogmatic teaching, including the Trinity, the Incarnation, and the sacraments of baptism and penance.

In spite of his rugged style, which was the expression of a passionate nature, he may be credited with having created the language of Western theology. Some of his statements have become part of the Church's literary history. Addressing the pagan persecutors, he told them, "The more you put us to death, the more we increase; blood is the seed of Christians."

SPECIALLY RECOMMENDED

Apologetical Works
Disciplinary, Moral and Ascetical Works

5. St. Cyprian

St. Cyprian, Bishop of Carthage and martyr, was an extraordinary person. Baptized at thirty-five, he was decapitated in 258 in the presence of all his people, after less than ten years in the episcopate.

Best known for *On the Unity of the Church,* Cyprian symbolizes the human side of Catholic belief in the primacy of the Bishop of Rome. The specific issues dealt with therein are whether Christians who deny their faith under persecution must be rebaptized and whether baptism conferred by heretics is valid.

The Popes held that neither repentant apostates nor converts from heresy had to be rebaptized, but Cyprian, as leader of the North African bishops, argued to the contrary. His correspondence with two Popes, Sts. Cornelius and Stephen I, was outspoken. Pope Stephen even threatened Cyprian with excommunication. But Cyprian not only never questioned the Pope's supreme authority but wrote the most explicit defense of papal primacy in patristic literature.

St. Cyprian's teaching on the sacrament of penance is a historical milestone. Three elements are necessary for this sacrament: the penitent must make a confession to a priest, the confession must include interior and secret sins, and the penitent must perform adequate satisfaction to expiate for the sins committed. Only then does the priest give absolution, which Cyprian variously called "peace," "remission," and "communication," and which the priest imparts by the laying of hands on the repentant sinner.

Above all, Cyprian was a moralist and pastor of souls. A fine synthesis of his spirituality is found in his short explanation of the Our Father. Running as a theme through this classic work is the stress on the necessity of prayer to obtain the graces we need to live up to the hard demands of the Gospel. Our aim should be, he said, to become more and more like Christ, for whom the will of God was the very food of His Life and the main object of His teaching.

Cyprian wrote during the peak of the Church's persecution. To be a Christian then meant to be ready for martyrdom. He did not have to cope with such heresies as Pelagianism, which denied the need of grace for salvation. But he laid the groundwork for St. Augustine and others to show how literally Christ meant His words to be taken when He said, "Without me, you can do nothing" on the way to heaven. When we pray, "Thy will be done on earth as it is in heaven," said Cyprian, we are not asking God to do what He will, but that we might be able to will what God wants.

St. Cyprian is being used to defend an independence of bishops from the Pope that has reached a critical stage in some countries in our day, but without justification. No doubt his baptismal controversy with two Popes while appealing to the body of bishops in North Africa lends plausibility to the charge of episcopalianism. No doubt, too, Cyprian's late conversion and rapid Christian formation made him less aware than he might have been of the latest heresy of bishops claiming superiority over the Bishop of Rome. But Cyprian's faith in the authority of the Pope over bishops was never in question. He spoke of the Bishop of Rome having primacy (Primatus), and by this he meant not only a primacy of honor but of active jurisdiction as the chief source for the preservation of Catholic unity. If Cyprian erred, it was an error of inconsistency between practice and what he strongly held in principle—namely, that "the primacy was given to Peter." Consequently, "if a man does not hold fast to this oneness of Peter, does he imagine that he still holds the faith? If he deserts the Chair of St. Peter, upon whom the Church is built, has he still confidence that he is in the Church?"

SPECIALLY RECOMMENDED

> The Lapsed, the Unity of the Catholic Church
> St. Cyprian on the Lord's Prayer

6. Lactantius

Among the early Christian writers, some are scarcely known, except by scholars. Yet, their contribution to an understanding of the true faith has been immense. Lactantius (c. 240–c. 320) is a classic example from the fourth century.

His full name was Lucius Caecilius Firminianus Lactantius. A pagan of North Africa, he taught rhetoric in Nicomedia, at the request of Emperor Diocletian. He became a Christian in about 303, lost his teaching position, and was reduced to destitution. He began to write to make a living, and providentially became a tutor to Emperor Constantine's son, Crispus.

Among his known writings were *The Workmanship of God,* a long poem; *The Wrath of God,* against the Stoics and Epicureans; *The Deaths of Persecutors,* in defense of the martyrs; and an explanation of the Phoenix legend and the Christian belief in the resurrection.

His most famous writing is on *The Divine Institutes,* a cryptic title for an elaborate comparison between Christian and pagan beliefs. It is instructive to read here how Lactantius defends the Providence of God in permitting the followers of Christ to be persecuted. He begins by setting down a general principle: God "allows persecutions to be carried on against us" so that "the people of God might be increased." This happens in four ways:

First, very many people are put to flight from the cults of the false gods by a hatred of cruelty. Who would not shrink from such sacrifices? Then, virtue and the faith itself are attractive to certain ones. Some suspect that not without cause is the worship of the gods thought to be evil by so many that they would prefer to die rather than do that which others do that they may live. Someone wishes to know what that good is which is defended even to death, which is preferred to all things that are pleasing or dear in this life, and from which neither loss of possessions, nor of light, nor pain of body, nor torture of its members deter. These are very strong, but those causes have always increased our number. The people standing around hear them saying in the very midst of torments that they do not sacrifice to stone statues made by human hands, but to the living God who is in heaven. Many know that this is true and admit it in their hearts. Then, as is accustomed to happen in uncertain matters, while they question each other as to the cause of this perseverance, many things which pertain to religion, being noised abroad and caught in turn, are learned. Since these things are good, they must please them. Besides, vengeance gained, as it always happens, strongly impels to belief. This is not a slight cause, either, the fact that unclean spirits of demons inhabit the bodies of many people, permission having been granted. When these have been ejected afterwards, all who have been cleansed adhere to the religion whose power they have felt. These many reasons, gathered together, marvelously gain a great multitude for God.

Lactantius has been criticized for being too close to the paganism from which he was converted to be an adequate exponent of Christianity. This is true only in the sense that the newfound faith had not been able to mature sufficiently to give a comprehensive account of his own religious convictions.

But he was an invaluable witness to the power of divine grace to change a successful rhetorician into a zealous Christian. He was also a witness to the power of revealed truth to change a whole empire (a process that began with Constantine) from the adoration of lifeless idols to the worship of the one living God, in the person of Jesus Christ.

SPECIALLY RECOMMENDED
   The Divine Institutes

The Patristic Age

The Fathers of the Church were those saintly writers of the early centuries whom the Church recognizes as her special defenders of orthodoxy. And the Patristic Age is the period during which they lived.

It is generally held that the last of the Western Fathers (Latin) was St. Bede the Venerable (673–735), and the last of the Eastern Fathers (Greek) was St. John Damascene (675–749).

Writers like St. Ignatius of Antioch and St. Irenaeus are, of course, Fathers of the Church. Nevertheless, it seemed wiser, for the purpose of this Lifetime Reading Plan, to distinguish some of the early Fathers who were outstanding witnesses to the faith in time of persecution. The authors here included are only ten out of an estimated ninety writers who qualify by their antiquity, orthodoxy, sanctity, and approval by the Church as belonging to the Patristic Age.

Why these ten? Mainly because their writings have been the most influential in shaping the minds and hearts of Christian believers. Every one of these ten has so deeply inspired future generations that he would qualify as father in spirit not only of Christian but of all human civilization.

7. *Eusebius*

Eusebius of Caesarea (265–339), the "father of Church history," had a checkered career. Baptized as an adult, he entered the ranks of the clergy and from his earliest days in the priesthood had an ardent desire for knowledge.

His greatest ambition was to enrich the library in Caesarea with new manuscripts. These provided him with the sources he later used to write his several histories. He was a close friend of St. Pamphilus, with whom he was imprisoned before Pamphilus' martyrdom. While in prison, the two composed the famous *Apology for Origen.*

After Pamphilus' death, Eusebius wrote his biography in three volumes. So devoted was Eusebius to his martyred friend that he began to call himself Eusebius Pamphili. Imprisonment and a narrow escape from death for his faith characterized Eusebius' years up to the Church's liberation under Constantine.

No sooner was the Church given political liberty than there arose the Arian heresy, which denied that Christ was truly divine. Throughout the Council of Nicea (325) and afterward, Eusebius would not accept the term *homoousios,* which Nicea used to define Christ as one in being with the Father. Although Eusebius signed the document of Nicea, as drawn up by the Pope's delegate, Hosius, he soon retracted it. In fact, he became one of the chief opponents of St. Athanasius, the staunch defender of the Council of Nicea. Thus, in 335 he was present at the "brigandage of Tyre," which condemned Athanasius. When Eusebius later wrote an account of the rebel meeting of bishops at Tyre, he did not even mention the name of Athanasius.

Some explanation is necessary for including Eusebius in the Catholic Reading Plan. He was very learned, a prolific writer, and a successful administrator as bishop, but he was also weak in character. Two aspects of this weakness that were especially grave were his unqualified admiration for Emperor Constantine and his uncontrolled desire to please his fellow bishops who would not accept the unqualified teaching of Nicea about the divinity of Jesus Christ.

Yet, Eusebius deserves to be included in this study of great Catholic writers. He was the pioneer Church historian of Christianity. His histories have proved substantially accurate. And he exemplifies the not uncommon failing of some Catholic prelates in the Church's history—namely, an absence of strength of mind and steadfastness of conscience in proportion to their vast erudition.

The *Ecclesiastical History* of Eusebius consists of ten books, composed over a period of about fifteen years. Were it not for this work of Eusebius, much of the first three centuries of the Church would be almost unknown to us. Its chief merit lies in the fact that it is drawn from reliable sources, sources that are often directly quoted by the author. Together with a mass of factual data, it contains numerous documents drawn from the state archives and extracts from other authors. Moreover, Eusebius' sincerity can hardly be questioned, even though his misplaced sympathies sometimes led him to make certain omissions. The great number of extracts also makes the work appear more of a collection than a history. These deficiencies, however, do not detract from Eusebius' claim to the title "the Christian Herodotus."

The following passage from one of Eusebius' orations before Emperor Constantine reveals the depth of his Christian faith. This is all the more remarkable because Constantine remained a catechumen all his life and was not baptized until shortly before he died.

The whole length of the day would fail me, my Emperor, if I should try to collect and combine into one account the manifest examples of Our Savior's divine power that are evident from effects still visible, since no one who ever lived either among Greeks or among barbarians ever exhibited such power of divine ability as has Our Own Savior. But why do I speak just of men, when of those who were called gods by all the nations not a one has manifested such a nature on this earth. If so, let anyone so inclined reveal him; let any philosopher at all come forward and tell us, what god or hero at any time or any place in all history has ever been said, as has Our Savior, to have transmitted to mankind salutary teachings about the eternal life and the heavenly kingdom, to have made countless masses throughout the entire inhabited world skilled in philosophic principles, to have persuaded them to concentrate on heaven and to hope for the pleasures stored up in heaven for God-loving souls? What god or hero ever has shined over and enlightened with the most brilliant rays of his teaching the area from the sun's rise to its setting, all but riding a circuit extensive as the sun's, so that every nation everywhere on earth discharges one and the same religious service to One God? What god or hero ever thrust aside all gods and heroes, Greek and barbarian, and ordained that not one god among those be believed to exist—and, having so ordained, prevailed. And what other when attacked by all, though He Himself was but One, ever destroyed the entire army of His enemies, conquering all the gods and heroes of the ages, so as to be Himself proclaimed by all peoples throughout the whole of human habitation the One Child of God? Who has ordained that those who inhabit the great earth, whether on continents or on islands, should assemble in the same place for the very same purpose every week on the day called after the Lord and have a holiday, and has accustomed them not to indulge their bodies but to rekindle their souls by divine study? What god or hero, being so attacked as was Our Savior, raised victory trophies over his enemies? For they from beginning to end never ceased from assailing His teachings and His people, but He who is invisible invisibly promoted His retainers, as well as their very houses of worship, to a fullness of glory. But why must we try to summarize in words that which surpasses all account, the divine powers of Our Savior, when even were we silent the deeds themselves would cry out to those who possess ears of the spirit, that the world of men has produced this truly strange and amazing and singular phenomenon, that the true Son of God has been seen on earth.

Perhaps the best estimate of Eusebius is to say he was a master of historical research but a poor defender of the true faith. His compromise with Arianism may have been the result more of his desire for peace and the influence of Constantine than of genuine conviction.

SPECIALLY RECOMMENDED
Ecclesiastical History

8. St. Athanasius

If there is one writer whose name stands for doctrine and whose life symbolizes fortitude, it is St. Athanasius. He died in 373, after forty-five years in the episcopate.

His extensive writings were mainly composed during the frequent exiles he suffered because of his defense of the faith. Like St. Paul, he was hounded by his enemies and was forced on one occasion to hide in the tomb of his father.

Unlike Cyprian, whom he resembled in many ways, Athanasius had to defend Christ's true divinity against heretical bishops. Still a deacon, he accompanied Bishop Alexander of Alexandria to the Council of Nicea in 325. Even then, his vigorous opposition to Arius, who denied that Christ had the same divine nature as the Father, earned for Athanasius the hatred of the Arians and their sympathizers. Three years after Nicea, the people clamored for his episcopal ordination, crying out, "He is a sincere, virtuous man, a good Christian, an ascetic, a true bishop."

St. Athanasius championed three principal doctrines of the Catholic faith: the divinity of Jesus Christ, the mystery of the Redemption, and the independence of the Church from the state in teaching the faith and in guiding the morals and worship of the faithful.

At first glance, Athanasius' writings may seem to be too polemical, as in his two main works, the *Discourse Against the Greeks* and the *Discourse Against the Arians.* But they are sober reminders to us that we should be more wary of errors in faith and more zealous in defending revealed truth in our day. If anything, ours is an age in which error flourishes, at least partly because those who possess the truth are too squeamish about safeguarding their possession from pollution by error. Athanasius spoke fearlessly about the servility of Arian bishops to heretical pressure and denounced as a crime the banishment of Pope Liberius by the Arian emperor.

Lacking the sharp theological vocabulary later developed by the Church, Athanasius yet remained clear in his understanding of the cardinal mysteries of Christianity. What he wrote at the end of *The Incarnation of the Word* summarizes Athanasius' whole approach to the faith. He saw in his day widespread confusion, especially among intellectuals, about the most basic truths of revelation. His recommendation in the fourth century is more than ever valid today: a deep study of the Scriptures and education are to be highly esteemed, but "an upright life, a pure soul, and Christian virtue are necessary if the soul, having practiced these things, would obtain and possess what it desires to learn, the Word of God, as far as this is possible for human nature."

It was Athanasius' conviction that if anyone hopes to reach the wisdom of the Church's great thinkers, "he must first draw near to the saints by resembling them in their actions." Only holiness of life gives light to the believing mind. This explains St. Athanasius' preoccupation with purity of morals. It also accounts for his writing the classic story of the hermit St. Anthony of Egypt. This book is a classic three times over: it is our earliest extensive biography of a saint; it emphasizes the need for prayer and mortification if the intellect is to remain humble in accepting the mysteries of the faith; and it explains the role of the devil in seducing souls through pride, even to the rejection of God.

SPECIALLY RECOMMENDED
The Incarnation of the Word
The Life of Saint Anthony

9. *Prudentius*

The Spanish Christian poet Aurelius Clemens Prudentius (348–c. 405) was a lawyer by profession. After two terms as provincial governor, he was summoned by the emperor to court, where he served with distinction. But jurisprudence did not really appeal to him. He finally gave up the practice of law altogether and gave himself up to a life of asceticism, for example, abstaining from food until evening and not eating meat.

In his spare time, he composed many poems, which are deeply religious and reflect the strong Catholic faith of the early Christians, following the liberation of the Church under Constantine. There is no question why Prudentius wrote his poetry. It was simply to glorify God and atone for his own sins. Scholars have divided his poems into three categories: the lyrical, the didactic, and the polemical.

His lyric poems cover a large variety of subjects, especially for the sanctification of the hours of the day or certain important feasts, such as Christmas and Epiphany. Some of his poems continue the liturgical tradition of St. Ambrose and are written in the Ambrosian iambic diameter. Others, especially his Christian burial poetry, follow the metric form of Horace. Not a few of his poems were written to glorify the Church's martyrs, like Sts. Peter and Paul, Cyprian and Agnes.

Prudentius' two principal instructive poems are on the mystery of the Holy Trinity and on the origin of sin. They are both examples of passionate, glowing exposition of revealed dogma combined with an extraordinary gift of poetic expression. There seems no doubt that Prudentius was at least partially influenced by Tertullian, whose mastery of language was superb. But, unlike Tertullian, Prudentius never wavered in his Catholic orthodoxy. Yet, even Prudentius is not free from occasional lapses, like his belief that only a small number of souls will be lost.

Among Prudentius' polemical poetry, outstanding is his invective against Symmachus. In it, he shows how the early Christians reconciled their patriotism with their faith. For Prudentius, the Church is the divinely planned fulfillment of the genius of the Roman government. As a Christian, he is impartial to his pagan fellow citizens for their services to the state. Prudentius is proud of the Roman Senate, seeing that by the end of the fourth century most of its members were Christians.

It is not surprising that so many of Prudentius' poems have found their way into the Church's liturgy over the centuries. Nor is it any wonder that he is considered the greatest among the Christian poets in the first millennium of Catholic history. What he also shows is the power of the faith to inspire literary genius, not only among priests and religious but among the laity involved, as Prudentius was, in the secular world.

SPECIALLY RECOMMENDED
Poems
Hymns

10. *St. John Chrysostom*

St. John Chrysostom had been Bishop of Constantinople for less than ten years when he died in exile in 407. But his place in history ranks among the giants of Catholic literature. He suffered intensely as bishop and was forced into exile because of his uncompromising defense of the Church's rights in conflict with the state.

He represents a new stage in the history of Christianity. The great writers who preceded him had to defend the true faith against heretical innovators, but Chrysostom had to protect the Church against political oppressors.

The epithet "Chrysostom" means "golden mouth" and identifies him as a powerful orator. He had a lively mind, a fertile imagination, a perfect sense of proportion, and an extraordinary depth of feeling. These features stand out even now, more than fifteen hundred years later, and are present in both his sermons and published writings.

His published oratorical works by actual count number over one thousand, some of which are extensive homilies on the New Testament. Among these are sermons on Genesis (67 homilies), on Matthew and John (178), and on St. Paul (250 homilies). The latter are considered the best commentaries on the Apostle of the Gentiles.

The nonoratorical writings are numerous and range across the spectrum of Christian faith and morals. The treatise *On the Priesthood* is the finest of his writings and perhaps the first really great pastoral work ever written, although he was only a deacon when he wrote this book. It stresses the dignity of the priesthood. The priest, it says, is greater than kings, angels, or parents. But priests are for that reason most tempted to pride and ambition. They, more than anyone else, need clear and unshakeable wisdom, patience that disarms pride, and exceptional prudence in dealing with souls.

Chrysostom's short *Address on Vainglory and the Right Way for Parents to Bring Up Their Children* is a treasury of practical wisdom that is still useful in our day. *On Virginity* praises marriage but points out that virginity is preferable, as taught by St. Paul in his letters to the Corinthians.

When he wrote in defense of the faith, his approach was unlike that of Athanasius. Chrysostom was above all a practical apologist. His classic *Against Julian and the Pagans* was a reasoned proof of the credibility of Christianity against the apostate Emperor Julian. He argued from the miracles of Christ and recent prodigies that occurred when the remains of Christian martyrs were being transferred to their permanent resting place.

A favorite theme of Chrysostom was the providential role of suffering. He wrote *To Those Who Are Scandalized Because of Adversity* and entitled one of his short books *No One Is Injured Except by Himself.* His argument is that suffering is an integral part of Divine Providence, that to be a true follower of Christ means to experience what Christ experienced—namely, opposition and the Cross.

It is a tribute to Chrysostom's genius that so much of what he said has been preserved over the centuries. One reason for this is that he used the Sacred Scriptures as the principal and almost only source of his ideas. In fact, he made them a law for every preacher. He preferred the literal method for explaining the Scriptures and concentrated on the moral teachings of the Bible.

It can safely be said that no other biblical commentator in history has ever brought together so much sound Catholic thought so calmly and sensibly, with such spiritual depth, and with such ease and skill as St. John Chrysostom.

SPECIALLY RECOMMENDED

> *On the Priesthood*
> *Address on Vainglory and the Right Way for Parents to Bring Up Their Children*

11. *St. Augustine*

St. Augustine, the greatest Doctor of the Church, has left us a library of Christian wisdom. His conversion to the faith in 387, at the age of thirty-three, was really the discovery of certain basic truths, which he spent the rest of his literary life defending:

- The world is essentially good because it is the work of God. It was the Holy Trinity who created the world out of nothing.
- There is order in the world, ruled by Divine Providence. Even evil has a place in the world. Physical evil, which is basically suffering, is the result of moral evil, or sin, which is the misuse of angelic and human liberty.
- Jesus Christ is true God, who became man to redeem a sinful human race. The humility of the Incarnation expiated man's pride, and the Crucifixion reconciled man with the offended God.
- As first created, Adam possessed not only a human nature but what are called supernatural and preternatural gifts. Original sin deprived Adam and his posterity of both gifts. Christ's passion and death merited the restoration of the supernatural life and provided the graces necessary to cope with the loss of the preternatural gifts. We are enabled, with divine help, to control our sinful desires and accept suffering and death. All the while, our free will, though weakened, remains intact, so that we can cooperate with the grace of God. If we cooperate, we shall reach heaven; if we refuse to cooperate, we shall be eternally deprived of the vision of God.

Augustine's contribution to Catholic thought made a universal and permanent impact on the Christian world. The underlying reason for this extraordinary influence was the fact that three of the most fundamental errors ever to plague Christianity were prevalent in his day. In fact, all three have continued to exercise their baneful influence down to the present.

Augustine did more than merely refute the errors. He explained the orthodox teaching so clearly that, in many cases, his explanation has been normative in Catholic thought. Three principal errors had to be answered, each having, by now, a famous name: Manichaeism, Donatism, and Pelagianism.

Having been a Manichaean himself for nine years before his conversion, Augustine drew on firsthand experience when he wrote in defense of the Catholic doctrine in *Nature of the Good Against the Manichees*. Where the Manichaeans claimed there were finally two gods, one the author of matter and the other of spirit, Augustine showed that all being, material and spiritual, is essentially good, since God, who is all-good, is its Author. Evil is always a privation or lack of what should be present. And all evil is finally the result of a misuse by a created free will of its God-given liberty.

Where the Donatists urged that the Church founded by Christ has only holy members, Augustine showed from Scripture that both good and sinful members were expected to belong to the Church on earth. This, in fact, is part of her universality, that she includes sinners who, in God's Providence, are to be converted before they die and, in the process, help to sanctify the good.

However, the main focus of Augustine's writing was to defend the idea that we absolutely need supernatural grace to reach our heavenly destiny, which the Pelagians denied. Because of his long struggle with sexual passions, Augustine had no illusions about man's inability even to live a morally good life without divine help. Pelagianism, he saw, was a deluded self-conceit. Twenty years of preaching and writing, to the day of his death, and some thirty volumes in a modern edition, testify to Augustine's zeal.

Running as a theme through his literary life was Augustine's firm allegiance to the Bishop of Rome. He constantly relied on the Roman Pontiff for approval of his own orthodoxy. In a statement that made history, he announced in a sermon on September 23, 417, that word had just been received from Rome: Pope

Innocent I had condemned Pelagius. "The case is finished," he declared. "If only the error would disappear!"

The writings of Augustine alone could constitute a Catholic Lifetime Reading Plan. Three books, however, should be read by anyone who wants to know Catholic thought, and not only that of the fifth century. They are essential for understanding authentic Christianity in any age.

The Confessions is not mainly a book of repentance but above all a book of praise. In Augustine's own words, "My *Confessions* praise the just and good God for all the blessings and all the misfortunes that have befallen me; they raise up to Him the mind and heart of man."

The City of God is the greatest story of world history ever written. It spans the providential action of God with regard to the whole of mankind, not only in the past but also in the future and into the next world.

Of True Religion is a short masterpiece in defense of Catholic Christianity. After showing the truth of the faith in contrast with paganism, it explains the two ways that Divine Providence provides for the salvation of the human family—namely, by authority and reason. It shows how God brings man to Himself through an examination of his vicious tendencies. The goal of these reflections is to lead his readers to Christian holiness, achieved in perfect liberty through contemplation of the truth and knowledge of Sacred Scriptures.

After the Bible, no other books are more widely read or have been more influential in shaping human thought than the writings of St. Augustine.

SPECIALLY RECOMMENDED
The City of God
The Confessions
Of True Religion
Enchiridion: On Faith, Hope, and Charity

12. *St. Jerome*

The Catholic Church honors St. Jerome as the heavenly patron of biblical studies. Ordained a priest about the age of thirty, his reputation as a scholar led to his appointment as secretary to Pope Damasus I. It was this Pope, who in 384, told Jerome to compose an official text of the Latin version of the Bible. As a result, Jerome spent most of the rest of his life—thirty-five years —in Palestine, working tirelessly on the work given him by the Pope. The translation into Latin was finished about 405.

After about two centuries, Jerome's version took the first place in the West. In the thirteenth century, it became known as the Vulgate, because it was the *vulgata editio* (edition in general circulation). By the sixteenth century, the Vulgate had appeared in several hundred print editions, with numerous variants.

The Council of Trent declared that the Vulgate "is to be held authentic in public readings, disputations and sermons and exposition," and ordered its careful revision. This meant that the Vulgate was to be the official biblical text of the Catholic Church.

Not satisfied with this monumental achievement, Jerome wrote extensive commentaries on the Bible. His approach to explaining Scripture may be described as spiritual. But he took pains to base his mystical interpretation on the literal sense of the inspired text. One reason for this caution was the rise of Origenism, named after Origen, the biblical scholar who was misled into thinking that hell might not be eternal, at least not for everyone.

Jerome may be said to have founded the history of Christian literature. His work *On Illustrious (Famous) Men* gives a library of information on one hundred and thirty-five writers from St. Peter to himself and includes some non-Christians like Philo and Seneca.

From a literary point of view, Jerome's correspondence is the most perfect of his writings. There are some one hundred and twenty-five letters, covering a vast range of subjects. Some deal with asceticism, others with controversy, and still others with personal matters. But all are so revealing of his own character and so outspokenly clear that over the centuries they have been considered masterpieces of the epistolary art.

St. Jerome typifies the paradox of a Doctor of the Church who was thoroughly sound on basic principles of faith and morals but who erred in some matters of Catholic doctrine. He seems never to have completely purged himself of Origenism, about the eventual salvation of all Christians. And he allowed himself to question the inspiration of the deuterocanonical books of the Old Testament.

Since the Church's magisterium had not yet made definite pronouncements on these matters, Jerome's ambiguity is less surprising. It was left to St. Augustine, one of his correspondents, to remove the uncertainty left by St. Jerome.

SPECIALLY RECOMMENDED
   Letters
   On Illustrious (Famous) Men

13. *St. Vincent of Lérins*

One of the least-known Fathers of the Church is also one of the most important. St. Vincent of Lérins, who died about 445, was of a noble family of Gaul. He gave up his military career to become a monk at Lérins Abbey, off the coast at Cannes. Ordained a priest, he wrote his famous *Commonitorium* on orthodox Catholic teaching.

Heresy was rampant in St. Vincent's day. He refers to Novatianism, Sabellianism, Arianism, Eunomianism, Macedonianism,

Apollinarism, Priscillianism, Pelagianism, and Nestorianism as examples of the subtle errors that were plaguing the Church in the early fifth century.

The problem was compounded, Vincent explained, by the fact that all the heretics were appealing to the Bible. They would quote the Scriptures in support of their erroneous teaching. "The same text," he said, "is interpreted differently by different people, so that one may almost gain the impression that it can yield as many different meanings as there are men."

How to cope with the situation? There must be some basic rule or standard by which to determine the true Catholic meaning of a biblical passage. What is this rule? St. Vincent's answer has become classic in the history of Christianity:

In the Catholic Church, *every care should be taken to hold fast to what has been believed everywhere, always, and by all.* This is truly and properly "Catholic" as indicated by the force and etymology of the name itself, which comprises everything truly universal. This general rule will be truly applied if we follow the principles of universality, antiquity, and consent. We do so in regard to universality if we confess that faith alone to be true which the entire Church confesses all over the world. We do so in regard to antiquity if we in no way deviate from those interpretations which our ancestors and fathers have manifestly proclaimed as inviolable. We do so in regard to consent if, in this very antiquity, we adopt the definitions and propositions of all, or almost all, the bishops and doctors.

What, therefore, will the Catholic Christian do if some members of the Church have broken away from the communion of universal faith? What else, but prefer the sanity of the body universal to the pestilence of the corrupt member? What if a new contagion strives to infect not only a small part but the whole Church? Then, he will endeavor to adhere to the antiquity which is evidently beyond the danger of being seduced by the deceit of some novelty. What if in antiquity itself an error is detected, on the part of two or three men, or even on the part of a city or a province? Then, he will take care to prefer the decrees of a previous ecumenical council (if there was one) to the temerity and ignorance of a small group. Finally, what if such an error arises and nothing like a council can be found? Then, he will take pains to consult and interrogate the opinions of his predecessors, comparing them with one another only as regards the opinions of those who, though they lived in various periods and at different places, nevertheless remained in the communion and faith of the One Catholic Church, and who therefore have become reliable authorities. As he will discover, he must also believe without hesitation whatever not only one or two but all equally and with one and the same consent, openly, frequently, and persistently have held, written and taught. [Italics in original]

It is impossible to exaggerate the importance of the foregoing norm of orthodoxy, especially of the first sentence, which is italicized.

Error has always been prevalent among Christians. The letters of Sts. Peter and Paul warn the followers of Christ against false teaching. The formula for distinguishing truth from error is the same today as it was in the days of Vincent of Lérins. Universality, antiquity, and consent are as valid norms of orthodoxy now as they were in the first half of the fifth century.

SPECIALLY RECOMMENDED
Commonitorium

14. *Boethius*

Boethius was the last great philosopher in the West before the close of the Patristic Age. Born in Rome about 480, he was executed by the Arian Emperor Theodoric about 526.

During the long imprisonment, awaiting execution, he wrote his famous work *The Consolation of Philosophy*. Written in the form of a dialogue, with short pieces of verse interrupting the text, the work builds on the author's Christian faith to find happiness in misfortune.

This classic is divided into five books. In Book 1, while the author is complaining of his misery, Philosophy appears to him as a noble lady. He confides to her his doubts about Providence. In the next book, Philosophy shows him the inconstancy of fortune. Nothing in this world can truly satisfy the human heart. Book 3 presents Philosophy's definition of beatitude as "the full and enduring possession of perfect good." Everyone is looking for beatitude, but most people look for it in the wrong place, here on earth. Full happiness can be found only in God, and then only in the vision of God in eternity. Answering Boethius' complaints in the fourth book, Philosophy explains the ways of Providence. No doubt the wicked may prosper here below, but order will be restored in the life to come, based on the merit we have earned by conforming to the laws of God during our stay on earth. In the final book, Philosophy concludes with a defense of God's wisdom and goodness. Provided we serve Him faithfully now, by the right use of our free will, He will not be outdone in generosity.

The book closes with a magnificent chapter on eternity. God's eternity is defined as "the perfect and simultaneous total possession of unending life." Rational creatures are destined to share in God's eternity according to the dispositions of His love.

Boethius accepts divine revelation, but then applies all the resources of cool reasoning to explain what the revealed truths actually mean. Thus, faith opens itself to man's intelligence with the help of philosophy.

The Consolation of Philosophy is one of the monumental works of Catholic thought and earned its author the soubriquet "founder of Scholasticism." Boethius was accepted as an authority second only to Aristotle by the Schoolmen of the Middle Ages, including St. Thomas Aquinas. It was left to Aquinas to subject the whole range of revealed truth to the same scrutiny that Boethius made of the mystery of Providence.

SPECIALLY RECOMMENDED
    The Consolation of Philosophy

15. *St. Benedict*

There are some writers who have left only one book to posterity. Yet, they deserve to be included in any Catholic Lifetime Reading Plan. St. Benedict of Nursia (480–550) is such an author and his Rule is such a work.

Born in Nursia, he was educated in Rome but found life there so licentious that he withdrew to nearby Subiaco. He lived there for some years as a hermit, where he founded some twelve monasteries with twelve monks each and with abbots appointed by him. Local jealousy prompted him to leave Subiaco about 529 and go with a small group of monks to Monte Cassino, where he remained for the rest of his life.

Although monastic life already existed, it was Benedict's genius to stabilize it and give it such form as has since affected all consecrated life in the Western world. Three qualities stand out in the Rule of St. Benedict, composed between about 530 and 540. It is at once exact and comprehensive. Instead of general maxims, it contains laws and so leaves the religious with no doubt as to his duties at any time of the day or night. The Rule reveals a rare wisdom in combining enough strictness to rein in human nature with such moderation as not to discourage those seeking Christian perfection. And the Rule introduced stability into community life by binding a religious to remain attached to the monastery of his profession until death.

Consistent with his logical thinking, Benedict built his monastic spirituality around three centers—namely, a hierarchy, work, and prayer. The hierarchy consisted of an abbot, who was elected by the community, had authority for life, and was assisted by officers of his choice, such as the prior, dean, and cellarer. The work was not definitively specified, but was obligatory on all during certain hours of the day; this work was manual for the most part, but could also be intellectual for some of the monks. Prayer, or the *opus Dei* (work of God), was to be the mainstay of the Rule, which meant the celebration of the Divine Office at stated times throughout the day.

Historically, the Rule of St. Benedict deeply and widely influenced not only the life of the counsels but all Christian living among the clergy and laity as well. Celebrating the Divine Office, in time, became mandatory for all priests. The administrative structure developed a sense of dependence on the hierarchy, culminating in the Bishop of Rome. And the necessity of work inspired the organized Christian towns and villages as the monks began to evangelize the barbarians of Europe.

SPECIALLY RECOMMENDED

The Rule of Saint Benedict

16. *The Venerable Bede*

St. Bede, called "the Venerable" (673–735), was the father of English history. Entering a Benedictine monastery as a young boy, he spent all of his priestly life as a tireless scholar and writer. He seems never to have left his native country, and he helped to consolidate the faith among the Anglo-Saxons by bringing them the knowledge of Christian antiquity.

The writings of Bede are numerous. Shortly before he died, he drew up a list of forty-five full-length works. Most of these treat of various branches of theology, but some also deal with secular subjects.

Bede is best known for his *A History of the English Church and People.* Divided into five books, it traces the religious, social, and political history of his nation from the first contacts between the Britons and the Romans down to the end of 731.

Persons and events of Church and state are carefully treated in a clear, concise style. The *History* is actually a chronicle or collection of stories in chronological order and dated according to Christian computation.

What stands out in this primary source of information is the remarkable industry of the author in collecting materials and his critical use of the assembled data. English translations from the Latin were begun by King Alfred, but after the invention of printing, no edition of the *History,* even in Latin, was printed in England until 1643; since then, several translations have been made.

Bede's commentaries on the Scriptures, although extensive, are in keeping with his historian's mentality. He relied heavily on Sts. Augustine and Jerome, being careful to echo their interpretation of the revealed text. When he did venture on his own, he favored a mystical explanation of the Bible, in the manner of his fellow monk Pope Gregory the Great. It is to St. Bede that we owe the story of Gregory's encounter with the fair Saxon slaves in the market, and the resulting decision to send St. Augustine to reevangelize the Anglo-Saxons.

SPECIALLY RECOMMENDED
A History of the English Church and People

Medieval Civilization

There are no fixed dates for the beginning and the close of the Middle Ages. Some would date medieval times from as early as 476, when Odoacer deposed Romulus Augustulus, the last of the Roman emperors of the West. Others would date the beginning to the opening years of the seventh century and the death of Venantius Fortunatus, the last representative of classical Latin literature. But since we are concentrating on Catholic writers, it seems only logical to date the start of the Middle Ages with the end of the Patristic Age—that is, the close of the eighth century.

All are agreed that the Middle Ages closed somewhere at the end of the fifteenth century, contemporary with the invention of movable type. But again, given our uniquely religious focus, it is only reasonable to date the end of medieval civilization with the massive breakdown of Catholic unity ushered in by the rise of Protestantism.

There is more than a coincidence in the timing of the invention of printing and the beginnings of Protestantism. Without exception, all the leading Protestant originators appealed to the Bible, the written word of God, as the only valid source of divine revelation. Yet, the Bible had by then been in existence and use for fourteen centuries. With the discovery of print and the ability to multiply the written word, however, it became plausible to say that all a Christian believer needed in order to know the mind of God was to have a copy of the Scriptures ready at hand.

Not surprisingly, the Middle Ages had for centuries been viewed, at least in the English-speaking world, as a sterile period. But they are now coming to be regarded as one of the most creative and fruitful periods in the world's history. For a person who wants to understand Catholic Christianity, it is the age that most nearly approached the realization of Christendom as a cultural unity.

17. St. Anselm

St. Anselm (1033–1109), who was born in Aosta, Italy, ran away from home after his mother's death because of his father's severe discipline. Traveling over the Alps to France, he entered the monastic school at Bec in Normandy. Taking vows as a monk, he became prior and then abbot. His first books were written during this period, notably *Monologium* and *Proslogium*.

Both these works are elaborate proofs, based on reason, for the existence of God. In the first, he assembled a series of arguments. In the second, he gave only a single proof, called the "ontological argument." Here he reasoned that the existence of the idea of God necessarily involves the objective existence of God. He urged that, since by the very notion of God we mean "that than which nothing greater can be conceived," if we were to suppose that God did not exist, we would be involved in a contradiction, because we could conceive of a Being greater than a nonexisting God—namely, a God who existed.

Anselm's periodic visits to England finally resulted in his appointment as Archbishop of Canterbury. Defending the rights of the Church against the English king, Anselm stood firm on such issues as clerical celibacy and lay investiture. Periodic exile gave him time to write some of his best-known books, including the masterful *Why God Became Man (Cur Deus Homo)*.

Like St. Augustine, Anselm saw in faith the precondition of, and for, the right use of reason. "I believe," he declared, "so that I may understand." In other words, we have a positive duty not only to believe but to use our intelligence to its limits, to try to grasp the meaning of what we believe.

Personally a very lovable man, he yet stood firm where the right of the Church to freedom from state control was involved. His extensive writings, especially in philosophy, have gained him recognition as "the very embodiment of righteousness and mercy."

SPECIALLY RECOMMENDED
  Prayers and Meditations
  Why God Became Man and the Virgin Conception

18. *St. Bernard of Clairvaux*

When St. Bernard (1090–1153) entered the monastery of Citeaux, he brought with him thirty young noblemen of Burgundy, including his own brothers. Two years later, he was asked by the abbot, St. Stephen Harding, to start a new monastery at Clairvaux. Under his direction, Clairvaux became one of the chief centers of the Cistercian Order, which by the time of his death numbered three-hundred and fifty abbeys. Clairvaux alone had seven hundred monks. Bernard was the inspiration of this movement.

He was remarkably active for a monastic contemplative: reforming religious orders and the clergy, healing the schism caused by two claimants to the papacy, defending the faith against such intellectuals as Peter Abelard, preaching the Second Crusade, and engaging in constant correspondence—of which more than five hundred letters have been published—St. Bernard is responsible for a library of books that have gained him the epithet "the last of the Fathers of the Church."

The most famous writings of St. Bernard deal with the doctrine of perfection, of how to become holy.

On Loving God is one of the classics of Christian mysticism. He insisted that God should be loved simply and purely because He is God.

In *Grace and Free Will,* he declares, "Remove free will, and there is nothing to be saved; remove grace, and there is no means of saving."

When one of his former monks became Pope Eugenius III, Bernard composed a work of *Reflections* to instruct the pontiff on the practice of virtue.

In the same strain, his manual *On the Conduct and Office of Bishops* is a blunt apostolic warning against ambition, luxury, and the spirit of disobedience. He stresses the duty of submission to the Bishop of Rome.

Bernard's life of St. Malachy, Archbishop of Armagh and a personal friend, is a masterpiece of hagiography. It is one of the most-finished works of the Abbot of Clairvaux.

Bernard's published sermons, numbering over three hundred, are models of eloquence. Among these, the homilies on the Blessed Virgin and on the Song of Songs contain the substance of his spiritual teaching.

SPECIALLY RECOMMENDED

> *The Steps of Humility*
> *On Loving God*
> *Magnificat: Homilies in Praise of the Blessed Virgin Mary*

19. *St. Francis of Assisi*

The founder of the Franciscan Order, St. Francis of Assisi (1181/2–1226), has left us very little of his deep spirituality in writing. Yet, few men in the Church's history have more widely influenced the literature of Christianity than he.

Born at Assisi in Umbria, the son of a prosperous merchant, Pietro Bernardone, he was named after France, where his father was on business at the time his son was born. While taking part in an attack on Perugia in 1201, he was made prisoner and kept as a hostage there for a year. This experience, along with a grave illness, started the process of his conversion. Yet, four years later he was on another military expedition, this time in Apulia. In a dream, Christ called him to His service. Francis returned and gave himself to the care of the sick. In still another vision, on April 16, 1206, Christ told him to rebuild the Church at San Damiano.

The result was that Francis completely abandoned his old life. When his father first imprisoned him and then hauled him before the bishop, he gave up all his possessions. In 1209 he was joined by two companions to whom he gave as a Rule three Gospel texts (Matthew 10:9 and 20:21, and Luke 9:23). When his companions numbered eleven, he wrote a short Rule (the last Primitive Rule) and led them to Rome to obtain the approval of Pope Innocent III.

In 1212 his ideals were accepted by a noble lady of Assisi, the future St. Clare. Meanwhile, Francis was able to inspire so many followers that by 1217 they had to be organized into provinces, with ministers appointed to supervise them. Gradually, Francis' direction of the Order passed into the hands of other friars. In 1221 he founded the "tertiaries," or faithful living in the world who agreed to adopt Francis' spirit as far as they could in their state of life. The formal Rule was authorized by Honorius III in 1223. A year later, Francis received the gift of the stigmata. He died in the chapel of the Portiuncula on October 3, 1226, and was canonized less than two years later by Pope Gregory IX.

One reason for the foregoing lengthy sketch is that the most eloquent biography of St. Francis was his own personal life. Yet, he did write, and there are more of his authentic writings than most people realize.

The best one-volume work that identifies Francis' written and spoken words is *The Words of St. Francis*, by James Meyer, O.F.M. The best collection of writings by and about St. Francis is the *English Omnibus of the Sources*.

The Testament of St. Francis, his two Rules for the Friars (1209, 1223), his Rule for the Poor Clares, and his Final Rule of the Third Order encapsulate the legacy that St. Francis left to posterity. Other writings of St. Francis, including his letters, canticles, and admonitions, fill out the portrait of a man whom posterity has called "the most lovable of the saints."

What may be overlooked from the writings of the "Poverello," or Little Poor One, is his simple and total commitment to the Catholic Church. The following quotations from his First Rule illustrate the depth of his commitment:

Let Brother Francis and whoever will be head of this order promise obedience and reverence to the Lord Pope Innocent. And the rest of the brothers are bound to obey Brother Francis and his successors.

Nobody is to be received contrary to the manner and form of Holy Church.

All the Brothers shall be Catholic and live and speak like Catholics. Should anyone, however, stray from the Catholic faith and life in speech or fact, and not amend, he shall be expelled from our brotherhood.

Let my blest brothers, both clergy and laymen, confess their sins to priests of our Order. Should they not be able, let them confess to other prudent Catholic priests, firmly convinced and aware that from whichever Catholic priests they receive penance and absolution, they will be absolved beyond doubt from those sins if they take care to comply humbly and faithfully with the penance enjoined on them.

All who within the holy Catholic and apostolic faith wish to serve God and the Lord. . . . all we lesser brothers and useless servants beg and entreat them that all of us may persevere in the true faith and in repentance, for there is no other way for anybody to be saved.

One book about him has become a classic of religious biography. *The Little Flowers of St. Francis* is a delightful collection of stories and traditions about him and his companions that bear witness to the enthusiasm with which the memory of the saint was preserved. In Italy it has enjoyed a popularity second only to the Bible and the *Divine Comedia* of Dante. The *Little Flowers* has been translated into nearly every European language. There are several excellent English versions.

SPECIALLY RECOMMENDED

The Writings of St. Francis of Assisi
The Little Flowers of St. Francis

20. St. Thomas Aquinas

St. Thomas Aquinas' works constitute a library all by themselves. Although he died at the beginning of his fiftieth year (March 7, 1274), his published writings amount to over one hundred volumes and span the whole range of Catholic faith and practice. If we were to identify one outstanding feature of Aquinas, it would be his originality, for he revealed a totally new horizon on the relationship of reason and revelation.

In the centuries between St. Augustine and St. Thomas, Catholic theology was wedded to the philosophy of Plato. This might have continued except for the rise of Islam and, within Islam, of a deep thinker named Averroës (or ibn-Rushd). Although a professed follower of Mohammed, Averroës discovered in Aristotle a man whose philosophy he used to undermine the foundations of all religion, whether Moslem or Christian. Averroism, as it came to be called, penetrated into Catholic circles with devastating consequences until the advent of Thomas Aquinas.

Among Aquinas' claims to glory is the fact that he, too, discovered Aristotle, but the real Aristotle, translated from the original Greek and purified of Averroës' pantheistic interpretation. In doing this, Aquinas placed human reason at the disposal of Christian revelation in a way that had never been done before and thus made the Christian faith credible, defensible, intelligible, and what may be called growable. In other words, thanks to Aquinas, we can prove from reason that God exists, that He revealed Himself in history as Jesus Christ. We can defend the validity of what we believe by showing there are no valid reasons against the truths of faith and every cogent reason in favor of the faith. We can grasp, to some degree, the meaning of what we believe; we can "make sense" of even the mysteries of faith. And we can grow in our understanding of this faith, through prayer and lived experience, as an anticipation of that perfect vision which awaits us in eternity.

There are several ways of approaching the treasure of St. Thomas' writings. They can be used for reference; as a base for studying the whole range of Catholic belief; or to give, in capsule form, an insight into one of the world's greatest minds wrestling with the world's deepest problems and thus the world's most reasonable solution.

On the first of these levels, different writings of St. Thomas should be used. Thomas Gilby's two-volume set of hundreds of select quotations from Aquinas' philosophical and theological writings is indispensable for quick reference. The fifty-page analytical index at the end of Volume 5 of St. Thomas' *Summa Theologica* (or *Theologiae*), in the Christian Classics edition, is also a valuable reference guide.

The best source for an in-depth study of St. Thomas is his *Summa Theologica,* now available in several modern translations. Taken as a whole, the *Summa* represents the clearest, most extensive, and most systematic development of Aquinas' thought. Yet, surprisingly, his intention was to provide a merely summary introduction to the whole of theology rather than a complete and exhaustive work. In his Prologue, he points out that in theology, as in the practice of virtue, there are "beginners" and the "advanced." And the *Summa* was written for beginners, who, like children, have need of milk rather than solid food (I Corinthians 3:1). The *Summa* uses the philosophy of Aristotle in the organized explanation of doctrine and morals.

The *Summa Theologica* was not completed by St. Thomas himself, for he died before he could finish. The last part on the sacraments was finished by his close friends, who used what he had written elsewhere on the subject. One thing to be noted about the *Summa* is that its theoretical tone should not mislead us into thinking it is merely a textbook. Its practical value, as a sure guide for the spiritual life, has been recognized for centuries.

Parallel with the foregoing is the *Summa Contra Gentiles* which ranks as the most powerful apologetical work ever written. Shorter than the *Summa Theologica,* it was written to gradually lead unbelievers to the acceptance of Catholic Christianity. Aquinas first sets out those truths that can be discovered by reason alone, although they are confirmed and their meaning deepened by revelation. He then goes on to higher truths, leading finally to the Christian mysteries of the Trinity, the Incarnation, the sacraments, and eternal life.

As for a cameo insight into St. Thomas as a person, G. K. Chesterton's *St. Thomas Aquinas: The Dumb Ox* is still the most illuminating volume. "This book," says Chesterton in his introduction, "makes no pretence to be anything but a popular sketch of a great historical character who ought to be more popular. Its aim will be achieved if it leads those who have hardly even heard of St. Thomas Aquinas to read about him in better books."

It is to be hoped, though, that more people will read St. Thomas himself. He is not difficult to understand and is immensely rewarding. He shows that the Catholic faith is not only reasonable but the only reasonable philosophy of life worth following. Why? Because it reveals that two agencies are at work in the world, reality and the recognition of reality. Their meeting is like a marriage that is fruitful, for it produces results—peace on earth among men of goodwill and perfect happiness with God in a heavenly eternity.

SPECIALLY RECOMMENDED
Summa Contra Gentiles
Summa Theologiae
The Catechetical Instructions

21. *St. Bonaventure*

St. Bonaventure (1221–1274) was born Giovanni di Fidanza, in Tuscany. His vocation to the Franciscan Order is attributed to his having been cured of a serious illness in childhood by the intercession of St. Francis. He and St. Thomas Aquinas received their doctorates on the same day (October 23, 1257) as a symbol of the right of the Dominicans and Franciscans to teach theology at the University of Paris. In the same year, Bonaventure was elected minister general of his Order. He remained in office until his death, while assisting at the ecumenical council of Lyons.

A prolific writer and orator, St. Bonaventure is best known for his mysticism.

His *The Journey of the Mind to God* was written on the mountain of La Verna as a guide to souls seeking contemplation.

The Triple Way teaches how persons may come to union with God through love, by meditation, prayer of petition, and a simple looking at revealed truth.

The *Soliloquy on the Four Spiritual Exercises*, in dialogue form, is a series of questions asked by the soul, with the interior man replying, on the results of sin, the fickleness of everything in this world, death as the dawn of eternity, and the last things.

In *The Tree of Life* are forty-eight meditations on the life and death of the Savior.

Bonaventure's two books about St. Francis of Assisi have become standards. The first is a model of religious biography; the second narrates the miracles obtained by interceding with St. Francis after his death.

Although Bonaventure and Aquinas were contemporaries, they differed considerably in their thinking and style of writing. This is mainly due to Bonaventure's reliance on St. Augustine. The true Master, Jesus Christ, found his ablest interpreter in Augustine, who gave the language of wisdom and knowledge. St. Bonaventure constantly refers to Augustine in his explanation of sacred doctrine and his counsels on the spiritual life. Thus, he gave a distinctive tradition to his Order. Since the time of St. Bonaventure, Franciscan theologians have assumed they are the disciples of St. Augustine.

SPECIALLY RECOMMENDED

> *The Journey of the Mind to God*
> *The Triple Way*
> *The Mirror of the Blessed Virgin Mary*

22. Bl. Jacobus de Voragine

The author of the single most popular volume of lives of the saints, Jacobus de Voragine (1230–98), was a Dominican friar. He taught theology and Scripture, was prior in Genoa, provincial of the Lombard Province, and died after six years as Archbishop of Genoa.

During his life as friar and archbishop, he became an eloquent preacher; an organizer of help to the poor; a builder of churches, monasteries, and hospitals; and a successful administrator who maintained clerical discipline.

He is best known, however, for *The Golden Legend*, which has appeared in hundreds of editions since it was first published in Latin in 1470. The term "legend" is misleading. Its Latin original *Legenda Sanctorum*, readings about the saints, more accurately describes the contents. It came to be called "Golden" because the people of those times considered it worth its weight in gold.

The author divides the ecclesiastical year into four periods, which he then compares to the four major periods of world history—namely, a time of deviation, renovation, reconciliation, and pilgrimage. The contents of the book, in one-hundred and seventy-seven chapters, are divided into five sections: from Advent to Christmas, from Christmas to Septuagesima, from Septuagesima to Easter, from Easter to the Octave of Pentecost, from the Octave of Pentecost to Advent.

Critics of *The Golden Legend* have dismissed the book as of no value from a historical point of view, and the readers of those days, as "extremely naive." Yet, the book has had phenomenal success. It is perfectly adapted to cultivate the reader's love and respect for God, to promote devotion to His saints, and to foster a desire to follow their example.

One evidence of the book's continued popularity over the centuries is not only the number of translations and editions but the fact that it has deeply affected the prose and poetic literature of many nations. It became the inspiration for many passionals during the Middle Ages and for religious poems in later times. The American poet Longfellow wrote his own "Golden Legend" and two other poems to form a trilogy entitled *Christus.* Not only the name, but many of Longfellow's ideas are directly borrowed from Jacobus de Voragine.

SPECIALLY RECOMMENDED
The Golden Legend

23. *Dante*

If there is one writer whose life bears deeply on his writing, it is the poet Dante (1265–1321). We do not know much about his early life, except that he lost his parents as a boy and made his philosophical studies under the Dominicans. His early love for Beatrice, whose family name was Portinari, became the inspiration of his first work, *Vita nuova* (1294), written four years after her death. For the rest of his life, Beatrice remained the mysterious figure who affected his thinking. It is she who dominates his *Divine Comedy,* or *Divina Commedia.*

When Dante took sides against those who supported the temporal authority of the Pope, he was defeated. Then began a restless life as a wanderer, from one Italian city to another. It was during these years of exile, as we may call them, that he wrote his less well known work *On the Monarchy* and his famous *Divine Comedy.*

On the Monarchy explains Dante's political views. This is not unimportant to an understanding of many sections of the *Commedia.* Dante advocated a universal monarchy that would hold all the temporal power independently of, but alongside of, the Pope. The Bishop of Rome was to be the supreme spiritual authority. As Dante viewed these parallel powers, they correspond to the twofold end of man, temporal happiness here on earth and eternal happiness in the life to come.

He spent the final years of his life completing and refining the *Divina Commedia,* which assured him the reputation of being one poet who belongs to all times and to all nations. On a deeply personal level, the *Divina Commedia* must be seen as the work of a man of faith who lived most of his adult life separated from all that he held dearest on earth. Forbidden even to enter his native city of Florence, he was not to see his wife Gemma after being exiled in 1302. Of his four children, we know that his two sons, Pietro and Jacopo, and one of his daughters, Beatrice, joined their father years later.

Dante's masterpiece is a trilogy whose parts correspond to the three realms of the next world—*Inferno, Purgatorio,* and *Paradiso.* The three poems are cast in the form of a vision that describes the journey of a soul from the state of separation from God to the ultimate goal of beholding God face to face.

The poet's purpose was to convert a corrupt society to righteousness. In his own words, he sought "to remove those living in this life from the state of misery and lead them to the state of felicity." It comprises one hundred cantos, written in a verse form called terza rima, consisting of tercets in which the second line of each rhymes with the first and third lines of the next. The poet purports to describe, nearly twenty years after the event, a vision that the Lord granted him during the Jubilee Year of 1300. In the vision, he passed for seven days through Hell, Purgatory, and Paradise. During the visit, he spoke with the souls in each realm and was told what God's Providence had in store for him and for the rest of mankind.

The *Commedia* is really *On the Monarchy* in poetic form. Virgil, the poet's guide through Hell and Purgatory, represents human philosophy acting in accordance with the moral and intellectual virtues. He guides Dante by the light of natural reason from the darkness of alienation from God to the gates of the earthly Paradise. This is a state of temporal happiness achieved only after spiritual liberty is regained by the sufferings of Purgatory.

In Paradise, Beatrice, representing divine philosophy enlightened by revelation, leads Dante up through nine moving heavens of intellectual preparation, into the true Paradise, in which perfect happiness is found in the beatitude of the sight of God.

There Beatrice's place is taken by St. Bernard, who typifies loving contemplation and who commends Dante to the Blessed Virgin, at whose intercession he obtains a foretaste of the beatific vision.

The poem closes with all the human powers of knowledge and love fulfilled and consumed in the vision of understanding the Divine Essence. There the human will is joined with the Divine Will, "the love that moves the sun and the other stars."

We may say that this trilogy gives us a complete picture of Catholicism at the end of the thirteenth century, often called "the greatest of centuries." It was a Catholicism, however, that was checkered by sharp contrasts. Dante denounced ecclesiastical corruption and condemned most of the contemporary popes (including St. Celestine V) to hell. Yet, he never wavered in his faith, as testified by the part played by the Blessed Virgin from the beginning to the end of this sacred poem.

Dante's son Pietro said that if anywhere the Catholic faith were extinguished, his father would restore it. As a matter of record, the *Divina Commedia* has had incalculable influence in popularizing Catholic belief and making it at least intelligible to untold thousands who would otherwise not know anything about the Catholic Church.

SPECIALLY RECOMMENDED

The Divine Comedy

24. St. Catherine of Siena

St. Catherine (1347–80), who was born in Siena and died in Rome, was declared a Doctor of the Church by Pope Paul VI in 1970. From early childhood she had mystical experiences and practiced severe mortifications. At sixteen she joined the Dominican tertiaries, and from 1366 she had what are called "spiritual espousals." By the time she was twenty, she began to work in caring for the sick, especially those suffering from revolting diseases. Because of her extraordinary supernatural gifts, she became adviser to the rulers of Church and state. She successfully brought about the return of Pope Gregory XI from Avignon to Rome (1376) and effected the reconciliation between Florence and the Holy See. During the Great Western Schism, she favored Pope Urban VI, the true claimant to the papacy.

She authored many lengthy letters, mostly of spiritual counsel and encouragement to her associates. But her principal claim to literary fame is her *Dialogue,* a masterful treatise on growth in holiness. Composed during the last stage of her life in Rome, the *Dialogue* was dictated to her followers as her spiritual testament to the world. Its four treatises are a treasury of Catholic wisdom capsulized in the revelation of God's infinite love in making the world out of nothing and redeeming a fallen human race only because He loves his sinful creatures. In St. Catherine's language, this divine love is symbolized in the Precious Blood of Christ, shed for us on Calvary.

What is most remarkable about her *Dialogue* is not only the depth of its author's insights but the clarity of her ideas. Thus, in explaining the work of Divine Providence, she describes how a repentant heart can satisfy the offended Majesty of God both for the guilt of sin and for the penalty due to sin. God is here speaking to His supernatural child:

> I have shown you, dearest daughter, that the guilt is not punished in this finite time by any pain which is sustained merely as something painful. What I mean is that the guilt is expiated by the pain which a person endures through loving desire and contrition of heart. What expiates the guilt of sin is not the pain itself but the soul's loving desire to undo the evil committed by sin, since this loving desire has value through Christ crucified.

We may therefore say that suffering endured out of love for God is part of our expiation for sin. But the heart of expiatory suffering is not so much the actual pain as the love of an offended God, for whom the pain is either voluntarily assumed or patiently borne.

Another basic insight of the *Dialogue* is the idea of what we call "external grace." In His ordinary Providence, God uses human beings as channels of grace to others. Our practice of virtue, then, is the normal way that God communicates His supernatural light and strength to everyone whose life we touch.

St. Catherine boldly stated that "every virtue is obtained by means of your neighbor" and every virtue that our neighbor obtains comes by means of us. This mystery of faith runs deeper than the familiar value of giving others a good example. Other people are supernaturally affected by every act of virtue we make in God's friendship. And we are correspondingly influenced by every morally good action that other followers of Christ perform. In fact, this is the highest form of charity we can practice, to be instruments of divine grace to other people.

Fundamental to St. Catherine's writings is the belief that growth in sanctity is possible only through humble obedience to the Church's divinely established authority. This explains her phenomenal zeal for bringing the papacy back to Rome after its years in "exile" in France. It also explains the paradox of her outspoken language to the Bishop of Rome, even as she humbly recognized him as the Vicar of Christ on earth.

Humility of heart in submitting to God's will and humility of mind in accepting God's revealed truth are the two virtues on which St. Catherine would say finally depends our eternal destiny.

SPECIALLY RECOMMENDED

The Dialogue

25. *Geoffrey Chaucer*

The father of English poetry, Geoffrey Chaucer (c. 1340–1400) was the son of a London vintner. While working as a page to the Lady Elizabeth de Burgh, he was in the military service during Edward III's last invasion of France and was taken prisoner at Rheims. Ransomed by the king, he was employed for thirty years on various diplomatic missions. Yet, in spite of his position and pension, he seems usually to have been in poverty.

Chaucer was married to Philippa de Roet, a lady in attendance to the queen. They had at least three children, two sons and a daughter. Frequent changes in politics and the uncertainty of a regular income pressed hard on the Chaucers. Then his wife died around 1387. It was during the last and most troubled period of his life that he wrote *The Canterbury Tales,* from 1386 to 1390.

The Canterbury Tales are unintelligible without knowing why they were written. They were written to relate the conversation that went on among the Catholic pilgrims to the Shrine of Canterbury. There was the Mother Church and primatial see of all England, from 597 until the death of the last Catholic archbishop before the Reformation, Cardinal Pole, in 1558. Pilgrims went long distances to Canterbury, to worship at the tomb of St. Thomas à Becket, who was martyred by Henry II on December 29, 1170.

Chaucer left ten manuscript sections of the *Tales,* of varying size. Editors have arranged these in what they consider the original sequence. The sections are currently designated Groups A to I, with Group B having two divisions (making ten altogether).

Chaucer's Prologue explains that each of about thirty pilgrims would tell two stories on the way to Canterbury and two more on the way back. He never completed the project and never had a chance to revise it.

The journey related by Chaucer lasted five days (April 16–20) and led to the outskirts of Canterbury. At that point, the poet closed his account with an apology for what might sound profane in his story.

Chaucer's *Canterbury Tales* is unique in world literature. It gives a coherent picture of a whole nation, high and low, young and old, men and women and children, lay people and clerics, educated and illiterate, saintly and sinful, persons from great distances and from nearby, from cities and small towns, but avoids extremes. Aside from the author's remarkable clarity and his eye for sharp detail, the most remarkable thing about the *Tales* is the normality of Chaucer's characters.

But these characters have one obvious feature in common, one seldom mentioned by commentators: they all share the Catholic faith. The pilgrims come from all over Europe, some from the writings of Chaucer's contemporaries. People are described as being from far afield, even the Orient.

It was not considered the duty of a fourteenth-century story-teller to make up tales of his own. What we have in Chaucer is what really took place, embellished, of course, by the imagination of each speaker and enhanced by Chaucer's poetic style.

Through five hundred pages of vivid description and dialogue, *The Canterbury Tales* remain a thoroughly human document. It is, in fact, so human that some have vainly tried to prove that Chaucer was at least an agnostic. Nothing could be further from the truth. He is certainly unsparing in his exposure of human weakness. But his Catholic faith was unquestionable. To settle any lingering doubts in readers' minds, the author wrote his own epilogue, called "Chaucer's Retractions," in which "the Maker of this Book" takes his leave. Here Chaucer begs mercy from Christ for his sins and "especially for any translations and editings of worldly vanities." He is sorry for the books that "tend toward sin," among which he includes *The Canterbury Tales.* Yet, even as he wrote this apology, he concludes it with this statement: "Here ends the Book of the *Tales of Canterbury,* compiled by Geoffrey Chaucer, on whose soul Jesus Christ have mercy. Amen."

Catholic scholars of English literature rate him as a great genius who may not have been a very spiritual person. But he had a most orthodox grip on his Catholic Catechism.

SPECIALLY RECOMMENDED
The Canterbury Tales

26. *Thomas à Kempis*

The author of the best-loved and most widely read religious book in the world, after the Bible, was Thomas à Kempis. His family name was Thomas Hammerken. Of German descent, in 1392 he entered a small community in Utrecht, founded by Gerard Groote, which concentrated on teaching Latin and copying and illustrating manuscripts. Groote's community had just become a religious institute following the Rule of Augustine and was known as the Brethren of the Common Life. Without taking formal vows, they lived together and specialized in producing books, handwritten and later printed, for the schools.

Some years after Thomas entered the Brethren, their community was forced to leave Utrecht and move to Lunenkerk. The people of Utrecht refused to obey the Pope in his appointment of the bishop. Since the community remained loyal to Pope Martin V, it had to disband. Thomas therefore knew from experience what the religious disorders of his time meant. The Brethren were in the vanguard, defending the Catholic faith by teaching in schools all over the Netherlands and later also in Germany. But they also knew that good teachers must be deeply spiritual.

This is what makes *The Imitation of Christ* so eminently practical. The controversies of Thomas' age became the seedbed of the revolution that was to follow in the next century. He rose above these controversies by stressing what is fundamental in Christianity—namely, the interior life of union with God, practiced by accepting the teachings of Christ, acknowledging one's own weaknesses and sins, resisting temptations with the help of God's grace, seeing His Providence in all the events of our lives, and receiving the Holy Eucharist with sincere devotion as the most powerful means we have on earth to remain faithful in the following of Christ.

Although originally written by a monk for monks, the *Imitation* has become the common possession of believers in every state of life. The reason is that it touches on all the essentials of Christian spirituality, which affect men and women in the world as much as persons in the cloister.

The book is divided into four parts. Part One contains twenty-five general counsels, beginning with an exhortation to follow Christ and ending with a plea to amend our lives by looking first to the health of our souls. Part Two has twelve explanations of such topics as "Inward Conversation," "The Love of Jesus Above All Things," "The Small Number of Lovers of the Cross," and "How Profitable Is Patience in Adversity." Part Three is the longest, with fifty-nine subjects dealt with under the rubric "The Inward Speaking of Christ to a Faithful Soul." The last part is a series of eighteen reflections, mainly on the Sacrament of the Altar.

It is impossible to exaggerate the value of *The Imitation of Christ* in shaping the spiritual life, not only in the West but also in the Orient. There are scores of English versions now in print. Among these the most accurate and satisfactory from a literary viewpoint are those based on the translation of Richard Whitford, printed in 1530. Whitford and St. Thomas More were good friends.

Regardless of the translation, however, *The Imitation of Christ* should be read, if only for a few minutes, every day. Thomas à Kempis set in motion what may justly be called modern Catholic spirituality. Christ is seen as the example we are to follow. By imitating His virtues as Man, we become more and more like Jesus, the Living God in human form.

SPECIALLY RECOMMENDED
   The Imitation of Christ

27. St. Catherine of Genoa

Married at the age of sixteen, St. Catherine of Genoa (1447–1510) found her husband, Giuliano Adorno, to be shiftless, unfaithful, and a spendthrift. After ten years of this, she became a Franciscan tertiary and converted her husband.

Catherine and Giuliano agreed to live a continent life together. They devoted themselves to working among the sick poor in the Great Hospital of Genoa. During the plague of 1493, she spent herself in the service of the plague-stricken and in organizing relief. She caught the plague when she impulsively kissed a dying man. Catherine recovered, but her husband died in 1497.

Her intense love of God cleansed her of every taint of self-seeking. Her fasts were extraordinary, not eating any solid food for twenty-three Advents and twenty-two Lents, yet active in serving others all the while.

Her mystical experiences were frequent and intense. She became the center of a small following of persons who remembered and recorded the profound sayings that she spoke as the result of her ecstasies. She has thus become one of the Church's outstanding teachers of mystical theology. All the while, she organized charitable works among the sick and poor, with the help of her spiritual counselors, Don Carrenzio and Don Marabotto, and her maid, Argentina. She also took care of her husband's illegitimate daughter, Thebia. Catherine's last years were difficult, as she suffered intense physical and spiritual pain and had to abandon the active apostolate.

After her death, her disciples put together a life and collection of her sayings, under the title of *Life and Doctrine.* In time, two sections of this work were published separately. One section, *Dialogue Between the Soul and Body,* was no doubt inspired by Catherine's experiences but is believed to have been actually composed by the daughter (herself a mystic) of one of Catherine's collaborators, Ettore Vernanza.

Certainly authentic is Catherine's *Treatise on Purgatory,* the second section of her original life and sayings. The state of the departed souls is seen in the light of its earthly counterpart—the purgatory of consuming love. This work is one of the classic writings on the Church Suffering.

"The souls in Purgatory," she wrote, "see all things, not in themselves, nor by themselves, but as they are in God, on whom they are more intent than on their own sufferings. . . . For the least vision they have of God overbalances all woes and all joys that can be conceived. Yet their Joy in God does by no means abate their pain . . . this process of purification to which I see the souls in Purgatory subjected, I feel within myself."

One aspect of Catherine's life that deserves emphasis is that for almost twenty-five years, though often going to confession, she was unable to open her heart for direction to anyone. It was not until the last part of her life that Father Marabotto was appointed her spiritual guide. To him she fully explained her states, past and present, and it was he who first compiled the memoirs on which all later biographies were based.

Also worth noting is the process of investigation before she was raised to the honors of the altar. The Holy Office, which examined her writings, pronounced that their depth and solidity of doctrine were such that, by themselves, they would be enough to prove her sanctity.

SPECIALLY RECOMMENDED

Treatise on Purgatory

The Catholic Reformation

"The Catholic Reformation" refers to the spontaneous resurgence of Catholic thought and spirituality that occurred from the sixteenth through the eighteenth century. During these three hundred years, the Catholic Church lost whole nations by their separation from the papacy. But she also experienced an unprecedented renewal in every aspect of divine faith, of moral fervor and personal sanctity, of religious education and missionary zeal, and of organized Christian charity in the practice of the corporal and spiritual works of mercy.

Men like Sts. Thomas More and Francis de Sales and women like Sts. Teresa of Avila and Margaret Mary were an integral part of the Church's realization that where sin abounded, there grace was even more abundant. The paganizing Renaissance of the late fifteenth century was characterized by a prodigious intellectual activity accompanied by widespread moral decay.

Under the guidance of the Holy Spirit, there arose such leaders in Catholic thought and piety as Christianity had not known since apostolic times and certainly not since saints like Francis of Assisi and Catherine of Siena had reformed the secularized immorality in the Church of their day.

There was such a litany of authors from which to choose for the Lifetime Reading Plan that some selective criterion had to be applied. I chose by preference those writers who had been founders of religious institutes, such as St. Ignatius; those who had used the art of print to reach the masses, like St. Francis de Sales; or those who had left a treasury of spiritual wisdom in writing, like St. Teresa of Ávila.

The three centuries of the Catholic Reformation were prolific in published works on every aspect of human life and worship. The bibliography of those books would amount to several thousand titles. Only about a dozen authors are here included, not because a hundred more could not be added but because I wanted to leave room in the Reading Plan for the final period, the modern age.

28. *St. Thomas More*

Lord chancellor of England and martyr for the faith, St. Thomas More (1478–1535) is one of the great writers of English literature. As a member of Archbishop John Morton's household at the age of thirteen, he early studied the Greek and Latin classics, and his lifelong friendship with Erasmus helped make him a master of languages. In rapid succession, he finished his studies in civil law, entered Parliament, married, and in 1529 was appointed by Henry VIII to succeed Thomas Wolsey as chancellor.

In 1516 he published *Utopia,* which remains one of the classics of the Renaissance. The book describes the fictitious travels of a certain Raphael Hythlodaye, who, in the course of a voyage to the newly discovered America, was left behind near Cape Frio. Then he wandered until he chanced to reach the Island of Utopia (Greek *ou,* "not," plus *topos,* "place"), where he found an ideal constitution in operation. The whole work is an exercise in fertile imagination with much clever satire on the world in which Thomas More lived. But real persons like Peter Giles, Cardinal Morton, and Thomas More himself engage in conversation with Hytholodaye. As a result, the work takes on such an air of reality that some critics have denounced it as a complete gospel of socialism. (Significantly, Pope Pius IX, in his encyclical condemning Communism, called it "Utopian Messianism.")

As the ideas of the Protestant Reformation penetrated England, Thomas More wrote a series of *Dialogues* on such varied subjects as the veneration of images and relics, praying to the saints, and going on pilgrimage. He wrote a number of lengthy treatises in defense of the Catholic faith. But his best-known spiritual work is *A Dialogue of Comfort Against Tribulation*, which he wrote during the fifteen months of his imprisonment in the Tower of London, awaiting execution. During this confinement, More wrote other works on prayer, penance, and spiritual devotion.

Accused of high treason because he opposed Henry VIII's claims against the Pope as spiritual head of the Church in England, Thomas More was beheaded on Tower Hill on July 6, 1535. This was just two weeks after St. John Fisher was executed for the same reason, as the only bishop in England who stood against Henry VIII to defend the papal primacy.

Three features stand out in the writings of Thomas More: strong convictions about the natural law, which is accessible to human reason; the clear expression of ideas, with no ambiguity of thought; and loyalty to the Catholic Church and her visible head on earth, the Bishop of Rome.

In reading More, we must of course distinguish between his *Utopia* and large correspondence with the humanists of his day, on the one hand, and, on the other, the dedicated Catholic defending his faith and drawing on its resources to strengthen himself (and others) in time of trial and persecution.

Also noteworthy is the great prudence that More showed in dealing with a monarch who was bent on dissolving his valid marriage with Catherine of Aragon. Thomas More kept his silence about his religious convictions, except to refuse to acknowledge Henry as the head of the Church in England. When a man perjured and falsely charged that the former chancellor had indeed denounced Henry's pretensions, Thomas More was finally condemned to death.

Only then did he make what has become a historic profession of faith in the Roman primacy: "For as much as . . . this indictment is grounded upon an act of Parliament directly repugnant to the laws of God and His Holy Church, the supreme government of which . . . may no temporal prince presume by any law to take upon him, as rightfully belonging to the See of Rome, a spiritual pre-eminence by the mouth of our Saviour Himself . . . only to St. Peter and his successor Bishops of the same See . . . it is therefore, in law, amongst Christian men, insufficient to charge any Christian man."

As he was about to be beheaded, he declared, "I die . . . the King's good servant, but God's first." Among the many biographies of St. Thomas More, two outstanding ones are by T. E. Bridgett and E. E. Reynolds.

SPECIALLY RECOMMENDED

A Dialogue of Comfort Against Tribulation
Thomas More's Prayerbook
Utopia

29. St. Ignatius Loyola

The author of the *Spiritual Exercises*, St. Ignatius Loyola (1491–1556), spent over thirty years composing and revising his masterpiece. Converted from a life of dissipation at the age of thirty, he spent a year (1522–23) in a cave at Manresa, in Catalonia, where he prayed, did severe penance, and began writing down his insights. His hope was that what the Holy Spirit told him would also be useful to others.

He went back to school to prepare himself for the priesthood and eventually founded the Society of Jesus. All the future members of the Society, including St. Francis Xavier, were formed by the *Spiritual Exercises*.

Since 1540, when the Jesuits were finally approved by the Pope (and the Council of Trent), the *Exercises* has become the basic structure for retreats for millions of the faithful in every state of life.

The *Exercises* opens with a plain statement of its meaning and purpose:

This expression, "Spiritual Exercises," embraces every method of examination of conscience, of meditation, of contemplation, of vocal and mental prayer, and of other spiritual activity. . . . For just as strolling, walking, and running are bodily exercises, so spiritual exercises are methods of preparing and disposing the soul to free itself of all inordinate attachments, and after accomplishing this, of seeking and discovering the Divine Will regarding the disposition of one's life, and thus insuring the salvation of his soul.

The one who is giving instruction in the method and procedure of meditation or contemplation should be explicit in stating the subject matter for the contemplation or meditation. He should limit himself to a brief summary statement of its principal points; for then the one who is making the contemplation, by reviewing the true essentials of the subject, and by personal reflection and reasoning, may find something that will make it a little more meaningful for him or touch him more deeply. This may happen as a result of his own reasoning or through the enlightenment of his understanding by Divine grace.

As this introduction by St. Ignatius makes clear, the *Spiritual Exercises* is not a book to be merely read. Nor is it simply a manual for prayer. It is a carefully organized program for in-depth spiritual assessment and communication with God. Its purpose is conversion: to change a person from a life of sin to the practice of virtue, to decide on one's state of life according to the will of God, or always to improve one's dedication to the service of Christ in selfless labor for the spiritual welfare of others.

Within the book are several sets of rules that can only be described as the work of spiritual genius. Two sets of these rules are especially valuable—namely, for the "Discernment of Spirits" and for "Thinking with the Church."

In the "Rules for the Discernment of Spirits," St. Ignatius provides directives, born of personal experience, for distinguishing between true inspirations of the Holy Spirit and seductive instigations of the evil spirit. All told there are twenty-two rules covering that many different situations in which people who are serious about their following of Christ may have to identify the divine or the demonic source of their thoughts and desires.

In the "Rules for Thinking with the Church," St. Ignatius gives eighteen norms for having "the proper attitude of mind in the Church Militant." The first and last of these Rules are typical of the rest:

> Putting aside all private judgment, we should keep our minds prepared and ready to obey promptly and in all things the true spouse of Christ our Lord, our Holy Mother, the hierarchical Church . . .
>
> Although the generous service of God for motives of pure love should be most highly esteemed, we should praise highly the fear of His Divine Majesty, for filial fear and even servile fear are pious and most holy things. When one cannot attain anything better or more useful, this fear is of great help in rising from mortal sin, and after this first step one easily advances in filial fear which is wholly acceptable and pleasing to God our Lord, since it is inseparable from Divine Love.

Centuries after the *Spiritual Exercises* was written, it is still what Pope Pius XI called "a most wise and universal code of laws for the direction of souls in the way of salvation and perfection . . . showing the way to secure amendment of morals and . . . the summit of the spiritual life."

SPECIALLY RECOMMENDED
> *Spiritual Exercises*
> *Letters and Instructions*
> *Autobiography*

30. St. Teresa of Ávila

Teresa Sánchez de Cepeda y Ahumada was born near Ávila, Spain, on March 28, 1515. She was reared in a strictly religious family; her mother died when Teresa was thirteen. At twenty-one, Teresa entered the Carmelite convent in Avila, but left it when her health broke down; she reentered it and then for fifteen years lived a very tepid spiritual life, as she herself admitted. At forty-one, she had a second conversion and began to experience mystical prayer, with visions and voices. By 1558, she decided to reform what she considered the unrecollected life of her own community of the Incarnation. She died at Alba de Tormes, Spain, in 1582.

Encouraged by the Franciscan St. Peter of Alcántara; the Jesuit St. Francis Borgia; the Dominican Fr. Bannez; and her own superior, Fr. Gratian, she established sixteen foundations of reformed Carmelite nuns, and with St. John of the Cross contributed to a Carmelite reform among the monasteries of men.

Under obedience to her confessors, she wrote a series of books that led to her declaration as a Doctor of the Church. She may also rightly be called the Doctor of Prayer.

Four of her books have become classics in spiritual literature. It is recommended that they be read in sequence—namely her autobiography; then *The Book of the Foundations*, in which she relates the history of all her houses; *The Way of Perfection*, where she gives directives to her own religious and to others; and finally her masterpiece, *The Interior Castle*. In this crowning work of her writing career, Teresa again explains the degrees of prayer, which she compares to the seven mansions of a castle. The "castle" is the soul, in which dwells the Holy Trinity. In the first three mansions, God dwells in the soul of a person engaged in active prayer, where the human will is mainly at work; in the last four mansions, God is present with increasing intimacy and the soul is more passive, though still cooperating, under the influence of divine grace. In the seventh mansion takes place what Teresa calls the "transforming union," which she personally experienced after years of opposition from others and interior trials from God.

The great value of reading Teresa of Ávila is her rare combination of spiritual depth and down-to-earth practicality. She never lectures like a professor but rather guides and instructs like a mother.

Living in an age of the Church's history when freedom of the human will was challenged, when obedience to ecclesiastical authority and especially to the Bishop of Rome was widely rejected, and when the very nature of man was being redefined as inherently corrupt, Teresa gave all future generations proof from personal experience that we are indeed free human beings, that obedience to the Church is of the essence of happiness, and that God literally transforms weak human beings into giants of moral strength, if only they cooperate with His grace.

Teresa is a valuable corrective to those who might attach undue importance to mystical phenomena, like revelations, mysteries, and supernatural locutions. She describes these phenomena from personal experience. But she is also careful to distinguish between the phenomena and the interior virtue of a person. Ecstasies, she insists, are no guarantee of sanctity! And sanctity is quite compatible with prayer that shows no signs of extraordinary gifts from God.

St. Teresa is also a constant reminder that we are only as pleasing to God as we practice that most fundamental virtue of humility. "I was once wondering," she writes in *The Interior Castle*, "why Our Lord so dearly loved this virtue of humility. All of a sudden—without my having previously thought of it—the following reason came to my mind. It is because God is Sovereign in Truth. To be humble is to walk in truth. For it is absolutely true to say that we have no good thing in ourselves, but only misery and nothingness. Anyone who fails to understand this is walking in falsehood."

Good English translations of Teresa of Ávila are readily available. Moreover, there are numerous commentaries on her writings, and whole volumes of studies of her spirituality. She tends to digress and sometimes goes into details that seem unrelated to the immediate subject of her writing. But she is never boring. She is natural, vivacious, and precise in the extreme. She is one of the most rewarding of writers to read. She makes the faith come alive and is living evidence of the marvels that God works in souls, including our own, if only we believe what Christ once told Teresa: "Ah, daughter, how few truly love me! If they did, I would not conceal my secrets from them."

SPECIALLY RECOMMENDED

The Life of St. Teresa (autobiography)
The Way of Perfection
The Interior Castle

31. *St. John of the Cross*

The interior life of St. John of the Cross (1542–91) cannot be understood without some knowledge of his exterior life. Biographers commonly divide his life into three periods: the time of preparation, when he was waiting for supernatural guidance; the period of spiritual growth once he knew God's will with regard to him; and the final period of activity, covered by his writings and reform of the Carmelite friars.

Not much is known about the first stage, except that St. John was born Juan de Yepes y Álvarez in Old Castile of a noble but impoverished family. In his youth he did various manual jobs like weaving and carpentry. Then he studied with the Jesuits of Medina and soon after joined the Carmelite friars in that town. Theology studies at Salamanca prepared him for ordination to the priesthood in 1567.

He then met St. Teresa of Ávila, who confided to him her plan of reforming the Carmelite nuns. John assured her he wanted to do the same for the friars. For nine years he held a number of important posts in the Order. Then, in 1577, he was taken from Toledo during the night of December 3 and thrown into a monastic prison by order of the Carmelite general, who favored a mitigated observance of the Rule. The physical and moral sufferings he endured, joined with spiritual trials, purified his soul and brought him to the transforming union with Christ. While in prison, he wrote the inspiring verses of the canticle on which he comments in several of his works.

After nine months he escaped from the prison and began setting up a reformed province. Successively rector, prior, and vicar-provincial, John never rose to prominence among his own reformed Carmelites. In fact, he died in disgrace in an Andalusian monastery. His constant prayer "to suffer and be despised" was answered literally. His writings known only among the Carmelites until they were published in 1618. Canonized in 1726, he was proclaimed a Doctor of the Church in 1926.

His main works are *Ascent of Mount Carmel* and *Dark Night of the Soul.* Two other writings, *A Spiritual Canticle* and *The Living Flame of Love,* are commentaries on two poems by St. John.

Both *Ascent* and *Dark Night* deal with the purification of the soul by the "night of the senses." Once detached from all sensible devotion, the soul is further spiritualized by divine grace. This normally involves intense sufferings to dispose the soul for the transforming union.

Ascent of Mount Carmel deals mainly with the active purification of the soul. This means that a person must actively practice mortification of the passions of the body and the mind. *Dark Night* concentrates on passive purification, where God sends trials, again to the senses and to the mind. But the purpose is the same: to further detach a person from creatures and turn the soul to God.

The state of a transformed soul is described in *The Living Flame* as a lyric commentary on four stanzas of verse. First, the soul expresses a strong desire for eternal union with God, and then are described the effects of this love, the tokens of love given to the well-beloved, and the indescribable rewards that God gives to souls united with Him.

A Spiritual Canticle was partly written during his imprisonment and treats of the mystical union of a soul with God—first the dispositions required, then the "spiritual espousals," and finally the union itself or the spiritual marriage.

Reading St. John of the Cross requires above all a sympathetic appreciation of his underlying principle of faith. He builds on the premise that the more generously we respond to God's grace, the more God will bless us in this life with a foretaste of the perfect happiness of heaven.

SPECIALLY RECOMMENDED

Ascent of Mount Carmel
Dark Night of the Soul

32. *Miguel de Cervantes Saavedra*

Cervantes, as he is commonly known, was born at Alcalá de Henares, Spain, in 1547 and died at Madrid in 1616. The story of his own life is as interesting as the most exciting novels of his writing career.

His biography covers a considerable stay in the suite of Cardinal Aquaviva in Italy; fighting in the famous battle of Lepanto (1571); where he suffered a wound in his hand from which he never recovered; fighting against the Moslems in North Africa; capture by pirates and captivity in Algiers; ransom and release to Constantinople; and his return to Spain.

Finally settled in Spain, Cervantes began a literary career that has few parallels in modern times for sheer output of production and lasting merit. His plays *El trato de Argel* and *El cerco de Numancia* are less well-known. More familiar are his twelve *Exemplary Novels*.

His chief claim to fame rests on the novel *Don Quixote*. It was frankly written to ridicule the romances of chivalry and to destroy the popularity of a literature that for more than a century had dominated the European literary scene. He succeeded so well that Byron could later write, "Cervantes smiled Spain's chivalry away, and therefore have his volumes done much harm."

Actually the books of chivalry, for all their idealism, created a sense of surrealism that was criticized by theologians and mystics as a dream world that once served a useful purpose in upholding knighthood and gallantry but was no longer a match for the stark reality of movements like the Protestant revolution.

The lasting value of *Don Quixote* is not to be found in its laying to rest the dream world of medieval chivalry. It is rather in the fact that Cervantes wrote a novel that can be rightly called a social document of the first order. It has not been surpassed as a literary classic in which the main interest is found in the complementary characters of Don Quixote and his squire, Sancho Panza. The creator of this contrast vividly portrays the behavior of people in a world of naturalism, where the ideals of the past enjoy but scanty respect.

Scholars have attempted to show that Cervantes had in mind certain individuals whom he intended to satirize. This is most unlikely. Without fully realizing what he was doing, Cervantes was depicting the rise of a new civilization—the modern world of flesh and individualism and the pursuit of worldly gain. But he also showed how there can be no continuity of a culture without preserving a deep devotion to its spiritual past, here the heritage of the Catholic faith.

This is brought out dramatically in the closing pages of *Don Quixote,* which describe the old knight's final hours and could not be more thoroughly religious in content and more sincerely repentant in tone:

> They looked at one another in amazement at Don Quixote's words and, though in doubt, were inclined to believe him. And one of the signs by which they concluded that he was dying was the ease with which he changed from mad to sane; for he said much more in the vein of his last utterances, so well spoken, so Christian and so connected, that they were finally resolved of all their doubts and convinced that his mind was sound. The priest made everyone leave the room, remained alone with him and confessed him. The Bachelor went for the clerk, and in a short time came back with him and with Sancho Panza, who had had news from Carrasco of his master's state and, finding the housekeeper and the niece in tears, began to blubber and weep himself. When the confession was ended the priest came out, saying: "Truly he is dying and truly he is sane, Alonso Quixano the Good. We had better go in so that he can make his will." This news gave a terrible start to the brimming eyes of his housekeeper, his niece and his good squire, Sancho Panza, causing them to break out into fresh tears and groans. For in truth, as has been said before, whether he was plain Alonso Quixano the Good, or Don Quixote de la Mancha, he was always of an amiable disposition and kind in his behavior, so that he was well beloved, not only by his own household but by everyone who knew him.

Among the items of Don Quixote's will is the closing one about his sorrow for the "many gross absurdities" he gave rise to. The confession is most revealing, especially since it makes "Master Priest" the first executor of Cervantes' will.

Item, I beseech the said gentlemen, my executors, that if by good fortune they should come to know the alleged author of a history circulating hereabouts under the title of "The Second Part of the Exploits of Don Quixote de la Mancha," they shall beg him on my behalf, with the greatest earnestness, to forgive the occasion I unwittingly gave him of publishing so many gross absurdities as are therein written; for I quit this life with an uneasy conscience at having given him an excuse for writing them.

In spite of his sometimes outspoken language about clerics, Cervantes always had a deep personal respect for the clergy, a childlike love of the Blessed Virgin, and a deep Catholic faith that even his most severe critics have been ready to recognize.

SPECIALLY RECOMMENDED
   Don Quixote

33. *St. Robert Bellarmine*

St. Robert Bellarmine (1542–1621) is among those great writers whose publications are almost unavailable in English. Nephew of Pope Marcellus II, Bellarmine was successively Jesuit priest, theologian, papal diplomat, bishop, and cardinal.

His small *Catechism* of the Catholic faith has been the most widely used in the history of the Church. For years, he taught at the Roman College, where he produced his major work, the many volumes of *Disputations*. So thorough was Bellarmine's defense of the Catholic faith that his contemporaries suspected a syndicate of scholars was responsible for the learned books published under his name.

Declared a Doctor of the Church by Pope Pius XI in 1931, Bellarmine's reputation in the English-speaking world is mainly due to the masterful two-volume biography by James Brodrick. But his writings deserve to be better known. His teaching *Disputations* were one of the main theological sources used by the First Vatican Council in drafting its definition of papal infallibility.

One feature of Bellarmine's scholarly writing is the extensive verbatim quotations from Luther, Calvin, Zwingli, and other

Protestant leaders that St. Robert used not only to defend Catholic doctrine but to clarify the whole spectrum of the Church's thinking.

Historians of political science trace to Bellarmine some of the basic principles of our American form of government. His ideas on the relationship of Church and state, though much refined since his day, gave strong impetus to the clear distinction between the spiritual authority of the Church and the temporal power of the state.

Besides his formal writing in positive theology, Bellarmine wrote some admirable works on the spiritual life. A number of these have been translated into English.

In *The Ascent of the Mind to God*, Bellarmine explains what we mean by the "depth" of God's practical wisdom, which consists in His Providence, predestination, and final judgment. Certain conclusions follow from this:

> We can gather that divine providence is worthy of all admiration from the fact that all things are under His immediate governance and are directed by Him to their proper ends. "He has equally care of all," says the Wise Man, that is, with no exception God looks after everything, so that not even a sparrow falls to the ground without the providence of God, as our Savior says.
>
> If you could count all the things that are in the whole universe you might have some slight idea of the vastness of God's wisdom that rules and directs each and every single thing. The Holy Father can rule the entire Christian world with a providence that is general, but not with a special providence that extends to each Christian; he has to call on a host of bishops to help him carry on the work of government.
>
> But God cares for each just as well as He cares for all. A sparrow is not forgotten by God. The hairs of our heads are numbered, and if any of these are not to perish, God's providence must be ever watchful over us. The young ravens may be abandoned by their parents, but not by God.
>
> How securely, O my soul, may you not rest in the bosom of so mighty a Father, even in the deepest darkness! No matter if you are surrounded by ravenous lions and dragons and be in the midst of countless legions of evil spirits, hold all the more fast to Him with true love, holy fear, unshakeable confidence and firm faith.

There was a rugged realism about Bellarmine's spirituality. In an age when so many denied human freedom and the need for cooperation with divine grace, he steered a clear middle course. No one can be saved without the grace of God, but God wants us to respond to the invitations of His love.

Yes, Catholics do believe in predestination, but a predestination whereby God eternally foresees how we would use our free will. Hence the admonition, "Strive, O my soul, by good works to ensure your vocation and your election." In other words, our destiny certainly depends on God but also mysteriously on us.

SPECIALLY RECOMMENDED

The Ascent of the Mind to God
The Art of Dying Well

34. *St. Francis de Sales*

Along with Teresa of Ávila and John of the Cross, St. Francis de Sales (1567–1622) is the great doctor of the spiritual life in the modern world. But unlike them, he allowed—emphatically— that the laity was capable of reaching high sanctity while remaining in the world.

Born at the Château de Sales at Thorens in Savoy and educated in Annecy, Paris, and Padua, he gave up the brilliant prospects of a legal career to embrace the priesthood. By the end of the sixteenth century, Calvinism had deeply penetrated France and the Low Countries. One result was that not a few people became infected with the virus of believing that God had eternally predestined some people for heaven and others for hell, irrespective of their own resisting or cooperating with God's grace. The young Francis was, for a time, obsessed with the idea that he was destined to become an eternal example of divine justice. He was near despair in thinking he was going to hell. He was freed from this obsession only when he became convinced that man does have a free will, which has the awful power of saying yes or no, even to the Almighty. This experience contributed greatly to shaping his whole future life. It gave his spirituality a strong human emphasis. Mysteriously, but truly, we *do* contribute to our destiny, both here and hereafter.

His two best-known books are the *Introduction to the Devout Life*

(1608) and the *Treatise on the Love of God* (1616). The *Treatise on the Love of God* is unparalleled for its depth of insight and originality of ideas. In twelve books, Francis deals first with the principles of divine love and then with their practical application. The core of the book is his testament of prayer, which, he says, is the principal means of attaining the love of God and the most effective way of growing in this love. No one has improved on his description of the true love of God and how it can give rise to extreme joy and intense pain at the same time:

All the terms of love are drawn from the resemblance there is between the affections of the mind and the emotions of the body. Grief, fear, hope, hatred, and the rest of the affections of the soul, only enter the heart when love draws them after it. We do not hate evil except because it is contrary to the good that we love.

This heart in love with its God, desiring infinitely to love, sees, notwithstanding, that it can neither love nor desire sufficiently. And this desire which cannot come to effect is as a dart in the side of a noble spirit; yet the pain which proceeds from it is welcome, because whosoever desires earnestly to love, loves also earnestly to desire, and would esteem himself the most miserable man in the universe, if he did not continually desire to love that which is so sovereignly worthy of love. Desiring to love, he receives pain; but loving to desire, he receives joy.

Better known is the *Introduction to the Devout Life*. It has made its author the greatest master of the spiritual life in the modern world. The origins of Salesian spirituality are found in the *Spiritual Exercises* of St. Ignatius, which first shaped the character of St. Francis' practical approach to the spiritual life. His own training in civil law led him to stress the need to have some form and structure in one's practice of virtue and dealings with God. At the same time, he warned against too much reliance on method or rigid form.

St. Francis de Sales is the great master of the "theology of temptations." His awareness of the role of human freedom in the pursuit of sanctity gives him a sure guide for steering between the error of pessimism (as we experience our sinful impulses) and the heresy of fatalism (by blaming God for our sins):

Even supposing that temptation to some particular sin were to last our whole life, it would not render us odious in the sight of God so long as we neither took pleasure therein, nor yielded our consent; and that, because in temptation we are not active but passive; and whereas we take no delight therein, neither can we partake of any guilt.

Even though our whole soul and body are disturbed, we still persevere in the resolution not to consent to sin or to temptation. The attraction which gratifies the outer man, displeases the inner man. And although it surrounds our will, it has not effected an entrance into it. We see that this attraction is involuntary and therefore not sinful.

St. Francis de Sales directed St. Jane Frances de Chantal and, with her, founded the Visitation Order of nuns in 1610. His published conferences to the community bring out the personal dimension of his spirituality. What he mainly stressed was not austerity but love, or what he called "the fervor of charity and the strength of a very intimate devotion."

SPECIALLY RECOMMENDED
  Introduction to the Devout Life
  Treatise on the Love of God

35. *Richard Crashaw*

The man who is known as "preeminently the English poet of the Counter-Reformation" was born in London and died in Loretto, Italy. Richard Crashaw (1613–49) entered the Catholic Church in 1645, but his Catholic sympathies go back to his early days.

Perhaps the single greatest influence on his life was St. Teresa of Ávila. Her canonization in 1622 created a large following outside of Catholic circles. "When the author was yet among Protestants," Crashaw wrote in the poem "An Apology for the Foregoing," her virtues moved him to unstinted admiration. He addressed her by saying, "Thine own dear bookes are guilty. For from thence I learnt to know that love is eloquence." His best-known poem is the "Hymn to St. Theresa." It and its sequel, "The Flaming Heart," express Crashaw's outlook, which he describes as "the Quintessence of Phantasie and discourse center'd in Heaven . . . the very Outgoings of the Soul."

It is not surprising that Crashaw would have strong admirers and equally strong critics. His admirers say that his "passionate outbursts with their flaming brilliancy and their quick-moving lines are hard to parallel in the language." His critics claim that "Crashaw more often gives positive offense by an outrageous conceit, by gaudy color, by cloying sweetness, or by straining an idea which has him squeezed dry."

The variant judgments on Crashaw are mainly due to his outspoken and very sensitive profession of Catholic beliefs long before he formally entered the Church. For this reason, it is true to say that Crashaw appeals mainly to those who fully sympathize with his religious sentiments and who are therefore not turned away by his baroque inspiration and "dazzling spray of associated images."

SPECIALLY RECOMMENDED
Poems

36. St. Margaret Mary Alacoque

The person most responsible for the modern devotion to the Sacred Heart was a cloistered nun. St. Margaret Mary (1647–90) was born in L'Hautecour, France, and died as a member of the Visitation Order at Paray-le-Monial. Bedridden as a child for five years, she had mystical experiences from the time she was twenty.

In 1675 she was first directed by Our Lord to promote devotion to His Sacred Heart. Basic to this devotion is the mystery of God's infinite love, especially as shown in His becoming man and dying on the Cross for the salvation of the whole human race.

She encountered great opposition, especially from the Jansenists. They held that Christ died only for the predestined, that we cannot resist divine grace, and that Holy Communion is to be received only rarely, by those who are completely detached from creatures. As a result, Margaret Mary's alleged revelations were dismissed as illusions. When Bl. Claude de la Colombière became confessor to the nuns at Paray, he approved her claims as truly supernatural experiences and helped to spread the devotion.

Her published writings are her *Autobiography* and her *Letters.* They reveal a soul that was extraordinarily tried by Providence, not excluding her being considered deluded by her fellow religious.

An excellent introduction to her spirituality is *Thoughts and Sayings of St. Margaret Mary,* compiled and translated by the Sisters of the Visitation. They are arranged for every day of the year. The following quotations from the first five days of January make clear how the saint stressed our free cooperation with the will of God:

> If you are faithful to do the Will of God in time, yours shall be accomplished throughout eternity. . . .
>
> You know that there is no middle course, and that it is a question of being saved or lost for all eternity. It depends on us: either we may choose to love God eternally with the Saints in heaven after we have done violence to self here below by mortifying and crucifying ourselves, as they did, or else renounce their happiness by giving to nature all for which it craves. . . .
>
> If you wish to regain the good graces of our Lord Jesus Christ, you must no longer commit any voluntary fault, otherwise you will seek for them in vain.

So the refrain runs through everything she wrote. On these terms, devotion to the Sacred Heart is our voluntary response of love to the imitation of God's love shown by the constant inspirations of His grace.

SPECIALLY RECOMMENDED

Autobiography

37. St. Louis Grignion de Montfort

St. Louis Marie Grignion de Montfort (1673–1716) was a popular missionary; he was educated at the Jesuit College of Rennes and, after ordination, devoted himself to a life of poverty and prayer. While chaplain at a hospital in Poitiers, he founded the Daughters of Wisdom, a community for nursing the sick and teaching poor children. Then, while giving missions in the countryside, he found his true vocation and established in 1705 the Company of Mary, a congregation of missionaries. Opposition from the Jansenists caused him much sorrow, and at his early death the two foundations he had established were almost extinct. They have since become flourishing religious institutes.

He is best known for his treatise *True Devotion to Mary* (or *True Devotion to the Blessed Virgin*). This small work was not discovered until 1842, but is certainly authentic and was first translated into English by Father Faber in 1862. Known to Cardinal Newman, it influenced the Marian poetry of Gerard Manley Hopkins and was fully examined and approved by the Holy See before St. Louis was beatified in 1888.

St. Louis relates his true devotion to Mary with her Divine Maternity. It is because she was, and remains, the Mother of God that she deserves to be honored, invoked and imitated beyond all other human persons. Except for her, we would not have Him. And because of her, we can best understand Him.

The logic of this Marian devotee is expressed in the opening words of his short classic. "All our perfection," he says, "consists in being confirmed, united and consecrated to Jesus Christ; and therefore the most perfect of all devotions is, without any doubt, that which most perfectly conforms, unites and consecrates us to Jesus Christ."

Christ is the goal and end of all our striving for perfection on earth. And the most effective way of reaching perfection is through Mary as the divinely chosen means. Thus, conformity to Mary's wishes leads to conformity with the will of her Divine Son. She knows best what He wants us to do. Provided we "do whatever He tells you," as she told the servants at Cana, He will in turn provide for everything we need, even to working miracles in our favor.

Provided we are united with Mary's mind and heart, we shall be united with the mind and heart of her Son. He is always in her thoughts, and she knows Him as no one else does in the Universe; and she loves Him as no other human being loves Jesus Christ. Through her, we become most like the One who is our perfect model to be followed if we are to be joined with Him in the life to come. Provided we are consecrated to her, we become totally dedicated to Him who is our God in human form.

The key word in St. Louis de Montfort's true devotion is the preposition "through." "This devotion," he explains, "consists in giving ourselves entirely to our Lady, in order to belong entirely to Jesus *through* her."

We must give her (1) our body, with all its senses and members; (2) our soul, with all its powers; (3) our exterior goods of fortune, whether present or to come; and (4) our interior and spiritual goods, which are our merits and our virtues, and our good works, past, present, and future.

Always the main focus is on Jesus Christ, who is the ultimate purpose of our devotion to Mary. The better we know and love her, the more we shall know and love her Son; the more often we invoke her, the more effectively she will intercede with Him; and the more faithfully we strive to become like her, the more surely we shall become like Him who is God, who became man through her, so that by imitating His humanity we can participate in His Divinity.

In his encyclical *The Mother of the Redeemer, (Mater Redemptoris)*, Pope John Paul II commemorated the bimillennium of Mary's birth. In closing the encyclical, the Pope singled out the *True Devotion* for spiritual practice by the faithful: "I would like to recall, among the many witnesses and teachers of this [Marian] spirituality, the figure of St. Louis Marie de Montfort, who proposes consecration to Christ through the hands of Mary, as an effective means for Christians to live faithfully their baptismal commitments."

Unlike many other books, the *True Devotion* is to be read and reread, in order to sustain one's motivation of giving oneself entirely to Jesus through Mary, in time and into eternity.

SPECIALLY RECOMMENDED
True Devotion to Mary

38. *Alban Butler*

The historian-author of the *Lives of the Saints,* Alban Butler (1710–73), was born in England and died in France. Ordained in 1735, he had studied at Douay and taught philosophy and theology there. Although he wrote a few other works, which were published after his death, his principal claim to fame is the collection of over 1,600 biographies, whose original title was *The Lives of the Fathers, Martyrs and Other Saints,* on which Butler spent thirty years of research and writing.

For two centuries, Butler's *Lives of the Saints* were recognized as a standard authority on the principal saints familiar to English-speaking Catholics. Then, in the early twentieth century, Herbert Thurston, S.J., was asked to undertake a revision and updating of Butler's *Lives.* Thurston worked for several years on the project, which was finally completed by Donald Attwater. The complete edition of Butler's *Lives of the Saints* is now published as "edited, revised and supplemented by Herbert Thurston, S.J., and Donald Attwater." The standard edition is in four volumes, with a general index in the last volume.

In his introduction, Francis Cardinal Spellman explains both the contents and the purpose of this collection of biographies:

Herein is a colorful galaxy of the lives of men, women and children challenged by difficulties and dangers, lives that triumphantly manifest the fulfillment of God's purpose in creating us: after this world's trials and torments heroically sustained and endured for the greater honor and glory of God, there comes the eternal reward of happiness with Him in heaven.

Reading these inspiring stories further demonstrates that Sainthood—the highest and noblest of all vocations—is not the rare privilege of a few but the desired destiny of all. This saintly hall of fame attests the democracy of God's Kingdom, for no class, no race, no profession has a monopoly on Sainthood. Sainthood, these useful volumes make abundantly evident, is everyone's vocation everywhere.

Certain rules were followed in revising Butler's original lives. The main purpose was to provide readers with a maximum of historically provable data within the space available—about twenty-five hundred pages. According to Attwater, "The exact knowledge of facts is of the greatest assistance to true piety."

The number of saints in the revised edition is 2,565, about a thousand more than in Butler's original collection. Moreover, the homilies that Butler added to the saints' lives were omitted. Finally, there has been so much development in the science of hagiology and so many persons have been beatified and canonized since 1800 that Butler's masterful work simply had to be revised.

Some readers may object that the revised *Lives of the Saints* is less inspiring than the eighteenth-century original. Certainly Herbert Thurston was well known for his hardheaded realism in dealing with popular piety. His *Physical Phenomena of Mysticism* is practically a manual on how to recognize pseudomystics and discard alleged revelations. Yet, Thurston accepted Butler's thesis that "the method of forming men to virtue by example is, of all others, the shortest, the most easy and the best adapted to all circumstances and dispositions. . . . In the lives of the saints, we see the most perfect maxims of the Gospel reduced to practice, and the most heroic virtue made the object of our senses, clothed as it were with a body, and exhibited to view in its most attractive dress."

Each biography has its own bibliography, not only of English works but of writings in other languages. Thus, *The Lives of the Saints* is in itself a lifetime reading program, not only in the biographies of holy persons honored by the Church but in the resources that each entry provides for further reading and spiritual inspiration.

SPECIALLY RECOMMENDED

   Lives of the Saints

39. St. Alphonsus de Liguori

The moral theologian and founder of the Redemptorists, St. Alphonsus de Liguori (1696–1787), began to publish only when he was almost fifty years old. Yet, he managed in his long life to write over one hundred volumes. His system of moral theology became the standard among priests and directors of souls into modern times. But better known are his innumerable devotional writings. They include *The Holy Eucharist, The Glories of Mary, The True Spouse of Jesus Christ,* and *The Way of Salvation and Perfection.*

In order to appreciate the depth of his writings, we must remind ourselves that they were composed by a man who suffered intensely for many years of his long life. Although he was founder of the Redemptorists, dissension plagued the institute he established. For twenty-four years, two former benefactors sued him in the civil courts. Some years before his death, his community was almost dissolved, and the crowning humiliation came when, unsuspectingly, he signed a document that changed the Redemptorist Rule beyond recognition. "You have founded the Congregation, and you have destroyed it," one of his priests told him. After a long process, followed by a formal decree in 1781, Alphonsus was removed from office by the same Pope who was later to declare him Venerable.

Alphonsus lived in this state of exclusion for seven years and in that condition died. He was made a Doctor of the Church in 1871 and declared the heavenly patron of spiritual directors.

There are three features of Alphonsus' writing that the reader should look for. They are his clear thinking, his practicality, and his understanding of man's freedom in cooperation with the grace of God.

The clarity of St. Alphonsus is especially striking in his frequent explanations of the Holy Eucharist. He understands Christ to have literally decided to be with us, all days, even to the end of the world. The Real Presence, he insists, means that the whole Christ—divinity and humanity, body and soul, bodily organs and emotions—is present in our midst in the Blessed Sacrament. That is why Alphonsus never tired of advocating prayer before the Holy Eucharist. That is also, he says, why "the saints experienced in this world such pleasure in remaining in the presence of Jesus in the Blessed Sacrament, that days and nights appeared to them as moments."

Alphonsus' practicality stands out in everything he wrote. We might almost say that his was the "Spirituality of the How." Always he gave specific directions and concrete examples of how the following of Christ should be lived out. One set of "Fifty Maxims for Attaining Perfection" includes such plain recommendations as these: "Always ask Jesus Christ for His Love; Often to visit the Most Holy Sacrament; To desire Paradise and death in order to be able to love Jesus Christ perfectly and for all Eternity; To honor Mary in order to please Jesus Christ; Not to do or yet to leave undone anything through human respect; To drive away melancholy." All that we know about Alphonsus de Liguori shows that he put into practice everything he urged others to do.

His defense of man's freedom in response to grace is striking. He recognized that while God wants everyone to be saved our salvation depends on our voluntary cooperation. In fact, most of Alphonsus' spiritual writing dwells on the power we have to resist or respond to the divine illuminations and inspirations, called actual graces. If we respond generously, we shall become saints.

SPECIALLY RECOMMENDED
   The Holy Eucharist
   The Glories of Mary
   The Passion and Death of Jesus Christ
   The Way of Salvation and of Perfection

40. *Anne Catherine Emmerich*

The Augustinian nun Anne Catherine Emmerich (1774–1824) was born and died in Germany. Her family was so poor that at the age of twelve she had herself bound to a farmer. Typical of her selfless charity, she took all the savings she had accumulated to enter a convent and gave the money to an impoverished organist's family for whom she worked as a servant.

At twenty-eight, she finally entered the Augustinian convent at Dülmen, where she was satisfied with the most menial tasks and was commonly regarded as the lowest in the house. Because of her deep piety and her ecstasies in church, in her cell, or while at work, she was envied by some of her fellow sisters and treated unkindly, even at times with cruelty.

When Napoleon Bonaparte closed the convent in 1812, she was forced to take refuge in a poor widow's house. The next year, she became bedridden, but continued growing in spiritual intimacy with God and having mystical experiences, including the stigmata. Her stigmata became external, so that she could not conceal them, as she was able to conceal the crosses impressed upon her breast.

Perhaps the dominant feature of her spirituality was an extraordinary compassion with the sufferings of others. This was especially true for sinners, whose state of soul she knew without being told, and for the souls in Purgatory, for whom she offered up her physical and mental sufferings.

Then followed what she most dreaded, an episcopal investigation into the phenomena that became widely known. The vicar-general of the diocese, Bernhard Overberg, and three physicians conducted the inquiry with scrupulous care and made their findings public. Her stigmata were declared to be genuine, and the sanctity of the "pious Beguine," as she was called, was declared to be authentic.

Some five years before her death, the well-known poet Clemens Brentano was urged to visit her. To his surprise, she recognized him and told him that he had been pointed out to her as the one who would carry out Our Lord's command to write down the revelations she had received. She dictated her experiences in the Westphalian dialect, and he immediately wrote them out in ordinary German. He would then read back to her what he wrote, and would change or remove what she wished until she gave her complete approval to his script. Consequently it is not true, as some of her critics have said, that it is impossible to determine in Brentano's writing what came from her and what came from the poet himself.

In 1833 appeared the first edition of Catherine's *The Dolorous Passion of Our Lord Jesus Christ, from the Meditations of Anne Catherine Emmerich.* In 1852 appeared *The Life of the Blessed Virgin.* Then, between 1858 and 1880, Father Schmoeger published three volumes, based on the preceding, under the title *The Life of Our Lord.* In the meantime (1867–1870), Schmoeger also authored a two-volume life of the stigmatic.

Her visions go into great detail, giving them a vividness that holds the reader's interest, as one graphic scene follows another, not unlike the meditations recommended by St. Ignatius in his *Spiritual Exercises.* Where other mystics are more concerned with ideas, she concentrates on events. Others stop to meditate aloud while reflecting on the mystery, but she leaves the facts untouched in their simplicity and brevity, not unlike the narratives of the Evangelists. The Christ she portrays is truly human and also authentically divine.

The rapid and silent acceptance of Catherine Emmerich's writings throughout the world is itself a powerful witness to their lasting value. Scholars of the stature of Dom Gueranger praise their merits in the highest terms.

SPECIALLY RECOMMENDED
The Lowly Life and Bitter Passion of Our Lord Jesus Christ and His Blessed Mother

The Modern Age

If we take the end of the eighteenth century as the beginning of modern times, we find an avalanche of Catholic writers who deserve to be recommended. A drastic limitation on their numbers had to be made. I have chosen to include those who have been most influential as witnesses to the Catholic tradition; whose writings have reached a wide cultural spectrum; who were unqualified in the profession of their faith; who were part of a chain reaction of what I call "genealogy of the spirit"; or who responded to the grave issues facing the followers of Christ, especially the rising tide of indifference and even hostility to the existence of a personal God.

One of the surprising features of modern Catholic publication is the role of the laity: their productivity has been phenomenal. There is no comparison on this score with any previous two centuries of the Church's history. Men of the stature of Maritain, Chesterton, Belloc, and Dawson and women of the rank of Sigrid Undset, Katherine Burton, and Alice Meynell have no counterpart in any two hundred years since the time of Christ. Even the Second Vatican Council's lengthy document on the laity simply highlights the fact that the Catholic laity has entered on a new era of involvement in every aspect of the Church's life, especially in her outreach to the secular world.

One thing should be specially emphasized: loyalty to the See of Peter has become, more than ever, a hallmark of Catholic authenticity. One reason for this is certainly the growing awareness that the Bishop of Rome is not only the custodian of doctrinal orthodoxy; he has also become in the last two centuries the most powerful voice still defending the indissolubility of marriage, the sanctity of unborn human life, and the liberty of all human beings to worship God without interference from civil authority.

41. *Frederick William Faber*

The Oratorian author Frederick William Faber (1814–63) came under the influence of John Henry Newman and collaborated with him in the Library of the Fathers series. He was ordained a priest in the Church of England (1839) but followed Newman into the Catholic Church in 1845. Together with other converts, Faber formed a small community, the Brothers of the Will of God. In 1847 he was ordained a Catholic priest, and the next year, he joined the Oratory of St. Philip Neri, which Newman had introduced into England.

As early as 1847, Faber began the publication of the Lives of the English Saints series, presenting the lives not as biographies but as witnesses to the power of grace to sanctify weak human nature. Then, between 1853 and 1860, he wrote eight works: *All for Jesus, Growth in Holiness, The Blessed Sacrament, The Creator and the Creature, The Foot of the Cross, Spiritual Conferences, The Precious Blood,* and *Bethlehem.* Soon after, he wrote two volumes of *Notes on Doctrinal and Spiritual Subjects.* Many of his hymns have become favorites, and his poems are included, along with essays, in a separate volume.

Faber is very quotable. His statements on the spiritual life are often included in anthologies, along with the great masters of asceticism. The following is a sample from *All for Jesus:*

One act of Divine Love is a more finished thing than a statue of Phidias or Praxiteles. It is more firm than the foundations of the Alps. It is more enduring than the round world which God made so strong. All things are bubbles to it. They have nothing in them. They mean little. They soon pass away. An act of love is a complete work, and has greater power and greater consequences than any other act. The mere act of dying is not equal to it. And yet this act of love can be made by a mental glance, quick as a lightning and piercing heaven. Such acts can be multiplied at will beyond our power of reckoning and in the midst of apparently the most distracting occupations.

Faber's unswerving loyalty to the Bishop of Rome and a strong devotion to the Mother of God come through almost everything that he wrote. This is not surprising. His conversion from Anglicanism was, in effect, a return to the faith of his forefathers. It was mainly the dogma of papal primacy that separated the English church from Roman Catholicism in the sixteenth century, but it was acceptance of the Pope's authority in spiritual matters that identified Faber and his associates in the nineteenth century. He (and they) would naturally want to share with others their rediscovered convictions about the Vicar of Christ.

The same is true regarding the Blessed Virgin Mary. For centuries England had been Our Lady's Dowry. Once Faber entered the Church, he would do all he could to restore their Marian heritage to his countrymen.

SPECIALLY RECOMMENDED
> Growth in Holiness, or the Progress of the Spiritual Life
> The Blessed Sacrament, or the Works and Ways of God
> Poems
> Spiritual Conferences

42. St. Peter Julian Eymard

Peter Julian Eymard (1811–68), born near Grenoble, France, from his earliest years had a deep faith in the Blessed Sacrament. Sickness forced him to leave the novitiate of the Oblates of Mary Immaculate. He then entered the diocesan seminary in Grenoble and was ordained at the age of twenty-three. Five years later he joined the Marist Fathers and remained with them for seventeen years, including time as rector and provincial.

He unsuccessfully tried to form within the Marists a group of men specially devoted to the adoration of the Holy Eucharist. Receiving dispensation from his vows, he founded in Paris in 1856 the Blessed Sacrament Fathers and remained their superior general for the rest of his life. Two years later, he established with Marguerite Guillot a cloistered community of nuns, the Servants of the Blessed Sacrament.

The main scope of Peter Julian's two congregations was to adore the Blessed Sacrament and to promote the apostolate of devotion to Christ's Real Presence in the Eucharist. He also established the Blessed Sacrament Confraternity, which has spread throughout the world.

Besides the constitutions that he wrote for his communities, his sermons and conferences have been published since his death and are widely circulated in many languages. He has become best known for what has come to be called the Eymard Library, which consists of nine titles, beginning with *The Real Presence* and ending with *In the Light of the Monstrance.*

Two features stand out in these books—namely, a clear faith in Christ's real, physical, bodily Presence in the Blessed Sacrament, and a strong sense of intimacy with Christ, now living on earth in the Eucharist. The union of these two elements is a unique contribution to Catholic spiritual literature. Not unlike St. Francis of Assisi centuries before, Peter Julian simply assumes that because Christ is now with us in the Eucharist, He continues the work He began in Palestine two millennia ago. A few paragraphs from *The Real Presence* illustrate the tenor of all his writings:

Adore and praise the immense love Jesus has for you in this Sacrament of Himself. In order not to leave you a lonely orphan in this land of exile and misery, He comes down from heaven for you personally, to offer you companionship and consolation. . . .

Express your wonder at the sacrifices He imposes on Himself in His sacramental state. He conceals the glory of His divinity and humanity so as not to dazzle and blind you. He veils his majesty so that you may dare to come to Him and speak to Him as friend to friend. He binds his power so as not to frighten or punish you. He does not manifest his virtues so as not to discourage your weakness.

Pour out your soul in thanksgiving to this good Jesus. Thank the Father for having given you his divine Son. Thank the Holy Spirit for having reincarnated Him on the altar through the ministry of the priest, and that for you personally.

See how obedient He is in the divine host. He obeys everybody, even his enemies, promptly and meekly. Marvel at his humility: He descends to the edge of nothingness, since He unites Himself sacramentally to worthless and lifeless species which have no other natural support, no other stability than that which His omnipotence gives them, sustaining them by a continual miracle. His love for us makes Him our Prisoner. He has housed Himself to the end of time in His Eucharistic prison, which is to be our heaven on earth.

By now millions have been inspired by this kind of believing elegance. St. Peter Julian's conferences are ideal books for prayerful meditation before the Blessed Sacrament.

SPECIALLY RECOMMENDED
> *The Real Presence*
> *Holy Communion*
> *Our Lady of the Blessed Sacrament*
> *The Eucharist and Christian Perfection*

43. *Alessandro Manzoni*

Alessandro Francesco Tommaso Antonio Manzoni (1785–1873) is considered "the noblest figure in the Italian literature of the nineteenth century." Manzoni wrote extensively, but his chief claim to fame rests on the only novel he published, *I promessi sposi* (The Betrothed).

After his studies in Italy under the Scolopi and the Barnabites, he joined his mother, who had left her husband and had been living in Paris. For some five years, he drifted away from the Catholic faith, as shown in his early hymns to liberty and reason and his open profession of atheism. However, not long after his marriage to a Swiss Calvinist girl, Enrichetta Blondel, his life changed drastically. She was a deeply religious person who became a Catholic two years after she married Manzoni. He then returned to the Catholic Church.

Convinced that he should go back to Italy, he took his family to Milan, where he began a lifetime of professedly Catholic writing. In 1819 he published a refutation of the Swiss historian Jean Charles Simonde de Sismondi, who had charged that Catholic doctrine was the main cause of Italian decadence. Then followed a series of biographies and poems, but all in the style of Romanticism, filled with heroic poses and allegories of vice and virtue.

Walter Scott gave Manzoni the inspiration to use the novel as the vehicle for deep religious convictions. But Manzoni differed radically from Scott in perspective. Instead of featuring the adventures, romances, intrigues and marvels so common in Scott, Manzoni concentrated on the interior, moral experiences of ordinary people. He believed that the deepest insights of human genius can best be expressed in the movements of a person's conscience, rather than in colorful and adventurous exterior events.

The first version of *I promessi sposi* was finished in 1823. Four years later, it was rewritten and published. He then spent another twelve years further editing it in order to achieve unity of style, order, and balance in his masterwork.

What is most remarkable about this novel is what might be called its objectivity. The author's concern was not with intrigues or passions but with the religious consequences of human conduct. He assumed that we have reason and free will and that God is constantly active with His grace in our lives.

The novel is set against the background of the Spanish oppression of the Italian people and the war of the succession of Mantua (1628–30). The story is of the love and fortunes of two young peasants. Around this core is a series of cameo portraits of men and women, all depicted with such unique realism that Walter Scott was moved to call Manzoni's work the greatest romance of modern times.

There is never any question about the author's earnestness of purpose, his delicate humor, or his moral intentions. Above all, he applies authentic Catholic morality to the study of life and history and harmonizes these with an artistic skill that never intrudes on the reader.

For the last thirty years of his life, he concentrated on writing a history of the French Revolution, numerous essays on the Italian language, and a work in philosophy. Critics who speculate that he gave up art for history because of moral scruples have been answered by Manzoni's defenders, who say the theory is groundless. One does not twice write a *Divine Comedy*.

SPECIALLY RECOMMENDED
The Betrothed

44. *Prosper Guéranger*

The liturgist Prosper Louis Pascal Guéranger (1805–75) is in many ways the father of the modern liturgical movement. He reestablished the Rule of St. Benedict at Solesmes, was elected the first Abbot of Solesmes, and was appointed superior general of the Benedictines of France by Pope Gregory XVI in 1837.

A devoted servant of the Church, Guéranger strove to establish more filial relations between France and the Holy See. He also undertook two extensive writing projects on the liturgy. The first was a three-volume work intended to correct some of the prevalent abuses in the liturgy. The second has come to be identified with the name of Guéranger. It was started in 1841 and its last, fifteenth, volume completed in 1866. *L'Année liturgique* has been translated into various languages and is commonly known in English as *The Liturgical Year*. Historians agree that this classic work began the liturgical renewal in the Catholic Church. For example, its German translation had a great influence in that country, which produced some of the leading spirits of authentic liturgical reform up to the Second Vatican Council.

It should be emphasized that Guéranger's reform was based on sound historical research and the Church's authentic interpretation of Sacred Scripture. Moreover, he insisted on a restoration of Gregorian chant. His modern critics have claimed that his view of the liturgy was too monastic and not sufficiently pastoral, but his defenders have pointed out that it was the monasteries of Europe that for almost fifteen centuries helped to preserve the Church's sound traditions, not only in the liturgy but in doctrine and Christian spirituality.

The Liturgical Year is a classic that is not archaic. Each volume begins by giving the background to the relevant liturgical feasts or seasons and then provides the appropriate texts of the liturgy. The purpose was to involve the whole mind and heart of the faithful in their worship experience. Thus, the way was opened for recovering the riches of the Church's liturgy, as found in the Scriptures and revealed tradition and developed by the magisterium since apostolic times.

A fair sample of Guéranger's approach is his explanation of the history of Christmas:

We apply the name of Christmas to the forty days which begin with the Nativity of Our Lord, December 25, and end with the Purification of the Blessed Virgin, February 2. It is a period which forms a distinct portion of the Liturgical Year, as distinct, by its own special spirit, from every other, as are Advent, Lent, Easter or Pentecost. One same Mystery is celebrated and kept in view during the forty days. . . .

The custom of celebrating the Solemnity of our Savior's Nativity by a feast or commemoration of forty days' duration is founded on the holy Gospel itself; for it tells us that the Blessed Virgin Mary, after spending forty days in the contemplation of the Divine Fruit of her glorious Maternity, went to the Temple, there to fulfill, in most perfect humility, the ceremonies which the Law demanded of daughters of Israel, when they became mothers.

The Feast of Mary's Purification is, therefore, part of that of Jesus' birth; and the custom of keeping this holy and glorious period of forty days as one continued Festival has every appearance of being a very ancient one, at least in the Roman Church. And firstly, with regard to our Savior's Birth on December 25, we have St. John Chrysostom telling us, in his Homily for this Feast, that the Western Churches had, from the very commencement of Christianity, kept it on this day. He is not satisfied with merely mentioning the tradition; he undertakes to show that it is well founded, inasmuch as the Church of Rome had every means of knowing the true day of our Savior's Birth, since the acts of the Enrollment, taken in Judea by command of Augustus, were kept in the public archives of Rome. The holy Doctor adduces a second argument, which he founds upon the Gospel of St. Luke, and he reasons thus: we know from the sacred Scriptures that it must have been in the fast of the seventh month that the Priest Zachary had the vision in the Temple; after which Elizabeth, his wife, conceived St. John the Baptist: hence it follows that the Blessed Virgin

Mary having, as the Evangelist St. Luke relates, received the Angel Gabriel's visit, and conceived the Savior of the world in the sixth month of Elizabeth's pregnancy, that is to say, in March, the Birth of Jesus must have taken place in the month of December.

Having established December 25 as the date for Christmas since the earliest times, Guéranger then goes on to explain the meaning of the Church's liturgical prayers for the Christmas season. The Fathers of the Church are quoted at length to bring out the meaning of the liturgical language, the season, and the implications for the spiritual life of Christian believers:

> "Let us, my Brethren, rejoice," cries out St. Augustine: "this day is sacred, not because of the visible sun, but because of the Birth of him who is the invisible Creator of the sun. . . . He chose this day whereon to be born, as he chose the Mother of whom to be born, and he made both the day and the Mother. The day he chose was that on which the light begins to increase, and it typifies the work of Christ, who renews our interior man day by day."

Guéranger is at pains to point out that the Church's liturgy is an integral part of revealed Christianity. Every detail of the words spoken, the ritual used, and the event commemorated partakes of the nature of a sacrament. Something sensibly perceptible is the divinely instituted channel of grace for the worshippers. Their intelligent cooperation in the liturgical experience contributes to their participation in the grace they receive.

SPECIALLY RECOMMENDED
    The Liturgical Year: Advent to the Last Sunday of Pentecost

45. *Orestes Brownson*

There are some Catholic writers in the Lifetime Reading Plan that I must qualify at the outset. Orestes Brownson (1803–76) is one of them. Successively Universalist minister, political activist, independent minister, Unitarian minister, and Catholic editor and propagandist, Brownson was one of the most admired—and most controversial—figures of the nineteenth century.

Moving from Presbyterianism at nineteen to Catholicism at forty-one, he looked for the best foundations to organize society. His personal life was seldom without inner turbulence, and his writing reflects this conflict.

The first deep influences on his thinking were the Deistic ideas of William Ellery Channing and Ralph Waldo Emerson. Then he took up the cause of the industrial proletariat, seeking to improve its status by philosophical discussion and political activity. Gradually he came to realize that human progress is a joint activity in which God's grace and man's voluntary cooperation must work together. This led Brownson to find in Christ the perfect example of combining the human and divine in one person. From Christ, he was led to see in the Catholic Church the living embodiment of Christianity, with a definite creed and moral principles, and the sources of grace—through the sacraments—for putting this creed and morality into practice. Once he became a Catholic, Brownson never wavered in his religious convictions.

As a Catholic, Brownson remained faithful to the Church's teaching. But he soon found himself at odds with some Catholics and with many Protestants. His strong advocacy of separation of Church and state and his criticism of what he called the political despotism of the Papal States did not endear him to many of his coreligionists. And his militant defense of papal authority estranged him from people outside the Catholic Church.

The only term to describe his literary output is enormous. He left the record of a vigorous mind grappling with the deepest problems of human existence. The mercurial quality of his thought requires careful selection from among his published writings. The following quotations from his critique of socialism reveal something of Brownson's mastery of language, and his incisive refutation of what he considered hostile to the teachings of the Gospel. Calling socialism "as artful as it is bold," he wrote:

It wears a pious aspect, it has divine words on its lips, and almost unction in its speech. It is not easy for the unlearned to detect its fallacy, and the great body of the people are prepared to receive it as Christian truth. We cannot deny it without seeming to them to be warring against the true interests of society, and also against the Gospel of our Lord. Never was heresy more subtle, more adroit, better fitted for success. How skilfully it flatters the people! It is said, the saints shall judge the world. By the change of a word, the people are transformed into saints, and invested with the saintly character and office. How adroitly, too, it appeals to the people's envy and hatred of their superiors, and to their love of the world, without shocking their orthodoxy or wounding their piety! Surely Satan has here, in Socialism, done his best, almost outdone himself, and would, if it were possible, deceive the very elect, so that no flesh should be saved.

What we have said will suffice to show the subtle and dangerous character of Socialism, and how, although the majority may recoil from it at present, if logically drawn out by its bolder and more consistent advocates, the age may nevertheless be really and thoroughly Socialistic. We know that the age seeks with all its energy, as the great-want of mankind, political and social reforms. Of this there is and can be no doubt. Analyze these reforms and the principles and motives which lead to them, which induce the people in our days to struggle for them, and you will find at the bottom of them all the assumption, that our good lies in the natural order, and is not attainable by individual effort. All we see, all we hear, all we read, from whatever quarter it comes, serves to prove that this is the deep and settled conviction of the age. If it were not, these revolutions [of 1848–49] in France, Italy, Germany, and elsewhere, would have no meaning, no principle, no aim, and would be as insignificant as drunken rows in the streets of our cities.

But the essence of Socialism is in this very assumption, that our good lies in the natural order, and is unattainable by individual effort. Socialism bids us follow nature, instead of saying with the Gospel, Resist nature. Placing our good in the natural order, it necessarily restricts it to temporal goods, the only good the order of nature can give. For it, then, evil is to want temporal goods, and good is to possess them. But, in this sense, evil is not remediable or good attainable by individual effort. We depend on nature, which may resist us, and on the conduct of others, which escapes our control. Hence the necessity of social organization, in order to harmonize the interests of all with the interest of each, and to enable each by the union of all to compel Nature to yield him up the good she has in store for him. But not all men are equal before God, and, since he is just, he is equal in regard to all. Then all have equal rights,—an equal right to exemption from evil, and an equal right to the possession of good. Hence the social organization must be such as to avert equal evil from all, and to secure to each an equal share of temporal goods. Here is Socialism in a nutshell, following as a strictly logical consequence from the principles or assumptions which the age adopts, and on which it everywhere acts.

Even the foregoing paragraphs from his *Essays and Reviews* are enough to explain why Brownson never left his readers either in doubt about his position or indifferent in their attitude toward his ideas. He was either ardently admired or vigorously opposed.

His great merit lies in the impact that the Catholic faith had on a first-rate intellect and Catholic morality had on a militant will.

SPECIALLY RECOMMENDED

Essays and Reviews Chiefly on Theology, Politics, and Socialism

46. *Matthias Joseph Scheeben*

Matthias Joseph Scheeben (1835–88), ordained in 1858, taught theology in the seminary at Cologne from 1860 to the day of his death. Unlike other theologians of his day, he was convinced that the laity needed to study and understand their faith to a degree far beyond that provided by ordinary religious instruction.

Scheeben did not write extensively. His devotional works include a Marian anthology, short lives of contemporary saints, and a prayerbook. His more profound writing is found in the three-volume German *Handbuch der Katholischen Dogmatik* (Manual of Catholic Dogma). But the classic publication of his life is *The Mysteries of Christianity*. It represents Scheeben's best scholarship and the peak of his theological development.

Central to *Mysteries* is Scheeben's conviction that Christianity is no mere philosophy nor even an exalted system of morals; it is a mystery. This means that, in the last analysis, Christ and His teaching would have been rationally inconceivable unless they had been divinely revealed. And since revelation, they remain rationally incomprehensible by the human mind.

Scheeben's first purpose is to show that without mysteries there would be no Christianity. The opening paragraphs set the stage for what follows:

Christianity entered the world as a religion replete with mysteries. It was proclaimed as the mystery of Christ, as the "mystery of the kingdom of God." Its ideas and doctrines were unknown, unprecedented; and they were to remain inscrutable and unfathomable.

The mysterious character of Christianity, which was sufficiently intelligible in its simplest fundamentals, was foolishness to the Gentiles and a stumbling block to the Jews; and since Christianity in the course of time never relinquished and could never relinquish this character of mystery without belying its nature, it remained ever a foolishness, a stumbling block to all those who, like the Gentiles, looked upon it with unconsecrated eyes or, like the Jews, encountered it with uncircumcised hearts. With bitter scorn they would ever scoff at its mysterious nature as obscurantism, superstition, fanaticism, and absurdity.

The greater, the more sublime, and the more divine Christianity is, the more inexhaustible, inscrutable, unfathomable, and mysterious its subject matter must be. If its teaching is worthy of the only-begotten Son of God, if the Son of God had to descend from the bosom of His Father to initiate us into this teaching, could we expect anything else than the revelation of the deepest mysteries locked up in God's heart? Could we expect anything else than disclosures concerning a higher, invisible world, about divine and heavenly things, which "eye has not seen, nor ear heard," and which could not enter into the heart of any man? And if God has sent us His own Spirit to teach us all truth, the Spirit of His truth, who dwells in God and there searches the deep things of God, should this Spirit reveal nothing new, great, and wondrous, should He teach us no sublime secrets?

Having shown that Christianity is filled with "sublime secrets," Scheeben proceeds to show that these divine secrets are more or less understandable. They are indeed incomprehensible. But they are not unintelligible. We do not know everything about the mysteries of Christianity, but we also do not know nothing about them.

The bulk of Scheeben's classic work is an examination of the major mysteries of our faith. With the help of God's grace, we can grasp something of the eternal truths they convey. There is only one condition: we must be humble in believing what we cannot fully perceive. I believe Scheeben's *Mysteries* will still be read a century from now and used by the faithful, especially the laity, as a superb one-volume synthesis of what Christianity really means.

SPECIALLY RECOMMENDED
> *The Mysteries of Christianity*
> *Mariology*

47. William Bernard Ullathorne

The autobiography of Ullathorne (1806–89) is appropriately called *From Cabin Boy to Archbishop*. Going to sea as a cabin boy at the age of thirteen, he lived to promote the restoration of the hierarchy to England, assist at the First Vatican Council, and become one of the strongest friends and defenders of Cardinal Newman.

After ordination to the priesthood, he volunteered for the Australian mission and went there as vicar-general of Mauritius. On returning to England, he worked zealously for the abolition of transporting criminals to Australia.

What is remarkable about Ullathorne is that his most important publication, *Groundwork of the Christian Virtues*, is a modern masterpiece on the virtue of humility. It contains over four hundred pages on the one virtue that his contemporaries might never have guessed he struggled to maintain while acquiring a reputation for hardheaded, aggressive realism in defense of what he considered to be God's will.

A prominent English prelate once reproved Ullathorne for allowing himself to be overawed by Newman's verbal logic and language. Ullathorne turned on the bishop to tell him he was no match for Newman's intelligence. Ullathorne's letters, especially those to Rome, reveal how strong-willed—and strong-minded—an English Catholic dignitary could be.

Yet, the picture we get of the real Ullathorne is quite different. His work on humility is no mere academic treatise. It is more like a classic on the one virtue that underlies all the rest—and without which no virtue can flourish or even survive.

Ullathorne spent a lifetime working on his own practice of humility. That is why his *Groundwork of the Christian Virtues* is so valuable. It is theology brought down to earth. The opening paragraphs are a fair sample of the whole work:

> God alone is independent; every creature is dependent on God. But as man is made for God, he has a vast capacity, and wants in full proportion to his capacity for God, and is therefore immeasurably more dependent on his Cre-

ator than the irrational creatures, whose wants are limited to this world. To be deeply conscious of this dependence is to have the soul filled with the most important moral truth with which we are concerned; and to enter with good-will into this truth is to place ourselves on the secure foundation of all justice. This dependence has its foundation in the divine pre-eminence and absolute sovereignty of God, and in His bountiful goodness, and in the need we have of receiving His divine help and bounty, that we may be united with Him, both as our first cause and as our final end: as our first cause, that we may receive His continual influence; and as our final end, that by His graces and blessings, as we are made to His image we may come to our Divine Original. So dependent is the ray of light upon the sun, that when separated it expires in darkness; and so dependent is our soul upon the divine beneficence, that when we are no longer subject to His gracious influence we decline into a moral death. As humility springs in the order of justice from the truth of our dependence on God, it is the virtue proper to the intellectual and moral creature, and the foundation of all those virtues whereby man is perfected unto God.

But as the pillar that led Israel from Egypt to the Land of Promise was both light and cloud, so this virtue of humility is light to the children of belief, whilst to the children of this world it takes the appearance of an obscure and unintelligible cloud. It enlightens the humble; it perplexes the proud. For the world without humility is the world without the sense of God, and consequently without the sense of dependence on God. But when for long ages pride had usurped the place of humility in human hearts, then came humility from Heaven in the person of God and the nature of man, that through its divine power and influence the souls of men might return to God.

In order to fully appreciate Ullathorne's book on humility, it should be read along with (or after) his autobiography. Having seen these works together, the reader will learn there are two demands on human nature, to avoid two extremes: on the one hand, we must be thoroughly humble in acknowledging that everything we have is a gift from God, and on the other hand, we must be humbly ready to use the gifts that God gave us. There are consequently two forms of pride that we are to avoid —the pride of self-conceit, which fails to give credit to God for what we have or achieve, and the pride of self-degradation, which fails to exercise the talents of nature and grace that we have received from God. Ullathorne struggled all his life to practice both forms of humility, neither to overreach himself by self-complacency nor underreach himself by self-debasement.

SPECIALLY RECOMMENDED
  The Groundwork of the Christian Virtues
  The Little Book of Humility and Patience

48. *John Henry Newman*

The life story of John Henry Newman (1801–90) constitutes more than a biography. It symbolizes the effective return of Roman Catholicism to England after its practical absence of almost three hundred years.

Newman was the leading spirit of the Oxford Movement, which began in 1833 with the first of a series of *Tracts for the Times.* The original purpose of the *Tracts* was to defend the Church of England as a divine institution, to prove that Anglican bishops are direct successors of the Apostles, and to show that the Book of Common Prayer is a valid rule of faith. In 1841, however, Newman published his famous "Tract 90," which was condemned by many Anglican bishops and led to his entering the Catholic Church on October 9, 1845. "Tract 90: Remarks on Certain Passages in the Thirty-Nine Articles" also closed the Oxford movement.

Almost immediately after, he published his *Essay on the Development of Christian Doctrine,* in defense of his change of allegiance. It is a very readable explanation (which took years to compose) of the single thesis that only in the Roman Catholic Church has there been true development of doctrine with no break in essential continuity from the time of Christ to the present day. "Doctrine," he says, "is where it was, and usage and precedence, and principle and policy; there may be changes, but they are consolidations and adaptations; all is unequivocal and determinate with an identity which there is no disputing."

Having been ordained in Rome, Newman established the Oratorians of Birmingham in 1849 and was rector of Dublin University from 1854 to 1858. During this time, he published *The Idea of a University,* which is regarded as the best defense of Catholic education in any language.

On his return to England, he became associated with *The Ram-*

bler, a periodical that published a negative review of Henry Manning's lectures on the temporal power of the Popes. Newman foresaw the loss of the Papal States, but his position estranged him from Manning. The result was a period of despondency for Newman.

Then came a marvelous release. A fiercely anti-Catholic writer, Charles Kingsley, published a scathing accusation of what he saw as Newman's treachery and deceit. Newman first engaged Kingsley in correspondence. But then he wrote in less than three months (April–June 1864) a unique specimen of religious autobiography, the *Apologia Pro Vita Sua* (Defense of His Life). Composed in white heat, the *Apologia* reveals the inner soul of Newman as nothing else he spoke or wrote. In eloquent prose, he tells the story of his religious change from early childhood to where years of study and prayer finally led him to "the one fold of Christ," the Catholic Church.

A year later, he wrote *The Dream of Gerontius,* a long poem not unlike Dante's, describing the journey of a soul to God at the hour of death. The *Dream* was inspired by the Requiem Mass and Liturgy of the Hours for the faithful departed. Thus, in 1865, he looked forward to his final pilgrimage, on which he would be "alone to the Alone."

While the First Vatican Council was in session, Newman finished his *Grammar of Assent,* which contains much of his ripest thought. It is especially noteworthy for its analysis of the role of conscience in our knowledge of God.

For twenty years, Newman was under a shadow in Rome, mainly because of misunderstanding about his attitude toward the papacy. But the new Pope, Leo XIII, in 1879 elevated the aged Oratorian to the cardinalate. In Rome for the occasion, Newman declared himself a lifelong enemy of liberalism, or "the doctrine that there is no truth in religion, but that one creed is as good as another."

The more than forty volumes of Newman's published works contain many sermons, several religious novels, and hundreds of letters. They are all superbly written. His motto as cardinal, Heart Speaks to Heart, was taken from St. Francis de Sales and reveals the secret of his genius as a man whose soul was always in tune with the Spirit of God.

SPECIALLY RECOMMENDED
Apologia Pro Vita Sua
Sermons and Discourses
The Idea of a University
The Dream of Gerontius

49. *Coventry Patmore*

The poet Coventry Kersey Dighton Patmore (1823–96) published his first verse, *Poems,* at the age of twenty-one. He was a writer by temperament, but to make a living, he worked for years as assistant in the printed book department of the British Museum.

At twenty-four, he married the daughter of a Congregationalist minister. She was a source of great inspiration to him and provided valuable criticism of his manuscripts. From 1854 on, there appeared parts of *The Angel in the House,* a series of poems on married love. As a panegyric of the joys and sorrows of marriage, they provided depth and charm to what might otherwise be considered trivial details in a loving home.

After the death of his wife in 1862, he went to Rome, where two years later he was received into the Catholic Church and married a second time. In 1877 he published *The Unknown Eros,* a collection of odes that are of great musical beauty and almost mystical in their spiritual depth.

In 1880 his second wife died, and the next year, he married for the third time. His last book, *The Rod, the Root, and the Flower,* was published a year before his death. It mainly consists of meditations along the same lines as *The Unknown Eros.* Historians of literature speculate that it is substantially the rewriting of an earlier work, *Sponsa Dei* (The Spouse of God), which he had destroyed. It represents his most mature religious insights and reveals the depths of his Catholic faith.

Patmore saw more than most writers the importance of knowing Christian revelation, of knowing what we believe. He made bold to say that the highest purpose of the works of creation is to provide analogies for understanding revealed mysteries. If we reread the Gospels in this light, we see how true that is. Everything created in space and time—birds and fishes and animals, sky and sea, trees and mountains, night and day, the seasons of the year—is used by Christ to teach us secrets of divine wisdom that, until God became man, remained hidden from the foundations of the world.

As a married man, Patmore drew heavily on the experiences of espoused life to bring out the mystical side of matrimony. I doubt if there is another Catholic author totally committed to his faith who has written more movingly on the meaning of marital love. He expressed himself so persuasively that even outside of Christian circles he is regarded as one of the fine English poets of modern times.

One example out of many that could be quoted illustrates the beauty of Patmore's language, the delicacy of his thought, and the simple-faith convictions that inspired his poetry. The following is entitled "The Toys":

> My little Son, who look'd from thoughtful eyes
> And moved and spoke in quiet grown-up wise,
> Having my law the seventh time disobey'd,
> I struck him, and dismiss'd
> With hard words and unkiss'd,
> —His Mother, who was patient, being dead.
> Then, fearing lest his grief should hinder sleep,
> I visited his bed,
> But found him slumbering deep,
> With darken'd eyelids, and their lashes yet
> From his late sobbing wet.
> And I, with moan,
> Kissing away his tears, left others of my own;
> For, on a table drawn beside his head,
> He had put, within his reach,
> A box of counters and a red-vein'd stone,
> A piece of glass abraded by the beach,
> And six or seven shells,

A bottle with bluebells,
And two French copper coins, ranged there with careful art,
To comfort his sad heart.
So when that night I pray'd
To God, I wept, and said:
Ah, when at last we lie with trancèd breath,
Not vexing Thee in death,
We made our joys,
How weakly understood
Thy great commanded good,
Then, fatherly not less
Than I whom Thou hast molded from the clay,
Thou'lt leave Thy wrath, and say,
'I will be sorry for their childishness.'

If there is one master theme in Patmore's poems, it is the mystery of Christ's love for the human soul as His espoused bride.

Coventry Patmore's essays are consistent with his poetry. In fact, they are the best commentary on his verse.

SPECIALLY RECOMMENDED

Poems

50. *St. Thérèse of Lisieux*

St. Thérèse, better known as the Little Flower, was born at Alençon in France in 1873 and died in the Carmelite infirmary of Lisieux in 1897. During these short years, she worked no miracles, had no reputation as a mystic, and lived in the obscurity of her cloister. Yet, she was canonized in 1925, within the lifetime of many of her contemporaries.

In the designs of Providence, the one book—if it may be called such—she wrote contributed more than anything else to her lightning rise to spiritual fame. Variously called *Autobiography, The Story of a Soul,* or simply *The Life of St. Thérèse of Lisieux,* the narrative of her spiritual reflections is utter simplicity.

What the book reveals is that Thérèse had a difficult nature to conquer. By early childhood, her pride and obstinacy had become evident. But, also in childhood, she resolved to become a saint. At thirteen, she thought she had never done her own will and had quite reached perfection. In the years that followed, she came to learn how much she needed God's grace to submit herself totally to the divine will.

Given to extreme timidity and an embarrassing tendency to cry, subject to scruples and black moods and to days of depression and a siege of difficulties against the faith, she struggled through all of this heroically. The most difficult part of her trials, as she admits, was that only she really knew of these interior conflicts. But she drew all the more closely to God, almost because of these sufferings.

What has come to be known as her Little Way was her complete surrender to the power of God. Her method, as it might be called, of coping with her weakness and self-will was the way of trust and total abandonment to the love of God. In the same way, she put her obsession with temptations against the faith into God's hands. All the while that her mind was being racked with objections to revealed truths, her will remained firm in believing.

Millions by now have been inspired by this one book of St. Thérèse of Lisieux. The most common way of benefiting from her words is to read them in the spirit in which they were written. They are not so much to be analyzed or scrutinized as personalized. By identifying oneself with the person who wrote her memoirs, we are able to see that, like us, she had all the human tendencies to pride and fear and self-conceit. But her total, childlike reliance on God enabled her to live with herself and trust Him, in His goodness, to love her in spite of herself. Why? Because what God mainly wants from us is our hearts—that is, our readiness to do, and endure, His holy will out of love.

SPECIALLY RECOMMENDED
Autobiography

51. *Eugene Boylan*

From lecturer and research scientist in physics, Eugene Boylan (born 1904) became a Cistercian monk and priest. He published his first book on his fortieth birthday.

As a Cistercian, Boylan admitted that "writing is a spare-time job, and a Cistercian has no spare time. The Divine Office takes six hours a day, and when the daily manual work is added to that, there is still a day's work of prayer to be fitted in. Cistercian silence and use of signs take away one's facility in the use of words."

Yet, this Cistercian monk has published some of the most influential books in Catholic spirituality. His two best-known works are *Difficulties in Mental Prayer* and *This Tremendous Lover*.

Boylan has written also for priests and religious, but his specialty has been to inspire the faithful laity to grow in sanctity. "There are those," he wrote, "and they are many, whose obligations tie them to the world. In fact, the majority . . . are to live in the lay state and God has His own ways of confirming them in their vocation."

This is the focus of his justly famous *This Tremendous Lover:*

All are called to perfection. Other things being equal—and they often are far from equal—the way to perfection is far from being impossible in the world. And at the moment, the crying need is for holiness among the laity. To be quite clear as to our terms of reference, let us say that we regard the married state as the normal one for the laity, and that it is the married man and woman whom we have particularly in mind throughout this book; we are not thinking in terms of lay recluses or hermits.

The basic theme of Boylan's writings is the belief that persons are more important than things and that the personal love of Our Lord matters more than any service, however great. Flowing from this fundamental premise are two convictions that Boylan passes on to his readers. The first is that the most urgent need of our times is the extension and intensification of the interior spiritual life among all Catholics and the application of its influence to every phase of their activity. The second is that, after the spiritual life, nothing is so necessary as the restoration of Scholastic philosophy to its proper place and influence in the intellectual life of Europe and America. He felt that no effort should be spared to provide suitable means of training Catholics, especially adult laymen, in the interior life and of instructing them in sound philosophy without unduly interfering with their secular careers.

SPECIALLY RECOMMENDED
> *This Tremendous Lover*
> *The Mystical Body; The Foundation of the Spiritual Life*

52. *Francis Thompson*

The poet Francis Thompson (1859–1907) went through a series of experiences that deeply influenced all his writing. Although his father was a physician, Thompson decided to study for the priesthood. After seven years in seminary training, he was advised to leave; he then spent another six years studying medicine. During his medical studies he acquired a drug habit. Leaving school, broken in health, he worked in various menial positions, but nothing seemed to help.

A year after he had submitted some poems and essays to the magazine *Merry England,* the editor, Wilfred Meynell, published them and went in search of their author. Thompson was found in the London slums and placed by Meynell in a hospital. Then he was placed under the care of the Canons Regular in Storrington. Cured of his addiction, he spent three years with the Capuchins in Wales. Returning to London, he remained there until his death.

Thompson's writings were originally published in three volumes. Two more volumes have appeared since. Among his works is an inspiring biography of St. Ignatius Loyola. His best-known poem, "The Hound of Heaven," is considered one of the world's greatest religious lyrics. It is autobiography at its best, as the opening lines reveal:

> I fled Him, down the nights and down the days;
>   I fled Him, down the arches of the years;
> I fled Him, down the labyrinthine ways
>   Of my own mind; and in the mist of tears
> I hid from Him, and under running laughter.

Thompson's writing proves that great literature is born of deep personal experience. In his case, it was depression, verging on despair, and the corresponding experience of divine mercy tracking down a sinner who was running away from a loving God.

SPECIALLY RECOMMENDED
Poems

53. *Robert Hugh Benson*

Robert Hugh Benson (1871–1914) was the youngest son of Edward W. Benson, Archbishop of Canterbury. After studies at Cambridge, he took Anglican orders in 1894 and was in charge of several parishes and missions until he entered the Catholic Church in 1903. A year later, he was ordained to the priesthood in Rome; he remained chaplain at Cambridge until 1908.

His published writings include plays, sermons, and essays, although he is best known as a novelist. His novels are remarkable for their vivid description of character and expression of fervent belief. *The Light Invisible* was published the year of his entrance into the Catholic Church. Then followed eight more novels in rapid succession: *By What Authority?, The King's Achievement, The Queen's Tragedy, The Sentimentalist, Papers of a Parish, Lord of the World, The Necromancers,* and *None Other Gods. Come Rack! Come Rope!* is in a class by itself as a historical novel in that it features the English martyr St. Edmund Campion.

Benson was probably the first son of an Anglican archbishop to become a Catholic since Jobie Mathew, son of the Archbishop of York, did so in 1606. His distinguished origin was soon forgotten in his own achievements. His short life was literally exhausted by the selfless service he gave to others. He had phenomenal success as a preacher. Not surprisingly, his strong faith drew thousands to hear him and brought many converts to the Church. He preached Lenten sermons in Rome in 1909, 1911, and 1913, and in the alternate years in the United States.

Everything he wrote was done with an avowed purpose and is marked by charm of style, subtle psychology, and appealing mysticism. Many of his novels are histories of a soul completely surrendered to God.

One thing that cannot be said of Benson is that he indulged in platitudes. His language was never ambiguous, as illustrated in the following passage from *Christ in the Church,* where he is writing about Judas:

> The Catholic Church has, I think, this characteristic in an almost unique degree, that while on one side she is capable of arousing the most passionate devotion that can ever be given to a Society, she also arouses, in those who leave her, the most violent opposition. An indifferent apostate is a very rare phenomenon.
>
> The very intensity with which the Church is assailed by those who were once her friends, and the lengths to which they will go—this is a mark of what she is as of all the sanctity of her saints.
>
> Of course, these ex-lovers of the Church found their accusations again and again upon what is objectively true. They know well her weakest lines of defense, and her very human Humanity. They have a private key to the door of the garden where she may always be found.
>
> Now, it is characteristic of Divine Truth alone to be treated in such a manner always and consistently. Human opinions are as incapable of calling out this white-hot antagonism, as they are incapable of drawing out the highest devotion. The really monumental crimes of human history are always concerned with really great principles; and the very pre-eminence of Judas' treachery is a sort of witness to the unique cause which it concerned. The whole world consents that the crime of Judas is the crime *par excellence* of human experience. Is not this very consent a witness to the unique character of the cause and the Person that were betrayed? Other traitors have betrayed other friends, but their names have not passed into proverbs as a consequence.

Robert Hugh Benson had no illusions about what it means to *be,* and not merely be called, a Catholic.

SPECIALLY RECOMMENDED
> *Christ in the Church*
> *The Light Invisible*
> *The Necromancers*
> *Come Rack! Come Rope!*

54. *Henryk Sienkiewicz*

Henryk Sienkiewicz (1846–1916) was born in a rural area of Poland, far from the major population centers, and died in Switzerland. Of Lithuanian descent, he spent most of his lifetime under czarist-Russian rule. After studies in Warsaw, he went into journalism and then began a career of publication that won him the Nobel Prize in literature in 1905.

He wrote short stories, including some about the emigrant Polish people in America, and novels. Among the latter is a trilogy based on Polish history. It appeared in English as *With Fire and Sword; The Flood* or *The Deluge;* and *Pan Michael* or *The Little Knight.* His best-known Catholic novel, *Quo Vadis?,* was published in 1896 and translated into English the following year.

The materials from which Sienkiewicz fashioned *Quo Vadis?* were the spectacle of the burning of Rome and the Roman amphitheater, where gladiators fought to the death and Christians were devoured by wild beasts. It was a civilization that boasted the greatest pomp and splendor since the dawn of history, but it was also a civilization on its way to historic decay. Sienkiewicz carefully researched the events and persons he used to weave into a powerful story. When first published in Poland, the book became a best-seller. It was translated into all the major European and several Oriental languages. For more than a generation, *Quo Vadis?* was one of the most widely read novels in the world.

It is not difficult to explain its popularity. Since the author lived in Poland under czarist domination, he knew from experience something of the meaning of oppression, so vividly described in *Quo Vadis?* Moreover, Sienkiewicz was a master at character portrayal. The Christians Lygia, Crispus, Peter, and Paul are portrayed as virtuous persons indeed, but thoroughly human nevertheless. The shrewdness of Petronius, the wickedness of Marcus, the cunning of Poppaea, the sensuality of Nero, the simplemindedness of Ursus, the hypocrisy of Chilon, and the puritan fanaticism of Crispus are clearly and carefully painted by the historian-novelist.

Quo Vadis? is a long book, over five hundred pages in a standard English edition. To call it fascinating would be an understatement; it is profoundly moving. The closing chapters depict the final days of Emperor Nero, who was putting untold numbers of Christians to death in the Colosseum because they were followers of Christ. The Christians would be led, one group at a time, to be devoured by the wild beasts, for the entertainment of Nero and thousands of spectators in the stands. At one point, the leader of a pack of lions at first hesitates when it sees a father on his knees trying to pull his trembling child from his neck to hand it to those kneeling further on, so as "to prolong its life even for a moment." The child's cry and the movement irritate the lion. "All at once he gave out a short, broken roar, killed the child with one blow of his paw, and, seizing the head of the father in his jaws, crushed it in a twinkle." This passage follows:

At sight of this all the other lions fell upon the crowd of Christians. Some women could not restrain cries of terror: but the audience drowned these with plaudits, which soon ceased, however, for the wish to see gained the mastery. They beheld terrible things then: heads disappearing entirely in open jaws, breasts torn apart with one blow, hearts and lungs swept away; the crushing of bones under the teeth of lions. Some lions, seizing victims by the ribs or loins, ran with mad springs through the arena, as if seeking hidden places in which to devour them; others fought, rose on their hind legs, grappled one another like wrestlers, and filled the amphitheatre with thunder. People rose from their places. Some left their seats, went down lower through the passages to see better, and crowded one another mortally. It seemed that the excited multitude would throw itself at last into the arena, and rend the Christians in company with the lions. At moments an unearthly noise was heard; at moments applause; at moments roaring, rumbling, the clashing of teeth, the howling of Molossian dogs; at times only groans.

Caesar, holding the emerald to his eye, looked now with attention.

But from the cuniculum new victims were driven out continually.

From the highest row in the amphitheatre the Apostle Peter looked at them. No one saw him, for all heads were turned to the arena; so he rose, and, as formerly in the vineyard of Cornelius he had blessed for death and eternity those who were intended for imprisonment, so now he blessed with the cross those who were perishing under the teeth of wild beasts. He blessed their blood, their torture, their dead bodies turned into shapeless masses, and their souls flying away from the bloody sand. Some raised their eyes to him, and their faces grew radiant; they smiled when they saw high above them the sign of the cross. But his heart was rent, and he said, "O Lord! let Thy will be done. These my sheep perish to Thy glory, in testimony of the truth. Thou didst command me to feed them; hence I give them to Thee, and do thou count them, Lord, take them, heal their wounds, soften their pain, give them happiness greater than the torments they suffered here."

Quo Vadis? deals with more than just persecution of the Christians by Nero. It is a tribute to the greatness of Sts. Peter and Paul, a denunciation of materialism, and a glorification of Christianity that has survived two millennia of oppression by godless civil powers.

SPECIALLY RECOMMENDED
> *Quo Vadis?*
> *With Fire and Sword*
> *The Deluge*

55. *Augustin Poulain*

The fame of some writers rests upon their only published book. Augustin Poulain (1836–1919) is such an author, and *The Graces of Interior Prayer* is such a book.

After completing his studies in the Society of Jesus, teaching mathematics, and directing an artists' guild, Poulain came out with *The Graces of Interior Prayer* in 1901 and surprised everyone. Even his friends did not know he had any special ability in the field of mysticism or the theology of prayer. Yet, in the author's own lifetime, the book went through nine editions and was translated into several foreign languages.

What makes the book a classic of spiritual writing is its clear explanation of the most-profound areas of mystical experience. Poulain maintained that there is a real difference between ascetical and mystical states.

The delicacy and difficulty of the subject did not deter the author from offering his readers a systematic treatise on prayer. At the same time, he provided guidelines for the growth in the spiritual life based on the Church's two millennia of supernatural experience.

Poulain makes clear at the outset that he is dealing with mysticism, not asceticism. In other words, he calls asceticism that form of the spiritual life which a person practices by being faithful to the graces received from God. Mysticism, however, is the spiritual life in which God confers extraordinary gifts on a soul. "I speak," he says, "of the things that God as King performs in certain souls, and not of those which these souls should themselves accomplish in order that God may reign in them." We might say that Poulain is mainly concerned with the special graces that God confers on some persons, called mystics, as distinct from the graces received by persons, called ascetics, who may, however, reach a high degree of sanctity.

Poulain's five preliminary criteria for appraising mysticism are a good synopsis of his famous book:

1. The mystic graces do not lift the soul out of the ordinary conditions of Christian life, or free it from the necessity of aiming at perfection. Whatever the state, whatever the road by which the soul is led, the way to show our love for God and to incline towards Him successfully, consists in avoiding sin, in the exercise of the practices of virtue; in renunciation and humiliation; in self-conquest, so that the heart may be emptied of self and a way made plain for grace; in a generous performance of the duties of our state. The paths of duty, or renunciation, and of humility are for all alike: there are no exceptions.

2. Mystical graces are not sanctity. They are merely powerful means of sanctification; but they must be received with humility and corresponded to with generosity. . . . One of the surest signs of the Spirit of God is an instinctive horror of any singularity of conduct, of exceptions, of privileges, of all that distinguishes the soul from other souls and attracts attention to her.

3. To pass our time in dreaming of the mystic ways is a dangerous error. If a desire for extraordinary graces of union is not forbidden as a general principle, if it may, theoretically speaking, be good, yet illusions are very easy and are not of rare occurrence. Certain souls flatter their self-love by making ready for these graces, as if there could be any preparation other than fidelity to all the

duties of our state, than the practice of the ordinary virtues, than the perfecting of our most common actions. By chimerical aspirations after blessings which are not in accordance with their actual dispositions, certain souls lose the graces of sanctity which God had destined for them. The practical course is to perfect ourselves in the ways in which our feet have been set; it is to correspond to the graces that we possess to-day.

4. One of the great advantages of St. Ignatius' method of spirituality is that it is a system of good sense and of action, a practical spirituality; and nothing could be more opposed to the illusion of chimerical desires and a vague sentimentality. It is in full accord here with true mysticism. And it is so also in a more positive way, by helping the soul to mount up with the aid of grace towards the highest sanctity by the gospel paths of renunciation and in the spirit of humility. Fixing its gaze lovingly upon the divine Master and Model, it removes all obstacles to the divine action, and prepares the soul in a marvelous way to feel its most delicate touches.

5. For all spiritual questions it is necessary to have a director. The more extraordinary the ways by which the soul is led, the greater, as a rule, is the need of direction.

When Poulain first published *The Graces of Interior Prayer* on the feast of St. Francis de Sales, he said, "I pray God that this book may accomplish the only end that I had in view: the good of souls. May it awaken within them an attraction for prayer and the need to unite themselves closely with the divine Master." All the evidence is that the author's hope has been realized.

SPECIALLY RECOMMENDED
  The Graces of Interior Prayer

56. *James Gibbons*

Some people may wonder why *The Faith of Our Fathers* by James Cardinal Gibbons (1834–1921) should be included in this Lifetime Reading Plan. There are several reasons. Gibbons was the recognized leader of the Catholic Church in America. His prudent guidance as Cardinal Archbishop of Baltimore, the mother church in the United States, won him the acceptance not only of believing Catholics but of persons outside the visible Church.

Gibbons' understanding of Catholicism in America was ex-

traordinary. As a priest, he knew that his first duty was to minister to the spiritual needs of the faithful. But he also saw the
larger need of preserving the Catholic faith in a culture that
gloried in its freedom and the bulk of whose population was not
Catholic. Against this background, it is easy to see why Gibbons
published *The Faith of Our Fathers* on the first centenary of America's independence (1876). Although covering every important
aspect of Catholic faith, morals, and worship, the book was pri-
marily written to explain Catholicism to non-Catholics. The
very title emphasized that the faith of Catholics is indeed the
same faith that was professed over the centuries since the time
of Christ.

Gibbons' opening paragraph of the Introduction to *The Faith of
Our Fathers* could not be more outspoken:

> Perhaps this is the first time in your life that you have handled a book in
> which the doctrines of the Catholic Church are explained by one of her own
> sons. You have, no doubt, heard and read many things regarding our Church;
> but has not your information come from teachers justly liable to suspicion?
> You asked for bread, and they gave you a stone. You asked for a fish, and they
> reached you a serpent. Instead of the bread of truth, they extended to you the
> serpent of falsehood. Hence, without intending to be unjust, is not your mind
> biased against us because you listened to false witnesses? This, at least, is the
> case with thousands of my countrymen whom I have met in the brief course of
> my missionary career. The Catholic Church is persistently misrepresented by
> the most powerful vehicles of information.

Then follow four hundred pages of explanation of what Catholics believe and why. The author's purpose is not polemical but
informative. The numerous printings through which the book
has gone testify to its lasting value.

SPECIALLY RECOMMENDED
   The Faith of Our Fathers
   The Ambassador of Christ

57. Alice Meynell

The English poet and essayist Alice Meynell (1847–1922) converted to the Catholic faith in 1870. Seven years later, she married Wilfrid Meynell and with him edited *The Pen*, which brought them into association with Browning, Rossetti, Ruskin, and Swinburne. She and her husband edited *The Weekly Register* from 1881 to 1898 and the monthly magazine *Merry England* from 1883 to 1895.

Her *Poems, Other Poems*, and *Later Poems* appeared between 1893 and 1902; *A Father of Women* in 1917; and *Last Poems* in 1923. She also published at least six volumes of essays, whose influence was widespread.

Her early poetry is musical and sentimental, but her later poetry is packed tight with faith and serious reflections. One of her first sonnets, "Renouncement," was described by John Ruskin as the most beautiful ever written by a woman. It begins:

> I must not think of thee; and, tired yet strong,
> I shun the thought that lurks in all delight—
> The thought of thee—and in the blue Heaven's bright height,
> And in the dearest passage of a song.

Among her collected essays is a volume with a long introduction by her son, Sir Francis Meynell. He says of his mother that "she was the most loved of women. She had the love of her husband, my father, now ninety-five years old, still in this year of her centenary celebration [1947] strongly alive in his faculties. She had the love of her family—seven children, who grew up in the most devoted and familiar relationship."

Coventry Patmore was almost an old man when he met her. She had the most fervent love for his poetry, and he for her womanhood.

Alice Meynell's devotion to the Blessed Virgin was deep and theologically oriented. In her essay "Mary, the Mother of Jesus," she wrote that "the mothers of all ages are those who have suf-

fered because others suffered; for each of them, self is less sensitive than the self of her child." Then she goes on to extend this
motherly compassion to the honor of a woman as the reflection
of a glory greater than her own:

The greatest honor ever given to a woman, or indeed to any creature, was
absolutely a reflective honour. Of all reflective glory the glory of the Mother of
Christ is the supreme example—so perfect an example that it might rather be
called the solitary pattern. Have some enthusiasts seemed—whether they were
poets writing sonnets in honour of the moon or Christians singing hymns in
honour of Mary—to give their more sensible tenderness to the secondary
splendour, have they seemed to forget that the moonlight is the sunlight simply returned, and Mary a moon to the sun of Christ, they have only seemed.
The consciousness of God, as the giver, the giver of all, lay immovably deep in
the heart of the peasant saying ten "Aves" to one "Pater Noster." Nay, the case
of Mary is singular in this entire humility and humiliation. For we may all
irrationally and nearly unconsciously attribute some glory of genius to the
poet, for instance, as though it were his own by origin; but in the case of the
Mother of Christ there is no such vague illusion. The little idolatries that are
offered to the poet or the soldier are withheld from her who is pre-eminent
only for sanctity bestowed, and distinguished only by her office assigned, the
preparation therefor, and the reward thereafter. And this similitude of Mary
and the moon is so perfect that it is a wonder the simple should need, or the
churches erect, images of the Virgin of Nazareth, the Virgin of the Annunciation, the Mother of the Seven Sorrows, or Our Lady of Peace, or the Mother of
Christ by His Cross, or Mary under any invocation whatever, when, month by
month, newly lighted every month, the moon presents her absolute similitude,
her image with the superscription of her Lord. And yet there is a nation with a
noble language that incredibly makes the moon masculine, facing—with ef-
frontery—a feminine sun.

It is no wonder that Alice Meynell's writing was so much
appreciated by the most exacting critics of her time. Nor is it any
wonder that she gave her husband so much help in his own
literary work.

SPECIALLY RECOMMENDED
   Poems: Complete Edition
   Essays

58. *Adolphe Alfred Tanquerey*

Adolphe Tanquerey, dogmatic and moral theologian (1854–1923), was born in Aix-en-Provence, ordained a priest, and entered the Society of St. Sulpice. His first teaching position as a Sulpician was at Rodez, France, but his longest was at St. Mary's Seminary in Baltimore (1887–1902).

Tanquerey did not write much. Most of his life was spent in the classroom, teaching seminarians. But his main claim to fame rests on three books: *A Manual of Dogmatic Theology,* in three volumes, later republished in two volumes; *Doctrine and Devotion;* and *The Spiritual Life,* which was originally published as *A Precis of Ascetic and Mystical Theology.* Among these titles, the one specially recommended here is the last one. It has gone through numerous printings since it first appeared in France in 1923. Though almost eight hundred pages in translation, *The Spiritual Life* is unsurpassed as the most detailed yet compact testament of Catholic spirituality available in English. Originally intended as a textbook, this volume has been the mainstay of thousands of priests, religious, and laypeople.

Certain of the book's features stand out. It is clear and lively, practical and nonpolemical. The author recognizes that the spiritual life is sound only insofar as it is based on divine revelation and in full conformity with the teachings of the Church. In his own words, this book is "first of all doctrinal in character and aims at bringing out the fact that Christian perfection is the logical outcome of dogma, especially of the central dogma of the Incarnation. The work, however, is also practical, for a vivid realization of the truths of faith is the strongest incentive to earnest and steady efforts toward the correction of faults and the practice of virtues."

Tanquerey draws on the spiritual wisdom of the ages, from New Testament times to the present century. He quotes hundreds of passages from hundreds of masters of the spiritual life. Yet, the whole work is carefully arranged in a coherent order in sixteen hundred sections, each subdivided and coordinated to form a composite literary whole.

The Spiritual Life is first of all an immensely useful book of information on almost every aspect of the pursuit of holiness. Its language is plain yet beautiful. Its terms are never ambiguous. Its many quotations are from classics of the spiritual life, and its references are a treasury of knowledge for further study and reflection. Above all, *The Spiritual Life* is a devotional treatise for spiritual reading. A single page or a single paragraph can be profitably meditated on. Through prayerful reflection, the truths explained by the author can become the foundation for growth in the spiritual life.

SPECIALLY RECOMMENDED
The Spiritual Life: A Treatise on Ascetical and Mystical Theology

59. *Joseph Columba Marmion*

Few people have rivaled the zealous monastic life of Joseph Columba Marmion (1858–1923). Marmion was born in Dublin of an Irish father and a French mother; ordained in Rome; entered the Benedictines; and, after fourteen years as abbot, died at Maredsous, Belgium.

His life was phenomenally apostolic. Besides guiding the monastery, he preached retreats, kept up an immense correspondence, and wrote books that promise to remain standards of Catholic spirituality for generations to come.

The spirituality he wrote about is very simple. In his own words, all he wanted to do was "to fix the eyes and the hearts of my readers on Jesus Christ and on His Word. He is the Alpha and the Omega of all sanctity and His word is the divine seed from which all sanctity springs."

His best-known books are *Christ, the Life of the Soul, Christ in His Mysteries,* and *Union with God.*

Implicit in Marmion's teaching is the conviction that what people most need is to hear the words of Christ, directly as recorded in the Gospels, and see Him as described by the Evangelists. Marmion believed that such an overlay of speculation and interpretation obscures the New Testament that for too many, even sincere believers, there is a barrier between them and the Master. However, the greatest obstacle to following Christ is people's own preconception and self-will. He describes such people in *Christ, the Life of the Soul:*

> They make holiness consist in such or such a conception formed by their own intelligence; attached to those purely human ideas they have formed, they go astray; if they make great strides, it is outside the true way marked out by God; they are victims of those illusions against which St. Paul warned the first Christians.
>
> In so grave a matter, in so vital a questions, we must look at and weigh things as God looks and weighs them. God judges all things in the light, and His judgment is the test of all truth. "We must not judge according to our own liking," says St. Francis de Sales, "but according to God's will."
>
> Divine Wisdom is infinitely above human wisdom; God's thoughts contain possibilities of fruitfulness such as no created thought possesses. That is why God's plan is so wise that it cannot fail to reach its end because of any intrinsic insufficiency, but only through our own fault. If we leave the Divine idea full freedom to operate in us, if we adapt ourselves to it with love and fidelity, it becomes extremely fruitful and may lead us to the most sublime sanctity.

Marmion never tires of repeating that Christ's plan for our sanctification is simplicity personified. The results of ignoring this fact can be disastrous. Ingenious and complicated "souls that have not understood the mystery of Christ lose themselves in a multiplicity of details and often weary themselves in a joyless labor. Why is this? Because all that our human ingenuity is able to create for our inner life serves for nothing if we do not base our edifice on Christ."

This stress on taking Christ and His teaching literally is the secret of the remarkable influence of Marmion's books. Basic, however, to following Christ literally is the faith conviction that the one we are following is God Himself in human form. He is at once the Author of our Redemption and the infinite Treasury of grace, the Model of our perfection and the Goal of our destiny— but only because He is the all-perfect God who became man to die for our salvation and to teach us how we are to reach heaven.

SPECIALLY RECOMMENDED
 Christ, the Life of the Soul
 Christ in His Mysteries

60. *Ottokár Prohászka*

The published writings of Ottokár Prohászka (1858–1927) fill twenty-five volumes. Most of them are still untranslated from the Hungarian. The best-known in English is his three-volume *Meditations on the Gospels.*

It is almost impossible to exaggerate the intellectual greatness of this man. Born in the year of the apparitions of Our Lady at Lourdes, he had a deep, childlike devotion to the Mother of God. When he suffered a fatal cerebral hemorrhage while preaching to a crowded university audience, he was still able to raise his left hand in blessing. "May Almighty God bless," he said strongly. The next day, he died.

When Cardinal Mazella ordained Prohászka in Rome at the age of twenty-three, he declared that the young priest's mind was so strong that it would impress millions. "If he were a heretic," the cardinal added, "he would disturb no fewer." As a priest, Prohászka combined the teaching of theology to seminarians and university students with an extraordinary devotion to meeting the needs of the poor. He visited the destitute on a regular basis and never tired of warning those who had more to share their possessions with those who had less. More than once, he deprived himself even of necessary food to feed the hungry.

Not long after his ordination, he began to write for publication. Under the pseudonym of Petho, he wrote for a magazine called *The Hungarian Lion.* Soon he took to writing books. His first independent work was *God and the World* (1892), soon followed by *Christian Repentance and Forgiveness.*

By the turn of the century, there was a popular demand for his elevation to the episcopate. Pope Pius X personally called him to Rome and ordained him bishop in 1905. He was given the very poor diocese of Székesfehérvár. As bishop, he intensified his apostolic and literary life. He would spend long hours in the confessional and urge his priests to do the same.

When Béla Kun's Communists gave the Church in Hungary a litany of martyrs, Prohászka did not flee. He survived that first Communist revolution, but was left destitute because he had given everything he had to care for the poor. His health began to fail. But no one was less an invalid. It was during these years that he wrote some of his most inspiring books on the Gospels.

Given the wide range of his published writing, it seems best to identify the main features of his thought. Prohászka was always practical. He never merely speculated. He would reduce the profound mysteries preached and lived by Christ to everyday life. For him, the Gospels were literally God's directives to the human race, as clear and definite in the twentieth century as they had been in the first.

Divine grace, Prohászka insisted, is never wanting. What is often sadly lacking is our willingness to work in cooperation with the grace we are receiving. Words like "labor," "energy," "work," and "effort" keep recurring in the bishop's writings. And St. Joseph is an excellent model:

St. Joseph is the faithful servant. A servant is anyone who works for others, or who exerts himself in the name and interest of others. Here upon earth St. Joseph was the shadow of God the Father; he carried out the Divine directions and decrees, and had no thought for himself. In this he resembled Eliezer, the servant of Abraham, who was sent to distant countries in the interests of his master, and who was entirely trustworthy. The Gospel has nothing to tell us about St. Joseph; he stands in the background of the Divine mysteries, and yet devout people are instinctively aware of the wealth and sanctity of his inner life. We too must serve God with faithfulness and constancy, and be, like St. Joseph, His faithful servants. This is man's noblest title.

St. Joseph, the faithful servant, served God to the fullest extent of all his spiritual and bodily powers; his soul was filled with troubles, cares and anxieties, yet God enlightened Him: "Fear not to take unto thee Mary, thy wife . . ."; "Fly into Egypt, and be there . . ."; "being warned in sleep retired into the quarters of Galilee." He had to earn bread for the Son of God by his own exertions, yet this manual labor sanctified his soul and brought him ever closer to God. Devout people, the artists of the Middle Ages, members of religious orders—all these understand this. And we can all imitate St. Joseph in this, no matter what our station and circumstances may be.

Yet, with all his strenuous exertion, Joseph never lost his peace of soul. "Tranquillity, humility and submissiveness characterize this faithful servant" was Prohászka's summary estimate of the foster father of the Son of God. This could also be a synthesis of all the writings of the Bishop of Székesfehérvár. He should be better known to English-speaking readers. Martindale does not hesitate to place him "intellectually above Newman, seeing that his range of interests was wider and his output more varied in theme."

One of my hopes for *The Catholic Lifetime Reading Plan* is that it will make writers of Prohászka's stature more familiar and their books more widely read.

SPECIALLY RECOMMENDED
Meditations on the Gospels

61. *Ludwig von Pastor*

The greatest historian of the papacy, Ludwig von Pastor (1854–1928), was born in Germany and died in Austria. During his lifetime, he taught Church history at Innsbruck, was director of the Austrian Historical Institute in Rome, and was the Austrian envoy to the Holy See for the last eight years of his life.

A prodigious writer who was also a meticulous scholar, Pastor published numerous works of history. But his chief claim to fame is the monumental *History of the Popes*. As I know from experience, reading *The History of the Popes* in forty volumes is a challenge. But it is most rewarding. In an age when the papacy is being widely attacked, it is deeply satisfying to know that, like Christ in the first century, the Vicars of Christ have been opposed in every century. Yet, they have maintained the integrity of the faith and have remained, in Pastor's words, "the most ancient and still the most vigorous of dynasties."

Why did Pastor write this exhaustive history of the papacy? His main reason was to make the papacy better known and appreciated. But there were other reasons, too, notably the fact that for the first time in the Church's history, the secret Archives of the Vatican were opened (by Pope Leo XIII) for use by scholars. Since authentic history depends on authentic sources, the opening of the Vatican Archives practically demanded that the history of the Popes during the previous four centuries be rewritten.

In addition to the secret Archives of the Vatican, Pastor also had access to the Consistorial Archives and the archives of the Lateran, the Inquisition, the Propaganda, the Sistine Chapel, and the Secretariat of Papal Briefs; the Library of St. Peter's; and the Angelica, Barberina, Casanatense, Chigi, Corsini, Vallicellana, Altieri, Borghese, and Buoncompagni libraries. He also used the archives of the Anima, Campo Santo al Vaticano, and Santo Spirito; the Roman princes; and the Colonna, Gaetani, Ricci, Odescalchi, and Orsini families.

The overwhelming mass of documents convinced Pastor that he should concentrate on the archives from the middle of the fifteenth century. He considered that period as the close of the Middle Ages and the beginning of modern times. In this way, too, justice would be done to the last century before the break in Christian unity caused by the Protestant Reformation. Moreover, the longest and most doctrinally prolific council of the Church, the Council of Trent, would be seen in its full historical perspective.

The truly remarkable feature of Pastor's volumes is that, while scholarly in the extreme, they are not stodgy or preoccupied with minor details. On the contrary, as I can attest from three years of reading *The History of the Popes* daily, these books are fascinating and most revealing. Footnotes direct the reader to further research on hundreds of topics. But the narrative itself reads like a best-selling novel, except that this is not fiction but historical fact. The human side of the papacy and of the Church stands out very plainly, but the divine side becomes equally clear and inspiring.

This massive history begins with Martin V (1417) and ends with Pius VI (1799). It was Pope Martin V whose election resolved the Great Western Schism that divided the Church when there were several claimants to the papacy, and it was Pope Pius VI who died in France as a prisoner of Napoleon Bonaparte.

Fifty-five Popes are covered by Pastor. He skillfully blends the inner life of the papacy with the political and cultural forces that affected the successors of St. Peter. An unspoken premise of the author is that only a believing Catholic can truly understand and interpret the papacy. Naturally, some historians have challenged this premise but without sufficient grounds. Whatever else may be said about *The History of the Popes,* it is not a panegyric of the papacy or an apologetic for Catholic Christianity. It is an objective, scientifically researched classic that, without intending to do so, shows how truly the promise to Peter has been fulfilled. The Bishops of Rome have been the Rock on which Christ built His Church, and the gates of hell have not prevailed against it.

SPECIALLY RECOMMENDED
The History of the Popes

62. *Jean-Baptiste Chautard*

Reformed Cistercian abbot and ascetical theologian, Jean-Baptiste Chautard (1858–1935) entered a Trappist monastery at the age of nineteen. From 1897 until his death, he was an abbot, first at Chambarand and then, for thirty-six years, at Sept-Fons. Besides the heavy responsibilities of his own monastery, he had the direction of several other monasteries of his order. In 1903, when other religious houses were being closed, Chautard pleaded so well before the French senate for his monks that the government reversed its decision and the Trappist order was allowed to continue in France.

As a busy administrator, Chautard did not have much time for writing. His main influence on the monks was through the daily conferences he gave them. He also carried on an extensive correspondence with people outside the monastery. Chautard, by nature and temperament a down-to-earth man of affairs, was put to the test during World War I, when many of his monks were conscripted into the armed forces. Chautard visited them regularly and worked incessantly to provide shelter for other monks who had been exiled by the war. He provided asylum for orphans and a home for the aged.

His life is a catalog of activities that would have strained the efforts of a member of the most active religious community in the Church. He had to purchase real estate; renovate the property; and, in one case, remake an old monastic building into a chocolate factory to provide some revenue for the monks of Aiguebelle.

It was therefore out of his own personal experience that he wrote *The Soul of the Apostolate.* The book was written with no concern for literary style but is filled with the fire of Chautard's spirit. Its great value lies in the proved value of the author's central theme: that our labor for the spiritual welfare of others is effective only insofar as we are united with God within ourselves. Chautard's thesis is that active apostolic work does not weaken the spiritual life. On the contrary, it deepens that life and contributes to the worker's sanctification. The basic principle is that "God wants active works." He wrote:

Consequently, if we were to view works, considered in themselves, as an obstacle to sanctification, and assert that, *although springing from the Divine Will* they *necessarily* slow down our advance towards perfection, it would be an insult, a blasphemy against the Wisdom and Goodness and Providence of God.

Hence, the following dilemma is inescapable: either the apostolate, no matter what form it takes, if it is *God's will,* not only does not bring about in itself as its effect any alteration in the atmosphere of solid virtue which ought to surround a soul that has a care for salvation and for spiritual progress, but it must also, and always, provide the apostle with a *means of sanctification,* so long as his apostolic work keeps within the *due conditions.*

Or else, the person whom God has chosen to work with Him, and who is therefore obliged to answer the divine call, will have every right to offer the activity, the troubles and cares undergone for the sake of the work commanded by Him, as legitimate excuses for his failure to sanctify himself.

Now it is a consequence of the economy of the divine plan that God *owes it to Himself* to provide his chosen apostle with graces necessary to make distracting business compatible not only with the assurance of salvation but even with the acquisition of virtues which can lead as high as sanctity itself. God *owes* the kind of help He gave to His St. Bernards and St. Francis Xaviers to the humblest of his preachers of the Gospel, to the lowliest teaching brother, to the most obscure nursing sister, in the measure required by each one of them. Such aid is a real *Debt of the Sacred Heart,* owed by Him to His chosen instruments. Let us not fear to repeat it over and over again. And every apostle, provided he fulfils the due conditions, should have an *absolute confidence in his inviolable right* to the graces demanded by a work whose very nature gives him a mortgage on the infinite treasure of divine aid.

This same principle of the divine economy applies also to the lay apostles of our day. It applies to parents, whose first and most important apostolate is to their children. It applies to husbands and wives in their apostolate to each other. It applies to the growing number of lay catechists, on whose zeal the future of the Church so greatly depends.

But Chautard brings out another aspect of this critical subject. By all the modern logic of efficiency, it would seem that education, professional training, and the acquisition of various skills are what a successful apostolate mainly requires. Not so, argues Chautard. All the skills in pedagogy or knowledge of the social sciences are unimportant when compared with a deep love of God and the spirit of prayer. The essence of the apostolate, Chautard affirms, is to be a channel of grace to other people. But no one gives what he does not have.

On these terms, therefore, the soul of the apostolate is a deep spiritual life. Nourished by prayer and the sacraments and deepened by the patient bearing of the Cross, the spiritual life of the apostle becomes God's chosen means of converting and sanctifying everyone with whom the apostle comes into contact.

SPECIALLY RECOMMENDED
The Soul of the Apostolate

63. G. K. Chesterton

The career of journalist, poet, and apologist Gilbert Keith Chesterton (1874–1936) can be divided into four separate phases.

During the first phase, before 1900, Chesterton struggled between materialism and balanced reason, but not always successfully. As a result, he destroyed many of his early manuscripts and left "an absolute command" that his surviving early writings never be published.

Then he married Frances Blogg in 1901, and this changed his life. The first of his more than one thousand essays in *The Illustrated London News* appeared in 1905. They were the prelude to a search for the full truth. As early as 1905, he published *Heretics,* and three years later he came out with *Orthodoxy,* which is a strong defense of Christianity.

The next phase lasted until he entered the Catholic Church. Chesterton became associated with Hilaire Belloc and engaged in public debate with H. G. Wells and George Bernard Shaw. During these years the four men were influencing each other and England, and indirectly other English-speaking societies.

Finally, in 1922, he converted to Catholicism at forty-eight. The conversion had been gradual but inevitable. He had carefully reasoned out this momentous step, which deeply influenced his writings. He became more serious in his thinking, and the books he wrote from then on will probably prove his most enduring. His poetry and plays have become part of English literature, and his Father Brown stories place him among the prominent writers of fiction in the twentieth century.

Four works of his Catholic period stand out: *St. Francis of Assisi, The Everlasting Man, St. Thomas Aquinas,* and his autobiographical *The Catholic Church and Conversion.* A few sentences from this last work will illustrate the tone of Chesterton's writing:

This is one of the very queerest of the common delusions about what happens to the convert. In some muddled way people have confused the natural remarks of converts, about having found moral peace, with some idea of their having found mental rest, in the sense of mental inaction. They might as well say that a man who has completely recovered his health, after an attack of palsy or St. Vitus' dance, signalises his healthy state by sitting absolutely still like a stone. Recovering his health means recovering his power of moving in the right way as distinct from the wrong way; but he will probably move a great deal more than before. To become a Catholic is not to leave off thinking, but to learn how to think. It is so in exactly the same sense in which to recover from palsy is not to leave off moving but to learn how to move. The Catholic convert has for the first time a way of testing the truth in any question that he raises.

The best word to describe Chesterton's writings is brilliant. His paradoxes almost overwhelm the reader with their extraordinary depth and what may be called "obviousness." He has been described as a plumed knight defending his lady, the Catholic Church, with a fidelity and sincerity of heart that cannot be matched by any other apologist.

Because Chesterton related everyday events and things to the eternal, his writings are sure to endure. Etienne Gilson called him "one of the deepest thinkers who ever existed." Pope Pius XI bestowed on him the rare title Defender of the Catholic Faith.

SPECIALLY RECOMMENDED
>   *St. Francis of Assisi*
>   *The Catholic Church and Conversion*
>   *The Everlasting Man*
>   *St. Thomas Aquinas*

64. *Fernand Cabrol*

The popular liturgical writer Fernand Cabrol (1855–1937) was born in France and died in England, and his life as a Benedictine monk also spanned both countries. He was prior at Solesmes (1890–96) and then founded St. Michael's Abbey in the English town of Farnborough, where he was abbot until his death.

Although Cabrol is commonly associated with popularizing liturgical writing, he was a scholar of the first magnitude. In

1900 he and Henri Leclercq began the *Monumenta Ecclesiae Liturgica* (The Liturgical Documents of the Church) as a collection of texts pertaining to the liturgy from apostolic times to Constantine. Volumes of this monumental work have been published and remain a permanent source of knowledge about the Church's liturgical teaching and practice in the Age of Persecution.

In 1903, Cabrol joined with his monks at Farnborough in the research that led to the publication of the *Dictionary of Christian Archaeology and Liturgy*, completed in 1953.

Best known of Cabrol's publications is *Liturgical Prayer: Its History and Spirit*. I consider it "must" reading for anyone who wants to understand what Our Lord meant when He said that where two or more are gathered in His name, He would be there in their midst. Through eight parts and over thirty chapters, Cabrol traces the history of the Church's communal prayer to the earliest Christian assemblies. But he does more than provide interesting data about the Church's liturgical development over the centuries: he analyzes, in depth and with spiritual fervor, such well-known prayers as the Our Father, the Gloria, the Te Deum and the principal Catholic creeds.

His section on "The Sanctification of Time" traces the origins and growth of the liturgical seasons, the Christian week and the Christian year. He goes into fascinating detail about the development of such practices as the consecration of churches, the use of holy water, blessed ashes, fire and lights, incense and bells.

The sacraments are placed into their ritual framework and seen in the context of the sacramentals that have surrounded them from ancient times. In fact, the sacramentals take on a meaning that would otherwise never have been seen. Since the first century, they have been the visual and audible vesture in which the sacraments were clothed.

Never ambiguous, Cabrol makes clear why the Church emphasized the use of sensibly perceptible things to teach and confer the things of the spirit:

In all times a symbolic meaning in harmony with their natural use has been attached to the great phenomena of nature and to material elements of universal utility.

Water, which has the power of cleansing and refreshing, is, in the language of signs as well as in that of religion, the symbol of purification. Fire not only burns, it also purifies like water: and again, it gives light. Oil softens, soothes, strengthens, renders supple. Salt gives flavour to food and preserves it. Every language contains expressions or metaphors derived from these words and based on these primitive ideas. For instance, we speak of fiery zeal, of the salt of wisdom; men endowed with a certain kind of eloquence are said to speak with unction.

The Church collected so carefully the traditions of the Mosaic worship and the golden nuggets buried in the mud of heathen religion, and borrowed so largely from the poetry of nature for her Liturgy, that she could not fail to adopt some of these profoundly expressive rites. That is why the ceremonies and formulas of the Liturgy so often stir us to the very depths of our being; they awake an echo in the human heart.

Reading Cabrol is not only informative; it is necessary. The Catholic liturgy has undergone many developments—which periodically occasioned not a few excesses. But always the liturgy has weathered the storms generated by its human creators.

SPECIALLY RECOMMENDED
   Liturgical Prayer: Its History and Spirit
   The Prayer of the Early Christians
   Mass of the Western Rites
   The Mass: Its Doctrine, Its History

65. *Ferdinand Prat*

Ferdinand Prat (1857–1938), Jesuit exegete, was born at Aveyron and died at Toulouse, France. After studies in Beirut and Paris, he taught Scripture in France, Belgium, Lebanon, and Rome. One of the first consultants to the Pontifical Biblical Commission, he contributed to the early decision on the historicity of the Bible and helped in the planning of the Pontifical Biblical Institute in Rome.

His most lasting publication is the two-volume *Theology of St. Paul* (1912), which has gone through numerous editions and translations. The first volume is a scholarly but very readable study of the life of St. Paul and of each of the letters that the Church associates with his name. Within each letter, Prat chooses the most important teachings of the Apostle of the Gentiles and analyzes them in their original historical setting. A good example of his approach is his treatment of the question of the indissolubility of Christian marriage, taught by St. Paul in his first letter to the Corinthians:

St. Paul proclaims with as much force as the Synoptists the indissolubility of Christian marriage, for the law that he promulgates on this subject has the same origin: "To them that are married, not I but the Lord commandeth that the wife depart not from her husband; and if she depart, that she remain unmarried, or be reconciled to her husband. And let not the husband put away his wife." By oral tradition Paul must have known the Lord's precept recorded by the three Synoptists; he here presents it in a form which resembles the text of Mark, yet with remarkable differences. By virtue of this divine command the wife is forbidden to *depart from* her husband *(choristhenai)*, and the husband is forbidden to *put away* his wife *(aphienai)*; this gives a very delicate shade of expression to designate marital authority both from the Jewish and the Roman point of view. The Apostle foresees, however, cases of bodily separation actually taking place, and lets us understand that this may be legitimate; but under no hypothesis is the marriage tie broken. In fact, the wife separated from her husband has only two alternatives, either to be reconciled with him, which shows that the bond still exists, or to abstain from marrying another, which also proves the continuance of the first union. The putting away of the wife by the husband is prohibited without any restriction or exception, because this *putting away (aphienai)* meant, for Jews as well as for Gentiles, an act which would have for its effect the legal annulment of the conjugal contract. Since this case must never arise, there is no need of building other hypotheses upon it. The indissolubility of Christian marriage has, therefore, no limits put upon it by St. Paul. As he loves to repeat, marriage is broken only by death. A woman will always be called an adulteress if she contracts a new marriage during the lifetime of her husband, and it would be the same with the man who remarried during the lifetime of his wife; for these two terms are correlative, and the Apostle establishes between husband and wife, from a conjugal point of view, perfect equality of rights and duties.

The second volume of *Theology of St. Paul* is an exhaustive analysis of the leading themes of Paul's revealed doctrine, notably the Redemption, the Church, the sacraments, morality and holiness, and the Last Things—that is, death, judgment, heaven, and hell.

Underlying all of St. Paul's letters is the fact of man's sinfulness and need of a Redeemer. Prat brings out the fact that, because of Christ, the tragedy of sin has become the occasion of graces that would otherwise not have come into this world.

SPECIALLY RECOMMENDED
> *Theology of St. Paul*
> *Jesus Christ: His Life, His Teaching, and His Works*

66. *Marie Joseph Lagrange*

The outstanding French biblical scholar Marie Joseph Lagrange (1855–1938) had a doctorate in law before he entered the Dominican Order. Since the Dominicans had been expelled from France, he finished his studies in Spain, where he was ordained in 1883. After ordination, he undertook Oriental studies at the University of Vienna and in 1890 was sent to the Holy Land to establish a biblical school in Jerusalem.

The name of Lagrange cannot be separated from that of Leo XIII. In 1893 the Pope published a historic document, *Providentissimus Deus* (The God of All Providence), on the study of the Bible. His purpose was to clarify the Church's teaching on the absolute truth of the inspired Scriptures. This document was not academic. Leo XIII anticipated the practical need of establishing a professional center for biblical studies in Palestine. Seeing the sad state of contemporary Catholic exegesis, he encouraged the Jerusalem foundation in 1890 of the École Pratique d'Études Bibliques. It was Lagrange who organized this school. In order to keep the Catholic world posted on the progress of Scripture studies during those turbulent years for orthodoxy, Lagrange founded (1892) the quarterly *Revue biblique*, which soon attained international recognition.

There is more than passing value in seeing Lagrange as a protégé of Pope Leo XIII. Lagrange was the pioneer in modern biblical scholarship and was always respectful of the Church's magisterium, even while he tackled some of the most vexing problems that have faced Catholic exegetes in modern times.

A complete bibliography of Lagrange's writings contains, by actual count, 1,786 titles. Some are shorter monographs, others are long scientific treatises, and many have appeared as books in print.

His most popular work, *The Gospel of Jesus Christ*, first published in 1928, is a synthesis of the best in biblical scholarship as well as a thoroughly Catholic understanding of the Church's magisterium in interpreting the revealed word of God. Every sentence of Lagrange's two-volume classic is a reflection of its author's contemplative-academic approach to the Gospels. In the following quotation, Lagrange is describing the angel's annunciation to Mary:

She was a virgin and was betrothed to Joseph, a man belonging to the house or family of David. She too appears to have been of the same lineage, as we are led to understand by St. Luke. But at the same time she was, as we know, a relative of Elizabeth, who, like her husband Zachary, was of the tribe of Levi. It was not uncommon to find marriage taking place between the members of one tribe and those of another: hence it seems that Elizabeth owed her descent to a union contracted at some unknown date in the past between a daughter of the tribe of Juda and a son of the tribe of Levi.

This was the second time within six months that the Angel Gabriel had been charged with a message from God: but the whole character of his interview with Mary shows that the content of the present message was of far greater import than that of the message to Zachary. Zachary had been troubled and afraid at seeing the angel. The angel had delivered his message without first addressing any greeting to Zachary. But, in the case of Mary, the angel seeks her out in her own home and greets her thus: "Hail, full of grace, the Lord is with thee"—words that ever since have been so often repeated by the faithful. This was as much as to tell her that she enjoyed the favour of the Almighty in the fullest degree possible. It was only then that Mary was troubled, and the sole cause of her trouble was amazement at such a high-sounding title as "full of grace." She was not afraid, however, even though the angel bids her fear not, for the object of his coming was to bring her a grace from God of even more remarkable a character than the graces she had already received. She was to bear a Son whom she should call Jesus, in Hebrew Jeshua, which means: "Jaho [the God of Israel] is a saviour."

This Son was to be great: He should be regarded as the Son of the Most High. He was also to be a Son of David, called by God to sit upon the throne of His father: not, however, merely to reign for a few short years, but for ever, because His reign was to last unto all eternity.

What seems chiefly to have struck Mary in the words of the angel was the announcement that the Messiah to be born of her was to be a son of David. Ought she to conclude from this that he was to be the son of Joseph her betrothed, who himself belonged to the house of David? Following the dictates of ordinary human discernment—what we like to call the principles of common sense—we should reply without hesitation: Why not? Would not that be the natural thing to expect? But, on the other hand, far back in the days of eternity God had disposed the order of things in a very different fashion; according to that order, the Son of God was to have no other father than God the Father. As for Mary herself, she was astonished by the angel's words and asked: "How shall this be, because I know not Man?"

We have to admit that this was a surprising question to ask; so much, indeed, does it appear out of place that many biblical critics want to strike it out of the text altogether. But it is clear that if we were to do this we should thereby completely lose what St. Luke chiefly intends to convey in this passage: it would be like taking away the diamond and leaving only the setting. An author like Luke, possessing such a delicate touch and skilled in the art of expressing delicate shades of meaning, could never have placed on the lips of this Virgin full of grace anything that savoured of excessive naïveté, could never have allowed her to interpose mere commonplace truisms in the midst of such a divine communication. Hence, what Mary wished to say was that she was, as the angel well knew, a virgin and intended to remain so: according to the interpretation of the theologians, she had made a vow of virginity and was determined to keep it. Nevertheless, she was far from presuming to oppose her own will to the will of God which He had just begun to reveal to her. Thus, on her lips "I know not man," means "I desire not to know." She did not say "I will never know," having no desire to thwart the designs of God. Hence, she awaits the outcome of her question.

Even this commentary for the general reader has explanatory footnotes to show that every significant insight has been scientifically investigated. Yet, the whole is totally within the Church's doctrinal tradition, made more clear and meaningful through years of research and exegetical analysis.

Except for Lagrange, there would be no Jerusalem Bible today. It was the original pioneer work of his School of Biblical Studies in Palestine that laid the groundwork for *La Bible de Jérusalem.*

SPECIALLY RECOMMENDED

The Gospel of Jesus Christ

67. Alban Goodier

Archbishop and spiritual writer Alban Goodier (1869–1939) was ordained a Jesuit priest in 1903. He was sent to India during World War I, when all the German Jesuits withdrew from Bombay University. After settling the university problems, he was appointed Archbishop of Bombay in 1919; he remained in that post until 1926. Given the delicate politicoreligious problems then stirring in India, he resigned his see and became titular Archbishop of Hierapolis in Phrygia and auxiliary bishop in London. For the rest of his life he devoted himself to giving retreats, lectures, and sermons and writing books on the spiritual life. His best-known books are *The Public Life of Our Lord Jesus Christ*, in two volumes; *The Passion and Death of Our Lord Jesus Christ*; and *An Introduction to the Study of Ascetical and Mystical Theology*.

Goodier's approach in his two principal works, *The Public Life* and *The Passion*, is clearly explained by the author. He distinguishes three different approaches to writing about the Savior. The first type of book is essentially devotional, where the emphasis is on the affective side of our relation to Christ, where He inspires believers to learn from Him and strive to imitate Him in the practice of virtue. Goodier calls the second approach the historical; here an author has done careful research into the words and events surrounding the life and sufferings of the Redeemer.

The third category, in which Goodier places his own efforts, describes the events of Christ's life and His sufferings as they really took place, but not only in their historical aspect. Rather, the emphasis is on how Christ's contemporaries and companions experienced the presence of Jesus in their midst, how their minds and hearts were affected by Him, and how He was affected by the people and circumstances in which He was the Central Figure.

As a result, *The Public Life* and *The Passion* are interweavings of

Gospel passages with a running commentary on how the event or episode in question shaped, and was shaped by, those who participated in the drama of God living and suffering, in order to inspire us to follow His example.

The opening paragraph of *The Passion and Death of Our Lord Jesus Christ* is typical of Goodier's two classic volumes. He strives to describe the Passion as it really took place, but in a unique way —as it occurred "in the minds and hearts of those who went through it, especially of Him who was the Central Figure." This explains "why those who have known it best, who have entered into it and lived it, have usually said least about it." Then Goodier states what one needs to write understandingly about the sufferings of Christ:

Understanding of the Passion demands active compassion, such compassion as cannot be expressed in words. It demands not only a power of deep sympathy, but active suffering of one's own; only by suffering ourselves can we understand at all what the Passion, apart from its effects, has actually meant to those who have gone through it. That is one at least of the reasons why the saints have always valued suffering and have asked for it.

Reading Goodier is like reading the mind of a person who has lived what he describes. There is stark realism in every sentence he writes. He shows that Christ not only had a history of which the Gospels are a faithful record but is even now part of our times and, indeed, the Lord of History, on whom depends the destiny of nations and by whom every human being is being directed to his eternal destiny.

SPECIALLY RECOMMENDED

The Passion and Death of Our Lord Jesus Christ
The Public Life of Our Lord Jesus Christ
The Prince of Peace

68. St. Maximilian Kolbe

There are not many modern writers who are also canonized martyrs. St. Maximilian Kolbe (1894–1941) is a famous exception. Born Raymond Kolbe at Zduńska Wola, near Łódź in Poland, he took the name Maximilian when he joined the conventual Franciscans. He founded the Militia of Mary Immaculate in Rome in 1917 and was ordained priest a year later. In 1919 he returned to Poland and founded the monthly periodical *Knight of the Immaculate*. In 1927, near Warsaw, he began the first of the so-called Cities of the Immaculate Conception, for several hundred dedicated persons, and later established similar centers in Japan and India.

The Nazis occupied Poland in 1939, and two years later Maximilian was arrested by the Gestapo and imprisoned in the notorious concentration camp at Auschwitz. He offered to take the place of a married man with a family, who was one of ten men arbitrarily picked to be executed in retaliation for the escape of one prisoner. After days of starvation, Maximilian was killed by an injection of carbolic acid. It was the eve of the Feast of the Assumption of Our Lady. Maximilian Kolbe was beatified by Pope Paul VI in 1971 and canonized by Pope John Paul II in 1982.

To understand St. Maximilian the writer, it is necessary to understand Kolbe the man. He began the publication of his magazine because he was determined that as many people as possible would read about the Blessed Virgin. "A working person," he said, "does not have the time" to read trash, but a worthwhile and reasonably priced book will find buyers. In the first year of publication, Maximilian changed printers five times because of rising costs and frequent strikes. The journal became popular from the first, and soon the printing was transferred to a private press that the crusading editor managed to house in a ramshackle friary near Grodno, on the border of Lithuania. From these humble beginnings and against almost impossible odds, Maximilian developed a worldwide Marian apostolate that culminated in his martyrdom at Auschwitz.

Since his beatification and canonization, the writings of St. Maximilian Kolbe have begun to be published in English. And the publications will continue. Their underlying theme is a generous, even heroic love of Christ, after the example of His Mother Mary.

"I insist," Maximilian told his brethren on one occasion, "that you become saints. Does that surprise you? But remember, my children, that holiness is not a luxury, but a simple duty. It is Jesus who told us to be perfect as our Father in heaven is perfect. So do not think it is such a difficult thing. Actually, it is a very simple mathematical problem. Let me show you on the blackboard my formula for sanctity. Then you will see how simple it is." On the blackboard, he wrote the equation $w = W$. "A very clear formula, don't you agree? The little w stands for my will, the capital W stands for the will of God. When the two wills run counter to each other, you have the Cross. So you want to get rid of the Cross? Then let your will be identified with that of God, who wants you to be saints. Isn't that simple? All you must do is obey."

And the pattern for perfect obedience is the Blessed Virgin, as seen in her answer to the Angel at the Annunciation: "Be it done to me according to your word."

SPECIALLY RECOMMENDED
> *Personal Letters*
> *Spiritual Writings*
> *Theological Writings*

69. Bl. Edith Stein

The philosopher contemplative Edith Stein came to international prominence when she was beatified by Pope John Paul II in 1987. Born at Wrocław, Poland, in 1891, she was reared in a devout Jewish home, but lost her faith as a young girl. Then she turned to philosophy, which she studied under Edmund Husserl, the father of phenomenology.

While studying at Göttingen University, she came to know about Catholicism through Husserl's former pupil Max Scheler. After many struggles, she finally entered the Catholic Church through reading St. Teresa of Ávila. Baptized on New Year's Day 1922, she left her university appointment as Husserl's assistant and for a while taught at a girls' school run by a group of Dominican tertiaries at Speyer.

Her writing career began with the translation of St. Thomas Aquinas' treatise *On Truth.* Then she spent several years completing her major work, *Finite and Eternal Being.* This was an inquiry into the meaning of being, in which she sought to synthesize the philosophy of St. Thomas with modern thought, especially with the phenomenology she had learned before her conversion to the Catholic faith.

In 1933 she had to relinquish her lectureship at the Münster Education Institute because of the anti-Semitic legislation of the Nazis. This occasioned her decision to carry out a years-long desire to enter the Carmelites. In the convent at Cologne, she took the name of Sister Teresa Benedicta of the Cross. It was in Cologne that *Finite and Eternal Being* was completed. On entering Carmel, she began to write *The Science of the Cross.* She had almost finished that work when she, along with other religious of Jewish origin, was seized by the Gestapo, in reprisal for a strong pastoral of the Dutch bishops condemning Hitler's persecution of the Jews. Sister Benedicta was taken to the concentration camp at Auschwitz and died in the gas chamber about August 10, 1942.

In the introduction to *The Science of the Cross,* she explains how we can legitimately analyze the meaning of the cross in a scientific—that is, philosophical—way:

> Here science is not spoken of in its ordinary sense. We do not have in mind a pure theory, a collection of true propositions considered as such, or an ideal edifice constructed by thought. We have in mind, certainly, a known truth, a theology of the Cross, but it is a living, existential and fruitful truth, resembling a seed cast into the soul. . . . It is this kind of theoretical exposition that

we find in the doctrine of Saint John of the Cross. We shall try to discover in his writings and in his life what gives them their unity and special character.

Then follows a closely reasoned study of St. John of the Cross in three parts. The first part, entitled "The Message of the Cross," describes the sequence of graces by which Christ progressively led St. John of the Cross to understand the mystery of His Passion and Death. In the second part, she closely examines the relation between the Cross and night, between the soul and faith, and between death and spiritual resurrection. This section closes with an analysis of the spiritual marriage of the soul. Sister Benedicta never finished the third part, which consists of quotations from St. John of the Cross and an account of his death.

Not the least feature of Edith Stein's spirituality is her associating the Cross of Calvary with the Sacrifice of the Mass, which enables us to carry the cross in our own daily lives:

> It is certain that whoever visits the Lord in his House will not always speak to Him about himself nor about his petty preoccupations, but will begin to interest himself in the concerns of the Saviour. Daily participation in the Sacrifice of the Mass draws us without our realizing it into the great current of the liturgical life. The prayer of the Church and the example of the saints penetrate the soul more and more deeply. The offering of the Holy Sacrifice renews it and brings it back to the essential mystery of our faith, the corner-stone which bears the world—the Redemptive Incarnation.

Besides *The Science of the Cross*, Sister Benedicta wrote a short biography of St. Teresa. The two works reveal the power of divine grace to enlighten the human mind in penetrating the deepest recesses of revealed wisdom.

SPECIALLY RECOMMENDED
The Science of the Cross
Essays on Woman

70. *Henri Ghéon*

Henri Ghéon (1875–1944), poet, dramatist, and hagiographer, was born Henri Léon Vangeon. Although baptized a Catholic and reared in the faith by his pious mother, he followed the example of his agnostic father and left the Church at fifteen. While practicing medicine, he also took to writing and became one of the founders of the *Nouvelle Revue française* (1909). He was converted to the faith of his childhood by the example of a saintly lieutenant commander of the marines. From Christmas Day of 1915, when he was reconciled with the Church, to his death almost thirty years later, Ghéon wrote almost exclusively on avowedly Catholic themes, notably lives of the saints and dramas modeled on the medieval miracle and mystery plays. Many of his publications have been translated into other languages, and his plays have been staged in several countries.

Ghéon believed that true theater exists only when there is a common spirit—really one faith—uniting playwright, actors, and spectators. He therefore organized a theater troupe, Les Compagnons de Notre Dame, dedicated to "the praise of God and the exaltation of His saints by means of art in the theater."

A fair sample of Ghéon's use of drama to "the praise of God" is his *Christmas in the Market Place,* a Nativity play in three acts. All the actors in the play are gypsies whose understanding of the faith is defective. In the following scene, a shepherd boy tries to help Mary and Joseph find lodging:

[*At this moment,* JOSEPH, *who has advanced slowly from the right, supporting* MARY, *stops near the young* SHEPHERD.]
JOSEPH: Excuse me, sonny.
SHEPHERD: Yes, sir?
JOSEPH: Do you happen to know an inn—a small inn—where we could stay the night?

SHEPHERD: There is this lady's hotel, but that is a big place, I think. Still—if she put in a word for you . . .

LADY: It is full, my boy, but even if it were entirely empty, it would not take them. My hotel does not cater for workmen.

JOSEPH: Yes, I am a workman. A carpenter, ma'am. I do fairly well at it. But journeys are expensive, and I have to watch the pennies.

LADY: My hotel is excessively dear.

JOSEPH: Then it is no good talking about it. But this is a special case. He that shall come . . .

LADY: He that shall come? . . . Oh! I see. Your wife is expecting.

JOSEPH: Yes, ma'am, any time now. She doesn't feel well. But if we are lucky enough . . .

LADY: Lucky? Well, that may be one point of view. I have no children. I should not want one, not for an empire . . .

JOSEPH: Maybe you are wrong. It is well worth one child—for the empire of the world.

LADY: What are you talking about?

JOSEPH: Yes . . . He that shall come . . . You would not understand.

LADY: Too stupid, I suppose?

JOSEPH: I didn't say that. But God works in a mysterious way . . .

LADY: God? . . . Oh, I don't believe in God! . . . Anyway, which God do you mean? You are Jews, are you not?

JOSEPH: Yes, we are Jews.

LADY: I can't bear Jews.

JOSEPH: Lots of people feel like that. They have their faults, I know. . . . Yet God chose them.

LADY: Really! What rubbish!—The prophets were all killed off. I shouldn't advise you to take to prophesying, or they may kill you . . . and this child you are expecting, if He resembles you.

JOSEPH: Heaven protect Him, sweet child! Shepherd, you live in these parts. Do you know any little inns? The Child must be born somewhere, and His poor mother must find a bed . . .

SHEPHERD: There are no beds to be had. They have put up notices saying all the inns are full. One of the townsfolk might squeeze you in, but most of them have friends or relatives staying.

MARY: Joseph! I cannot stand!

JOSEPH: Lean on me! Lean on me, Mary! Where can we go? Lord, where can we go?

SHEPHERD: Come along with me, and we will look together. It is all right now. The traffic is moving again.

LADY: About time, too. Drive on your flock, and let me go.

SHEPHERD: Good-bye, lady. The road is empty now. It only needed a bit of patience.

LADY: Patience! I have no patience! A lady of my rank does not need patience!

JOSEPH: } Good night, madam.
MARY: }

LADY: Good night.

SHEPHERD (coming back): Wouldn't you let her have your bed, if they cannot find anything? You could make yourself comfortable in an armchair for one night.

LADY: My bed! . . . My bed! . . . Oh! I shall remember Bethlehem! [She goes out.]

SHEPHERD (followed by JOSEPH and MARY): Sheep! . . . Sheep! . . . Sheep! . . .

[They go out.]

MELCHIOR: The whole world will remember Bethlehem! She spoke truer than she knew.—Isn't it so? The world remembers it still. (Reading.) "But the little shepherd found no lodging for them, nor for himself,—not even in his sheepfold, which had been taken by a nomad tribe, who stayed there for lack of other shelter. They ate, drank, swore and told stories: and Joseph and Mary went on their way, while the young shepherd, leaving them regretfully, lay down in a field with his flock."

[Again we hear "Baaa! . . . Baaa! . . ." offstage, and the young SHEPHERD comes on again with his flock.]

Ghéon's lives of the saints are in a class by themselves. Four of the best-known are short biographies that capsulize the spirit of each, and the title of each begins The Secret of . . . —in sequence, *the Curé d'Ars, St. Margaret Mary, the Little Flower,* and *St. John Bosco.* Always in view is the author's purpose to select those facts in the hagiography that highlight the subject's saintly personality.

SPECIALLY RECOMMENDED
> *Secrets of the Saints*
> *Three Plays*
> *Christmas in the Market Place*
> *The Art of the Theatre*

71. *Edward Leen*

The inspiration to publish came to Edward Leen (1885–1944) while he was a student in Rome as a member of the Congregation of the Holy Ghost. Bedridden with illness, he was reading a theological treatise on divine grace. Suddenly he had the inspiration "to give to the ordinary Catholic reader, should I ever get the chance, a glimpse into the wonderful life that God opens for souls." After his ordination, Leen carried his resolution into practice.

Born in Ireland, Leen spent most of his life there, giving retreats and teaching philosophy, ethics, and psychology. For two years he was secretary to the vicar apostolic of southern Nigeria. The experience directed his attention to catechetics and education.

His first book was *Progress Through Mental Prayer,* surely one of the great writings on prayer in this century. This work, which appeared in 1935, was followed in rapid succession by six other volumes. Among these, I would consider *In the Likeness of Christ* and *The Church Before Pilate* outstanding.

Leen makes much of the need for faith to grow in the likeness of Christ by reading the four Gospels:

> Admiration for a man can exist even when he is known only by fame or by history; but such admiration is but bloodless and uninspiring, compared with that which is begotten by seeing and hearing him. Can we know Jesus only

through hearing about Him, and is our admiration for Him to be restricted to the academic kind that is generated by mere history? In a certain true sense we can see and hear Jesus. The pages of the Gospel enable us to do so. But they do this only for those who read them with a firm faith in the divinity as well as in the humanity of Jesus Christ. Those who have not that faith may draw from the study of the inspired pages a great enthusiasm for the moral beauty of the person portrayed in these pages—but that admiration is powerless to exercise any supernaturalising transformation. It is but the admiration that can be extended to any historical person whose greatness stirs the imagination and wins the approbation of the reader. To faith, Jesus is not merely a historical person who has lived and is no longer; He is a person Who has lived and yet lives. Hence for faith He lives and moves and breathes, and is seen in the pages of the Gospel. It is the study of these pages; it is viewing in faith what is set forth there that will transform the soul to the likeness of Jesus and so adapt it for the inflow of the divine life which is stored in the Sacred Humanity as in an immense reservoir.

Leen's small book *The Church Before Pilate* extends this necessity of faith from Christ to the Church which He founded. Once we believe that Christ not only was a historical person who has lived but is a person who lives now, it becomes more clear why the Church He founded and with which He identifies Himself should go through the same experiences that He had during His mortal stay on earth:

There is perhaps nothing so explicable as the hatred of men for the Church of Christ. It is just as explicable as the hatred of men for Christ Himself. He said to His Church: "If the world hate you, know ye, that it hath hated me before you. If you had been of the world, the world would love its own: but because you are not of the world, . . . therefore the world hateth you. Remember my word that I said to you: The servant is not greater than his master. If they have persecuted me they will also persecute you." It has been truly said that never has a man been loved with such intensity, with such ardent loyalty, and in a spirit of such utter sacrifice, as Jesus Christ, Son of Mary. . . . But those who thus love Him were not of the *world*. They were the few and the exceptions.

If it is true that nobody has been so intensely loved, it is also true that no one has been so intensely hated. And this is His fate at the hands of vast numbers with varying degrees of intensity. He is hated by the world and the world is very numerous, very widespread and very influential. The world is as lasting as time and as widespread as space. And the world guides the destinies of the nation. And this world hates Jesus Christ. Is it explicable?

At any rate it cannot be said to be unexpected. It was foretold from the very beginning as inevitable.

Leen sustains this powerful thesis throughout the book. He shows how logical—even normal—it is for the Church to expect at the hands of the world what her Founder experienced in His personal life and what He predicted would befall His Spouse until the end of time.

SPECIALLY RECOMMENDED
> *Progress Through Mental Prayer*
> *In the Likeness of Christ*
> *The Church Before Pilate*
> *The Holy Ghost and His Work in Souls*

72. *Alexis Carrel*

Not many modern Catholic writers have the list of distinctions of Alexis Carrel (1873–1944). He was a world-renowned surgeon, biologist, Nobel Prize winner, and member of the Pontifical Academy of Science. Born and educated in France, he came to the United States in 1905, working especially at the Rockefeller Institute for Medical Research. In 1912 he was awarded the Nobel Prize in physiology or medicine for his discoveries in the suturing of blood vessels and transplanting living organs. During World War I, he helped develop new methods of treating wounds. His discoveries contributed to the saving of countless lives and preventing amputations.

Although not a practicing Catholic during most of his life, he was fully reconciled with the Church before his death. Yet, his deeply Christian attitude was evident in the books he published. Carrel illustrates the fact that a Catholic philosophy can pervade a person's whole life, provided the individual maintains a spirit of humility and the practice of prayer.

In 1935 he published *Man the Unknown,* which has gone through more than thirty editions and been translated into some twenty languages. It is, by all odds, one of the great books of the twentieth century. When the book was written, the author's description of himself was slowly beginning to change:

Absorbed in his scientific studies, his mind had been strongly attracted to the German system of critical analysis and he had slowly become convinced that outside of the positivist method, no certainties existed. His religious ideas, ground down by the analytic process, had finally been destroyed, leaving him only a loving memory of a delicate and beautiful dream.

He had taken refuge in tolerant scepticism.

What began to change this tolerant skeptic into a believer was the experience he narrates in *The Voyage to Lourdes,* the manuscript of which was found after his death. The Preface to this masterful tribute to the power of grace through the Blessed Virgin was written by Charles A. Lindbergh. In Lindbergh's words, "In this work, Carrel lets the young Dr. Lerrac (Carrel spelled backwards) represent him in a moving and personal account of his own experience at Lourdes in 1903. The observations he made then, early in his career, had a deep effect on his outlook toward science and religion during his entire life."

The eight pages (out of fifty) in which Carrel recounts what happened at Lourdes are unrivaled in medical history. They tell how a thoroughgoing religious skeptic and budding scientist was shaken to the roots of his being on seeing Marie Ferrand, dying of tubercular peritonitis, suddenly cured before his eyes. The miraculous cure did not then and there convince him. But his candor in describing the experience reveals the working of grace that would take many more years before it would finally bring a doubting genius back to the faith of his fathers.

SPECIALLY RECOMMENDED
  Man the Unknown
  The Voyage to Lourdes

73. *Sigrid Undset*

The Norwegian novelist Sigrid Undset (1882–1949) became a Catholic in 1924, just four years before she received the Nobel Prize in literature. Her first novel, *Fru Marta Oulie,* composed in diary form, appeared in 1907. Three others followed in rapid succession—*Happy Youth, Jenny,* and *Spring*—all centered on the theme of family life in the contemporary world with its painful loneliness and questioning of authority. In order to write her trilogy, *Kristin Lavransdatter (The Bridal Wreath, The Mistress of Husaby,* and *The Cross*), she read deeply in the Catholicism of medieval Norway. It was this research that finally led to her conversion. *The Longest Years,* an autobiography, and *Saga of Saints* reveal Undset's spiritual journey. It is not surprising that her books were banned by the Nazis nor that she had to escape to America in 1940 after doing radio service for a while with the Norwegian government in exile.

We get some idea of her outlook on life from her observations on the Church's veneration of saints. They are proof that we cannot equate worldly success with authentic achievement. Devotion to the saints excludes "the veneration of those people who have got on well in this world, the snobbish admiration of wealth and fame." Then a caution:

This does not mean that a person who apparently has succeeded in the world and has led a happy life is necessarily a bad Christian who must be prepared for a painful settlement with his God and Judge when he comes to die. But it does mean that the religious business instinct which has caused people to imagine that the material welfare of individuals or nations is a sign of God's special favour, or to see in disasters and defeats a punishment from God—that this is opposed by the Church in her veneration of saints. There is a story of a well-known Norwegian shipowner—I have heard it connected with more than one name, so I dare say it is apocryphal, made up to fit into a fairly common line of thought—anyhow the story goes that the man did not insure his ships; this was supposed to be a proof of his trust in God. Then one day he received news that one of his ships had sunk in spite of this. The man looked up at the ceiling and sighed: "O Lord God, what have I done wrong?" It is human to think in this way, all too human—and of course a great number of Catholics yield to the temptation of thinking so. But it is a line of thought which the Church herself disclaims; whenever she celebrates Mass in red vestments it is a protest against this. And even among those saints who did not become martyrs there are relatively few who in their lifetime achieved a victory for the cause for which they had been fighting, if that cause was of such a nature as to demand realization in external forms; as, for instance, has been the case with most missionaries and founders of Orders.

One of the unique merits of Sigrid Undset's writing is her ability to depict human characters. She saw them as more than weak human beings struggling with a cold, impersonal Fate. In fact, it was this search for meaning in human life that led her to the Catholic Church. Her exploration into the pre-Reformation history of her country led to a remarkable discovery: that there is a loving Providence at work in the world which can draw good out of evil, even great good out of great evil. Long before she became a professed Catholic, she sensed that we have a purpose in life. This purpose is to use our free wills to cooperate with the grace of God. We can actually be generous in our response to God's will and, in the process, become saints.

SPECIALLY RECOMMENDED

> *Kristin Lavransdatter*
> *Saga of the Saints*
> *The Longest Years*

74. *William Thomas Walsh*

William Thomas Walsh (1891–1949) should be better known among the American authors of the twentieth century. A master of the English language, a meticulous scholar, and a devoted Catholic, Walsh had been a journalist in his early days in Waterbury, Philadelphia, and Hartford. While head of the Department of English at the Roxbury School in Cheshire, Connecticut, and then professor of English at Manhattanville College, he combined his teaching with publishing.

His novel, *Out of the Worldwind;* his play, *Shekels;* his *Lyric Poems;* and his essays are carefully crafted pieces of literature. But his main claim to fame is a series of biographies: *Characters of the Inquisition, Isabella of Spain, Philip II, St. Teresa of Ávila,* and *Saint Peter the Apostle.*

His deep Catholic sense enabled him to write about Spain and its history with an understanding that previous biographers simply did not have. In his Foreword to *Isabella of Spain,* he admits that "for nearly a century, the 'official' biography has been Prescott's *History of the Reign of Ferdinand and Isabella.* He was a careful and patient scholar to whom we owe a debt of no small size. Yet he was incapable of understanding the spirit of 15th-century Spain, because with all his erudition he could never wholly forget the prejudices of an early 19th-century Bostonian."

A fair sample of Walsh's literary biography of Isabella describes what happened when, early in 1492, Columbus made his first—unsuccessful—plea to Ferdinand and Isabella to finance and authorize a voyage across the Atlantic to reach the Indies. Columbus' proposal was rejected as preposterous:

Columbus left the Court in anger and sorrow, decided to go to France, and started on his way to the seacoast. Fortunately he stopped once more at the Franciscan monastery of La Rabida, overlooking Palos. The good Prior, Father Juan Perez, was delighted to see him again, to talk cosmography with him, to hear the latest tidings of the Crusade that was thrilling all Europe. It has been conjectured that Columbus in his bitterness may have described his plans more frankly to the priest than he had at the Court. At any rate, Friar Juan declared that his going away was preposterous; nor could he believe that the Queen would permit Castile to lose so much glory. He called in a learned physician of Palos, Garcia Fernandez, and Father Antonio Marchena, the astronomer, who heartily agreed. They sent a sailor to the Queen with a letter.

Fray Juan wrote that Columbus was undoubtedly right in his hypothesis, that whoever sent him would gain glory and riches, and the eternal reward of those who propagate the Faith; for he was convinced that Columbus was as sincere in his piety as he was daring and sound in his speculations. Such an opinion from her old confessor, confirming her own impressions, influenced the Queen so profoundly that she sent back 20,000 maravedis in gold florins by the messenger, that Columbus might buy new clothes and a mule; and she bade him return to Court.

"Our Lord has listened to the prayers of His servant," wrote Fray Juan Perez with joy. "The wise and virtuous Dona Isabel, touched by the grace of Heaven, gave a favorable hearing to the words of this poor monk. All has turned out well."

Columbus returned to Santa Fe supremely confident that nothing remained but to sign the contract and assemble his crews. Looking back on that time in his old age, he wrote, "In all men there was disbelief"—by no means an accurate statement—"but to the Queen, my lady, God gave the spirit of understanding and great courage, and made her heiress of all as a dear and much-loved daughter."

As it turned out, there were still some grave obstacles to overcome, but Queen Isabella was convinced that Columbus should be authorized to set sail that year—in what proved to be the discovery of America.

Given his great love of Catholic Spain, it is not surprising that

Walsh should have been signally honored by the Spanish government.

Walsh's most popular book, *Our Lady of Fatima*, was published in 1947, on the thirtieth anniversary of the apparitions in Portugal. It has done much to promote the Fatima devotion in English-speaking countries.

SPECIALLY RECOMMENDED
> *Isabella of Spain*
> *Characters of the Inquisition*
> *Our Lady of Fatima*

75. *Owen Francis Dudley*

After four years in the ministry of the Anglican church, Owen Francis Dudley (1882–1952) became a Roman Catholic in 1915 and two years later was ordained a Catholic priest. He was appointed a British army chaplain during World War I, saw service in France and Italy, and was wounded while ministering to the soldiers in battle. He joined the Catholic Missionary Society after the war and labored untiringly throughout the British Isles, expounding Catholic truth in "town hall, theatre, Hyde Park, or mining clubroom." Dudley added to this strenuous work what he called "motor missioning," which he described as "packed with human interest," for he could meet "humanity in the raw, hungry, restless, seeking" for the truth.

In 1933 he was elected superior of the Catholic Missionary Society, which Herbert Cardinal Vaughan had founded in 1902 as an association of priests set apart by their bishops for the work of conversion of England and Wales. After Dudley's visit to Australia, a similar society was founded there for the conversion of non-Catholics.

Dudley is best known as a powerful novelist. His aim, he said, was "to bring Catholic philosophy and theology before the public in a popular form." Six of his novels have become standard in English Catholic literature.

Will Men Be Like Gods is an answer to humanitarianism. It takes issue with the popular notion that serving the needs of others is to "play God," rather than fulfill the sacred duty of Christian charity.

The Shadow on the Earth is the answer of Christian revelation to the presence of moral and physical evil in a world that God has created good.

The Masterful Monk is the Catholic reply to the modern attacks on man's moral nature; man is indeed weakened by the Fall, but his nature is essentially sound and, with God's grace, he is capable of rising even to high sanctity.

The Pageant of Life is a moving story of moral cowardice, to which human beings may succumb without losing their basic human dignity.

The Coming of the Monster is a powerful Christian refutation of Communism, provided the followers of Christ are willing to pay the price that the Savior expects of His disciples.

In 1940, Dudley published a sequel to his earlier novels, entitled *The Tremaynes and the Masterful Monk*. His own introduction to this classic is also a good example of his way of thinking:

> The Tremaynes and the Masterful Monk is a character study. May I mention, by way of apologia, that I have not hesitated to reveal the character of Gordon Tremayne in all its naked ugliness; otherwise the full nature of his redemption would be missed.
>
> We are apt, rather smugly I think, to place certain characters beyond redemption. My choice of Gordon Tremayne has been deliberate, for the reason that humanly he seemed unredeemable. In the event he proved otherwise— owing to the monk acting on the principle of the potentially reclaimable deep down.
>
> The Gordon Tremaynes of this world are not uncommon, whose cruelties cry to heaven for vengeance, and yet remain untouched by law.
>
> Beyond human reach they may be, but not beyond reach of the Divine.

World War II gave Owen Dudley further opportunity to bring hope and courage to the suffering. Instead of writing novels, he cared for the wounded and dying in the hospital wards of London. "All around," he wrote, "is a haunted scene of death and desolation." His books are a permanent expression of these same sentiments. They reveal in graphic language how the true faith provides light and strength to the "poor, banished children of Eve, suffering and weeping in this valley of tears."

Dudley's works have been serialized, translated into various languages, and transcribed into braille.

SPECIALLY RECOMMENDED
> *Will Men Be Like Gods? Humanitarianism or Human Happiness*
> *The Tremaynes and the Masterful Monk*

76. *Hilaire Belloc*

The historian, essayist, poet, and biographer Joseph Hilaire Pierre Belloc (1870–1953) was born in France but moved to England. In 1896 he married an American, Elodie Hogan, from California. When she died in 1914, he was left with the responsibility of raising their five children.

One of the most voluminous writers in the Catholic Church, Belloc published more than 150 books. Among these some were controversial, like the *History of England*. Others were critical studies, like the biographies of Danton and Marie Antoinette. His *Path to Rome* is a travelogue that has been reprinted many times.

Two of Belloc's writings may be singled out as most typical, *The Servile State* and *Europe and the Faith*. Both these works have a fundamental thesis with which the name of the author is identified. In *The Servile State,* Belloc argues that "if we do not restore the institution of property, we cannot escape restoring the institution of slavery; there is no third course." He concludes that "the re-establishment of the Servile Status in industrial society is actually upon us." But he does not predict what the future of Europe or America shall be. "There is a complex knot of forces underlying any nation once Christian, a smoldering of the old fires." God may, and Belloc hopes he will, rekindle those fires and save the nations that recover their weakened (or lost) Christian heritage.

Europe and the Faith is built on the same theme, but the theme is expressed more forcibly and applied more universally. According to Belloc, "the Church is Europe; and Europe is the Church." He does not mean that there is no European civilization without the Catholic Church, but he does claim that it was the Catholic Church which first civilized the Continent and gave its people a sense of unity based on a common faith. He believes that the future, not only of Europe but of the Americas, depends on the degree to which the basic moral and religious values of the Catholic Church are rediscovered.

Implied in all of Belloc's writing is the thesis that the Church which Christ established was an institution; He was not merely starting a new movement nor even just founding a religious philosophy:

That is what history has to say of the early Church in the Roman Empire. The Gospels, the Acts, the Canonical Epistles and those of Clement and Ignatius may tell a true or a false story; their authors may have written under an illusion or from a conscious self-deception; or they may have been supremely true and immutably sincere. But they are contemporary. A man may respect their divine origin or he may dispute their claims to instruct the human race; but that the Christian body from its beginning was not "Christianity" but a Church, and that that Church was identically one with what was already called long before the 3rd century the *Catholic* Church, is simply plain history, as plain and straightforward as the history, let us say, of municipal institutions in contemporary Gaul.

Belloc's own quality of being "straightforward" has created many enemies. What no one can dispute, however, is the logic of his thinking.

SPECIALLY RECOMMENDED

The Path to Rome
The Servile State
Europe and the Faith
Marie Antoinette

77. Paul Claudel

The French poet and dramatist Paul Claudel (1868–1955) had four Christian names, Paul Louis Charles Marie. Although he was baptized a Catholic and made his first Communion at the age of twelve, Claudel soon lost his faith and became, in his own words, an inmate of the "materialists' prison" of science. He then went through a period of "suffocation and despair" because scientific dogmatism did not satisfy his inquiring mind.

The person who finally led him to return to his Catholic heritage was his oldest sister, Camille. Books that she gave her brother, including Dante, and having him attend the Christmas services at Notre Dame in Paris proved decisive. He recalls exactly what happened. It was the Vespers: "Near the second pillar by the entrance to the choir, on the right, in the direction of the sacristy," the years of skepticism dissolved in grace. "In one instant," he confessed, "my heart was touched, and I believed."

But a four-year struggle was still to follow. Again, he took to reading on his sister's urging, from the Bible, *The Imitation of Christ,* and St. Thomas. He addressed God in a prayer he composed, "I was before Thee, as a fighter who yields." The final victory took place (again) on Christmas Day of 1890, when Claudel made his second Holy Communion. These biographical details are important to make a proper estimate of his prodigious writing in the many years that lay ahead.

Claudel's fame rests chiefly on his poetry and a powerful series of mystery plays, the central theme of which is the consecration of the world to God in Christ. Among the most beautiful of his plays is *The Tidings Brought to Mary,* a canticle on the spiritual meaning of voluntary suffering and expiation levied on the gentle Violaine, who thus becomes the channel of grace to others.

Better known to English readers is *The Satin Slipper.* This play is set in sixteenth-century Spain. Its theme is as old as the *Confes-*

sions of St. Augustine: that God uses even sin to achieve the goals of His Providence. Dona Prouheze is married to one man but loves another. She offers her slipper to the Virgin Mary while praying in a strange way.

(DON BALTHAZAR *holds the mule's head and* DONA PROUHEZE *climbs up on the saddle; taking off her shoe she puts the satin thing between the hands of the Virgin.*)

DONA PROUHEZE: Virgin, patron and mother of this house, protectress and surety of this man whose heart lies open to you more than to me, and companion of his long loneliness,

If not for my sake then at least for his, since this bond between him and me has not been my doing but your intervening will:

Keep me from being to this house whose door you guard, O mighty extern, a cause of corruption:

Keep me from being false to this name which you have given me to bear, and from ceasing to be honourable in the eyes of them that love me.

I cannot say that I understand this man whom you picked out for me, but you I understand, who are his mother and mine.

See, while there is yet time, holding my heart in one hand and my shoe in the other,

I give myself over to you! Virgin mother, I give you my shoe, Virgin mother, keep in your hand my luckless little foot!

I warn you that presently I shall see you no longer and that I am about to set everything going against you!

But when I try to rush on evil let it be with limping foot! The barrier that you have set up,

When I want to cross it, be it with a crippled wing!

I have done so much as I could; keep you my poor little shoe,

Keep it against your heart, tremendous Mother of mine!

Claudel should be better known in the English-speaking world. No less than eighty of his writings are listed in *Books in Print*, of which less than half are in English. All the rest are offered to American readers in their original French. Claudel is Catholic to the core; and it takes a Catholic mentality to appreciate, and be inspired by, his poetry and drama.

SPECIALLY RECOMMENDED

The Satin Slipper
The Tidings Brought to Mary: A Drama
The Book of Christopher Columbus: A Lyrical Drama
Letters from Paul Claudel, My Godfather

78. Johannes Jørgensen

The Fyn Island home of Svendborg, Denmark, was always dear to the heart of Johannes Jørgensen (1866–1956). Reared in a deeply religious Lutheran family, Jørgensen began to explore other religions at an early age. He read Goethe's *Faust* and Longfellow's *Golden Legend*. He looked into cabala and theosophy. He felt very lonely and summed up his feelings in these early years by coining the motto I Suffer, Therefore I Am.

As a student at the University of Copenhagen, he was exposed to the radical ideas of Ibsen, Strindberg, and Zola. Inspired by socialist leaders, he neglected his studies and soon became an ardent follower of the biologists Ernst Heinrich Haeckel and Thomas Henry Huxley, both prophets of Darwinism. What most tormented him was the thought that there was no life after death. On the verge of despair, he turned to Nature and was attracted by pantheism.

In the meantime, he began to write. His first book of prose, *Legends of Spring* (1888), was followed by the *Tree of Life*, which critics denounced as "a Catholic book." This alienated him from his former friends, and in 1894 he uttered his first prayer since early childhood.

A convert from Judaism, Møgens Ballin, introduced Jørgensen to Catholic writers. This in turn moved him to visit Italy. He spent months at Assisi and La Rocca, struggling with divine

grace. Finally, in 1896 he entered the Catholic Church at Stenos-
gade, in Denmark.

In 1895 he published *The Book of the Journey*, which has been
compared to Huysmans' *En Route*, and *Bekendelse*, a collection of
poems. But after his conversion, his literary output was prodigious. He translated *Little Flowers of St. Francis* and wrote *The Book
About Rome*, a two-volume work of apologetics. In the novel *Our
Lady of Denmark*, he wrote a series of essays in philosophy, politics, and religion around his hero, a Christian democrat. Unfortunately these and other writings of Jørgensen are not available
in English.

While researching the life of St. Francis, he went to Assisi and
published a companion volume, *The Pilgrim Book*. His biography
of the Poverello was followed by the great work of his old age
on the greatest saint of Scandinavia, St. Bridget of Sweden. Although he lived for many years in Assisi, his first affection was
for Denmark and Sweden. His great hope was to restore as much
as he could of Catholic culture to his own people. Friendly admirers, although not Catholic, were grateful. "You have taught
us Danish to make the sign of the cross," one of them declared.
"Your books have the effect of deliverance and help," another
writer said. "Young men and young women breathe the air of a
new Christianity in your writings, that are refreshing and vivid,
like yourself."

SPECIALLY RECOMMENDED
　　Saint Bridget of Sweden
　　Saint Catherine of Siena
　　Pilgrim Walks in Franciscan Italy
　　Jørgensen: An Autobiography

79. *Pierre Pourrat*

There are not many first-rate historians of the spiritual life.
Pierre Pourrat (1871–1957) is one of the best. One of six children in a thoroughly Catholic family, Pourrat responded early to

his vocation to the priesthood. As a member of the Society of St. Sulpice, Pourrat spent almost thirty years teaching dogmatic theology at the seminary in Lyons, France, and was superior of the Solitude, the quasinovitiate of the Sulpicians at Issy-les-Moulineaux until shortly before his death.

This combination of a strong foundation in sacred doctrine and the experience of dealing intimately with souls equipped him for writing the two main publications of his career. The *Theology of the Sacraments* is a concise analysis of the Church's teaching on the sacraments as channels of divine grace. *Christian Spirituality*, in four volumes, is a classic synthesis of the life and teaching of the Church's saints and spiritual masters over the centuries.

A quotation from *Christian Spirituality* will illustrate his approach:

Jansenism was the child of a particular conception of Christian life, one vitiated by pushing on Augustinian pessimism to its limits. This rigorist conception that underlies the theology taught by Bishop Jansen of Ypres in his *Augustinus* can be found especially in Saint-Cyran's letters. So Jansenism issues from a false spirituality; and once again we see the influence of spiritual doctrines on the development of theological systems, whether orthodox or heterodox, that are concerned with grace and the state of fallen man. We need only to recall the origins of Pelagianism and the controversies between Pelagius and St. Augustine, men inspired by opposed conceptions of Christian life.

Quietism, . . . even more than Jansenism, dominates the history of spirituality from the middle of the seventeenth until the nineteenth century. During this time the rigorism arising from the heresies of Jansen and Saint-Cyran made its mark, but the excesses to which Quietism led were more disturbing to spiritual theology.

Quietism is not restricted to the gross errors of Molinos, derived from those of the Spanish *Alumbrados*, or to the famous controversy between Bossuet and Fénelon. There was a spirituality of Quietist tendencies in Spain, Italy, and especially in France, before Molinos; and it prepared the way for, and helped spread quickly, Quietism properly so-called. Before the birth of a heresy there is always a period of incubation, during which the minds of men are prepared for the errors that are to come. The writers who foster this mentality may be in good faith; several of those who opened the way to Quietism left a reputation of holiness. They erred by excess . . . and were so concerned with the "interests" of God that they totally misconceived those of men. They so emphasized abandonment to God that they fell into a sort of spiritual idleness; pure love excluded all self-interest, even that of one's salvation.

One of the great benefits of Pourrat's history of Christian spirituality is that it provides balance and perspective. This applies not only to the past but also and especially to the present. There is such a thing as orthodoxy and heresy of spirituality. In fact, Pourrat would say that soundness of doctrine in matters of faith depends absolutely on soundness of doctrine in morals and the spiritual life. The great leaders of both orthodoxy and heterodoxy have been persons whose ideas grew out of their personal lives and whose writings were a reflection of their own relationship with God.

SPECIALLY RECOMMENDED
   Christian Spirituality

80. *Ronald A. Knox*

The biblical scholar Ronald Arbuthnott Knox (1888–1957), was the youngest son of the Anglican bishop of Manchester. Educated at Eton and Oxford, he took Anglican orders and became chaplain of Trinity College, Oxford. Knox's strong Anglo-Catholicism brought him into conflict with the Anglican hierarchy. Finally, in 1917, he was received into the Catholic Church and published his reasons in *A Spiritual Aeneid.* Ordained a Catholic priest in 1919, he first served as Catholic chaplain at Oxford University (1926–39). But he found that he needed more time to concentrate on his literary work, especially the production of a modern English Bible. In 1958 his translation of the Old and New Testaments was published and approved by the English Catholic hierarchy.

Among his many books, the best known is *Enthusiasm,* which is an in-depth analysis of religious vagaries over the centuries of Christian history. Through six hundred pages of fascinating reading, he traces the uninterrupted history of enthusiasts and their attempts to break through the barriers of cold institutional

Christianity (as they called it) and experience an inward communication with the Divine.

Knox's purpose in writing this classic on the search for the experience of God was not, he says, to criticize it. He was, rather, intent on trying to help his readers understand it.

No doubt one of the basic reasons for the periodic breaks in Catholic unity has been the desire to be free of the Church's moral restraints. Those we call heretics wanted freedom from ecclesiastical authority in such deeply human areas as marriage and sexual morality. But Knox believes there is another element at work—namely, the desire for "being oneself also in relation with God." As a result, he finds the rise of enthusiasm to be partly the fruit of the hunger for religious experience—with emphasis on experience. This is revealed by the fact that the same phenomenon has taken place among Christians who are not professed Catholics.

The closing paragraphs of Knox's *Enthusiasm* are both a summary of what he calls "the Philosophy of Enthusiasm" and a warning:

But my aim is to interpret enthusiasm, not to criticize it. If we would interpret it rightly, there is one point that must be seized on above all the rest—in itself enthusiasm is not a wrong tendency but a false emphasis. Quietism exaggerates only a little the doctrine of the mystics about simplicity in prayer, about disinterested love. Quakerism does but enthrone in dangerous isolation the truth of God's presence within us. Jansenism is the vigilant conscience of Christendom overshadowed by a scruple. Methodism is the call back to Christ in an age of Deism. What men like Pascal, Fénelon, and Wesley saw clearly was something true and something valuable; the exaggerations, the eccentricities, were hatched by the heat of controversy. The sympathy which those names evoke is not the index of a rebel spirit in us, who read of them; it is not because they fell foul of authority, and imperilled unity, that we attribute to them greatness. It is not surprising if those who are most sensitive to the needs of their age find their way, sometimes, on to the wrong side of the calendar. Fine instruments are easily spoiled.

One distinction I have slurred over, all through this book; I hope not to the scandal of my readers. I have written in the same breath about people like the Vaudois, who broke away from the unity of the Catholic Church, and people like the Methodists, whose movement took its origin in a Reformation culture. I have done so advisedly, because it seems to me that the enthusiast will always react against any form of institutional religion, whether it be Catholic or Protestant, and there is no Christianity with a hundred years of history that does not become, to a more or less degree, institutional. Waldensianism and

Wesleyanism have their points of resemblance, their points of difference, but where they differ, it is not because the background was Catholic in the one case, Anglican in the other. Fundamentally, either has the same point of departure; a suspicion, not ignobly entertained, that a church in alliance with the world has unchurched itself.

More than all the other Christianities, the Catholic Church is institutional. Her enemies too easily conclude that she is thereby incapacitated from all spiritual initiative, David in Saul's armour; history makes short work of the conclusion. New things as well as old she keeps in her treasure-house; you will find current coin there, not only obsolete doubloons. But there is danger in her position none the less; where wealth abounds, it is easy to mistake shadow for substance; the fires of spirituality may burn low, and we go on unconscious, dazzled by the glare of tinsel suns. How nearly we thought we could do without St. Francis, without St. Ignatius! Men will not live without vision; that moral we do well to carry away with us from contemplating, in so many strange forms, the record of the visionaries.

Ronald Knox knew better than most people that the great danger to the Catholic Church is not from outside her ranks but from within. He realized how seriously Christ meant what He said when He told His followers to be the salt of the earth. "But if salt becomes tasteless," He warned, "it is good for nothing, but can only be thrown out to be trampled underfoot by men" (Matthew 5:13).

SPECIALLY RECOMMENDED
> *Enthusiasm*
> *A Spiritual Aeneid*
> *The Belief of Catholics*
> *A Commentary on the Gospels*

81. *Paul de Jaegher*

The author of *One with Jesus* was born in Belgium and died as a missionary in India. Paul de Jaegher (1880–1958) entered the Jesuits in 1903 and for most of the rest of his life was a busy missionary among the people of Chota Nagpur and elsewhere in the Indian subcontinent. His busy labors as builder, catechist, and pastor allowed him little time for writing. But he was inspired by men like Raoul Plus and Dom Marmion to put some of his thoughts about sanctifying grace on paper. As he explained, "It was not without great difficulties that I managed to write my spiritual books. What encouraged me in this difficult work was my opinion that there was a real need for more Catholic literature on some subjects. I would never have written anything on matters which have been abundantly treated, as spiritual life in general, prayer, mortification and kindred subjects."

His first book has also remained the best known. Its original French edition, *La Vie d'identification au Christ-Jésus,* was translated into English as *One with Jesus.* It has since been translated into most European languages, as well as into Malayan and Japanese.

After the warm reception of his first book, de Jaegher said, "I noticed that little had been written on the virtue of trust." So he composed *Confiance,* which became *The Virtue of Trust.* This was followed by *Anthology of Mysticism* and *The Lord Is My Joy.* All of these works have appeared in English and other languages. They have also inspired many readers, among the laity and persons living in the cloister.

SPECIALLY RECOMMENDED
   One with Jesus
   The Virtue of Trust

82. *Francis Trochu*

The author of the classic biography of the Curé d'Ars (St. John Vianney), Francis Trochu (1877–1967) was ordained a priest in 1901. He taught in French colleges and published over thirty volumes, mainly the lives of saintly men and women.

A number of his books have been honored by the French Academy and translated into many languages. Their special merit consists in being written according to a strict historical method. Thus, in writing the life of the Curé d'Ars, Trochu relied mainly on the documents of the Process of Beatification and

Canonization. Among the persons interviewed for the Church's investigation into the sanctity of St. John Vianney were his sister Marguerite, the playmates of his childhood, his fellow students at the seminary, his parishioners, his brother priests, and many other people whose lives he touched. All of them were convinced Catholics and bound under oath to tell only what they were sure was the truth. The cause of St. John Vianney was begun immediately after his death.

Through almost six hundred pages, Trochu traces the life of the Curé d'Ars with painstaking detail. He lays the groundwork by explaining the situation of the Church in France after the tragic French Revolution. Priests faithful to the Church and the Bishop of Rome had to live in hiding. They lodged in different houses and, as a precaution, took up some trade. They went out only at night and avoided the highway when going to whichever house had been chosen for the celebration of Mass. Young Vianney admired these priests in disguise and hoped one day to be like them. His parents constantly distinguished the faithful from the unfaithful priests, and his one ambition was to become "a good priest."

Trochu's narrative of John Vianney's first confession is worth quoting. It illustrates the preciseness of his writing and the warmth of affection for the subject of his biography:

> With what emotion and reverence did not little Vianney look up to these men as they stood at the altar? They had grown old before their time, and their faces bore the tell-tale traces of the labours and privations which they had endured for the love of souls. The priests themselves ended by noticing the bright-eyed lad whose fervour and recollection were so manifest. One day, in the year 1797, M. Groboz came to the village of Dardilly and called at the house of the Vianneys. After blessing the children one by one, he asked Jean-Marie: "How old are you?"
> "Eleven."
> "How long is it since you last went to confession?"
> "I have never yet been to confession," the boy replied.
> "Well, let us set right this omission at once."
> So Jean-Marie and the priest were left alone together, and the lad began his first confession. "I remember it well," the saint related in later life, "it was at home, at the foot of our clock." What could he have to confess? The priest, to be sure, must have marveled at the whiteness of this beautiful soul. However, the boy was in need of further instruction. This he could receive from the lady catechists who had been secretly established at Ecully. M. Groboz experienced

no difficulty in convincing the parents; they saw no reason why Jean-Marie should not spend a few months in a village that was quite near and in the house of Marguerite Beluse, his aunt, who was the wife of François Humbert.

Another masterpiece of Trochu is his biography of St. Bernadette Soubirous. While giving due attention to her early years and her extraordinary prudence under trial after the revelations at Lourdes, the author dwells on Bernadette's interior life as a member of the Sisters of Nevers. As Sister Marie Bernard, she was tried beyond description. Among others, her directress of novices, Mother Marie-Thérèse, did everything in her power to keep Bernadette humble. The directress was said to have "had passion for shaping souls." Trochu explains:

> She employed a quite particular severity towards Bernadette. The Mistress of Novices could not be judged harshly for trying to counteract the fame of the Massabielle visions in order to keep her novice humble: such a practice is not contrary to the teaching of the spiritual writers. But severity and coldness are two different things. When a fair-minded child feels it is being punished from a motive of love, any suffering there may be is attributed to the correction, not to the mother's deliberate harshness; if on the other hand the punishment seems to the child to be tinged with ill-will, especially if the rest of the children in the family are treated with noticeable affection, it will experience much more acute distress because the mother's attitude then seems to result from lack of love. Is it possible that for some ten years or so, first as a novice, then as a professed nun, Sister Marie-Bernard had to bear an affliction such as this? Yes! But did it prove a misfortune for her? No!

Trochu had the rare genius of using minute detail to bring out the full meaning of a person's character. Yet, he never becomes trivial.

SPECIALLY RECOMMENDED
> *The Curé d'Ars: St. Jean Marie Baptiste Vianney*
> *St. Bernadette Soubirous*

83. *John Peter Arendzen*

If there is one quality that characterizes the work of John Peter Arendzen (1873–1954), it is clarity. An expert in Semitic philosophy and languages, Arendzen could write so clearly because he had a thorough command of the Catholic faith and an extraordinary facility, for a native of Holland, in expressing the most profound speculative theology in everyday English words.

Ordained at twenty-two, he edited the "Question Box" in *The Catholic Gazette* for many years; was spiritual director of St. Edmund's College in Ware, England; and was a canon of the Metropolitan Chapter of Westminster. He was the last surviving member of the first three foundation members of the Catholic Missionary Society.

His book *The Holy Trinity* is a masterpiece of simple explanation for modern laymen of the primary mystery of Christianity. His three works in the Treasury of Faith series—on heaven, hell, and the sacrament of anointing—have remained in print for more than a generation.

Arendzen drew on his knowledge of Semitic languages to defend all the basic mysteries of the faith as revealed in the four Evangelists. Even the titles of his books reveal the concern he had to establish the historical validity of the New Testament narrations and to discount the wild speculation of those whom he called "the Modernists." *The Gospel: Fact, Myth, or Legend* is a superb defense of the facts in the life of Jesus Christ. If the Gospels cannot be trusted as sound history, Arendzen concluded, then no events of comparable antiquity are credible and historical skepticism is the only alternative.

Prophets, Priests, and Publicans is a readable study of such fascinating areas as the prophecy of Mary's virginity in Isaiah, the competing schools of Hillel and Shammai, which occasioned Christ's uncompromising doctrine on the indissolubility of marriage, and a penetrating study of the characters of the men who plotted the death of Christ. His chapter on Judas Iscariot could only have been written by one who thoroughly understood the Jewish people in the first century of the Christian era.

Two professedly apologetic works, *Reason and Revelation* and *Faith and Commonsense,* are as timely today as when originally published in the first half of the twentieth century. So far from being a competition with faith, reason is its greatest ally. The only precondition is that a person must look at the facts of revelation with a mind that has no bias against miracles and the supernatural.

However, it is especially in exploring the mysteries of faith that Arendzen is at his best. In the following passage from *What Becomes of the Dead?* he stresses that there should be growth. Indeed, even in heaven there can be no monotony of perfection:

God remains unfathomable even to the greatest of His saints. They see Him, but none can see to the very depths of His divine being. God is a world, a wide universe, which none of the Blessed has ever totally explored. Even after millions of cycles of ages, neither Mary, the Queen of heaven, nor Michael, the Prince of the heavenly host, shall exhaust the greatness of the divine majesty. It is an ocean on which the little craft of creative intelligence can forever press forward in all directions, for it is a sea without a shore. As a pretty, many-colored insect on swift wings floats on the summer breeze and allows itself to be driven along in the seemingly boundless air; as a lark rises in the apparently boundless sky, so do the Blessed roam about in the limitless wideness of God.

The nearest that any modern writer comes to Arendzen's clarity and depth of thought is Frank Sheed. But Arendzen has the advantage of a wider range of theological knowledge and years of contact with the original languages and culture in which Christianity was born.

SPECIALLY RECOMMENDED

The Holy Trinity
Reason and Revelation
What Becomes of the Dead?
Purgatory and Heaven

84. *Giuseppe Ricciotti*

One Italian biblical writer whose books are widely available in English is Giuseppe Ricciotti (1890–1964). Ricciotti, a native of Rome, was for years the abbot of the Congregation of the Canons Regular of the Lateran. Studies in theology, Oriental history, and literature, and wide travels on archaeological missions in

Asia, from Palestine to China, gave Ricciotti a rare mastery of the world in which the Old and New Testaments were written.

He served as chaplain of the D'Annunzio regiment during World War I. He was near death in a field hospital when he resolved that if he survived, he would write a life of Christ. "His Gospel," Ricciotti remembered, "was on the straw mattress beside me, and its pages, with splotches of blood crossing the Greek letters like rubrics, seemed a symbolic pattern of life and death."

Ricciotti recovered, and by the early 1950s his *Life of Jesus Christ* had gone through fourteen editions. It has been translated into many languages. His other published titles read like a library of biblical scholarship. Unlike many other writers on the Scriptures, Ricciotti hides his erudition, especially in books intended for the general public. Moreover, there is an extraordinary coherence, unity, and effective emphasis in his books. He never gets lost in details, yet he uses details profusely to bring out features in the biblical narrative that might otherwise be overlooked.

The History of Israel, in two volumes, is a gold mine, not only for understanding the Old Testament but for a deeper appreciation of the Gospels. The introduction to his chapter on Herod the Great is typical:

> If the title "Great" should be awarded a prince who, with little at his disposal, carried on an obstinate struggle in the face of extraordinary difficulties and attained to enormous power, Herod fully merits the title. If, however, there enters into the judgment a consideration of the means whereby that power was attained and exercised, then Herod can still be called "the Great," but only in irony.
>
> He was a very complex type of person. Endowed with exceptional qualities of mind and body, he was insensible to fatigue, adept in the handling of arms, a good leader of soldiers, and capable of prodigious activity. In political questions he had a clear grasp on reality which, aside from any abstract ideology, pointed out to him where his practical advantage lay, and in the attaining of this, his steely temperament did not know the meaning of fear or distraction, nor was he ever hampered by any sort of moral considerations.
>
> Herod's dominant characteristic was an obsession for power. Everything in him was subordinated to the power of his scepter and the glory of his throne. He had a family, he was a father, he had his human affections, but when his mind, driven by that fixed idea, was crossed by a fleeting suspicion of opposition between his affections and his scepter, he did not hesitate to kill relative

after relative, son after son, in order to allay that suspicion. *Regnare necesse, vivere non necesse* (It is necessary to rule, it is not necessary to live.)

Ricciotti's description of Palestine after the fall of Jerusalem in A.D. 70 is brief but illuminating:

Life was not pleasant in Palestine for the Jewish survivors of the catastrophe. Most humiliating and galling to their religious sensibilities was the knowledge that the two drachmas which they had formerly contributed to the Temple were now being sent to the Temple of Jupiter Capitolinus at Rome. Moreover, the holy city of Jerusalem had been reduced to rubble, and its ruins were profaned by the presence of the Roman legion. The Sanhedrin, once the supreme authority of the nation, was dispersed and no longer functioned. The Temple was gutted by fire, the perpetual sacrifice had ceased, the priests, of course, could no longer fulfill their duties. The victorious Messias who was to have appeared to guide the nation to triumph, and to establish his reign of happiness, had not been seen and was nowhere to be found. What did the future hold for Israel?

For one thing, there remained the task of gathering together the precious records of the past with a view to the future. From 68 on, a group of learned scribes, assembled at Jamnia with the permission of the Romans, had been silently laboring to reconstruct amid the ruins the future spiritual fortress of Judaism. Thus was gathered together that immense body of tradition which was later fixed in the Mishna and the Talmud.

The masterpiece of Ricciotti's writing career is *The Life of Jesus Christ*. The inspiration to write the book came when he thought he was facing imminent death. Yet when actually writing the *Life*, he decided to produce "an exclusively historical and documentary work. I have studied the ancient fact and not the modern theory, the solidity of the documents and not the flimsiness of any interpretation presently in fashion. I have even dared to imitate the famous dispassionateness of the canonical Evangelists, who have neither an exclamation of joy when Jesus is born nor a word of lament when He dies."

Illustrative of this dispassionateness is the effect of Mary Magdalen doing what the risen Savior told her, "Go to my brethren and say to them, 'I ascend to my Father and your Father!' " Ricciotti wrote:

She did immediately as she was bid: "Mary Magdalen came, and announced to the disciples: 'I have seen the Lord, and these things he said to me' " (John 20:18). But her jubilant announcement met an utterly humiliating response: "And they, hearing that He was alive and had been seen by her, did not believe it" (Mark 16:11).

In fact, the first Christians consistently accorded the women witnesses of the Resurrection a very cold reception. When the pious women returned from the sepulcher and said they had found it empty and repeated the message of the angels, they were told they were talking "nonsense." Here, when Mary Magdalen reports that she has seen and spoken to Jesus, she fares no better. But even later, when the Apostles and the whole Church were unshakably and officially convinced of Jesus' resurrection, there still persisted a certain unwillingness to appeal to the testimony of the women. In fact, not one woman is mentioned in the famous passage in which Paul lists, not all certainly, but many of the witnesses of Christ's resurrection: "He rose again the third day, according to the Scriptures, and . . . appeared to Cephas, and after that to the Eleven. Then He was seen by more than five hundred brethren at one time, many of whom are with us still, but some have fallen asleep. After that He was seen by James, then by all the Apostles, and last of all, as by one born out of due time, he was seen also by me" (1 Cor. 15:4–8). All these witnesses were men. Probably the official attitude of the Church was prompted by alert prudence so that Jews and idolaters might not be able to accuse it of being too quick to accept the tales of overimaginative women.

It is certain in any case that the immediate disciples of Jesus, as we shall see presently, were anything but ready to believe anyone—man or woman—who said that he had seen Jesus alive again.

This is the key to Ricciotti's genius. He wants to make sure that the mysteries of faith he describes are mysteries beyond human comprehension. But he also wants to show that our faith is not mythological but grounded on the solid rock of history.

SPECIALLY RECOMMENDED

> The Life of Jesus Christ
> The History of Israel
> Paul the Apostle
> The Age of Martyrs: Christianity from Diocletian to Constantine

85. Gerald Vann

During his relatively short life (1906–1963), the Dominican moralist and spiritual writer Gerald Vann published some twenty books. He was born and educated in England, except for his theological studies in Rome at what was then called the Collegio Angelico.

His best-known work, *The Divine Pity*, is a study in the social implications of the Beatitudes and reveals the author's shrewd practical counsel combined with deep theological insight. Three paragraphs that introduce the book also summarize its contents:

There is surely a connection between the superficiality and the arrogance of much of our modern manner of life and thought, and the decay in our times of the sense of sin. We like to think that human nature is capable, of itself, of dealing with the problems that confront it and of securing its own happiness; and so we fight shy of the deep places with which we cannot deal, and perhaps we pretend that the deepest problems do not really exist at all. But if we live on the surface of life, we miss the meaning of life. There is only one way to know reality fully and to live fully: we have to die and be re-born.

In the mythologies and folklore of the peoples of the world . . . you find the same theme constantly recurring: the hero must make his long journey through the darkness of the sea or the night, he must slay the dragon or the serpent, he must come through death to the new life, the new birth. And in the Christian story which is the fulfilment of these secular dreams of humanity . . . you will find the same theme in its highest form in the sacrificial death of the Word who was made flesh and dwelt among us that we might be re-born to the sons of God. And what was done in and by Christ must be done also in a different fashion in and by ourselves; in us, too, the dragon must be slain and we, too, must pass through death to the new life.

What is this death . . . and how are we to be re-born? The death is the false self, the self in rebellion to God . . . and the re-birth is the finding of our true centre, which is God. We find God through making for ourselves the long sea-journey—in the company and in the power of Him who made it for us first.

If there is one underlying motif in all of Vann's books, it is the belief that twentieth-century man is isolated and lonely because he is so completely absorbed in himself and his earthly needs. There is only one remedy, Vann insists, and that is to return to friendship with God. The result is predictable: an experience of such happiness already in this life as only those who have their hearts set on eternity have a right to expect.

There is nothing superficial about Gerald Vann's writing. It is the Catholic faith expressed in depth but also with such inspirational form that everyone, and not only Catholics, can enjoy and profit from what he says.

SPECIALLY RECOMMENDED
> *The Divine Pity*
> *The Seven Swords*

86. Réginald Garrigou-Lagrange

The Dominican philosopher and theologian Réginald Garrigou-Lagrange (1877–1964) was born at Auch in France and died in Rome. For fifty-three years of his long life he taught fundamental, dogmatic, and spiritual theology at what is now the Pontifical University of St. Thomas Aquinas in Rome and served as a consultant to the Holy Office and other Roman congregations.

After 1904, when he began to publish, he produced scores of books and several hundred articles. As a zealous promoter of the doctrine of St. Thomas Aquinas, he combined a deep respect for the past with a keen appreciation of the needs of modern times.

When Modernism became a threat to sound doctrine, he reaffirmed the validity of the philosophy of being, of moderate realism, and of Thomistic metaphysics based on Aristotle. Garrigou-Lagrange stressed the fact that the human mind grasps objective reality and therefore possesses the truth. He carefully distinguished between supernaturally revealed truths, found in Sacred Scripture and Sacred Tradition, and naturally knowable truths that we can obtain by the use of our reason reflecting on God's creation. He also distinguished between growth in revelation and doctrinal development. There was growth in revelation as God manifested Himself ever more, from the dawn of human history to the end of the apostolic age. But development of doctrine is the Church's ever deeper and clearer understanding of God's essentially unchangeable revelation.

Garrigou-Lagrange never wavered in his position that apologetics is a theological, rather than philosophical, science. He understood apologetics as a rational defense of divine revelation made by reason under the positive direction of faith.

In spiritual theology, he insisted on the universal call to holiness. He therefore defended the idea that infused contemplation and the mystical life are the normal ways of holiness and of Christian perfection. Among his most basic works in this field are *Christian Perfection and Contemplation, The Three Ways of the Spiritual Life,* and *The Three Ages of the Interior Life.*

A sample of his clear thinking from *Christian Perfection and Contemplation* also illustrates his hardheaded realism. He is speaking of prayer and goes out of his way to explain that our prayer does not change God, either by enlightening the divine mind or by changing the divine will:

We have our Lord's words in the Gospel: "Ask, and it shall be given you; seek, and you shall find; knock, and it shall be opened to you." Prayer is not a force with its first principle in ourselves; it is not an effort of the human soul trying to do violence to God to make Him change His providential disposi-tions. At times these human ways of expression are used metaphorically. In reality, the will of God is absolutely immutable; and precisely in this immuta-bility lies the source of the infallible efficacy of prayer.

It is puerile even to conceive of a God who would not have foreseen and willed from all eternity the prayers we address to Him, or of a God who would incline before our will and change His designs. Not only all that happens has been foreseen and willed, or at least permitted, in advance by a providential decree, but the way things happen, the causes that produce events, all have been determined from all eternity by Providence. In all orders, physical, intel-lectual, and moral, in view of certain effects, God has prepared the causes that must produce them. For material harvests, He has prepared the seed; to make parched soil fertile, He willed abundant rainfall. He raises up a great military leader to bring about a victory which will be the salvation of a people. To give the world a man of genius, He prepares a superior intellect served by a better brain, by special heredity, by a privileged intellectual environment. To regen-erate the world in its most troubled periods, He decided there should be saints. And to save humanity, divine Providence prepared from all eternity the com-ing of Jesus Christ. In all orders, from the lowest to the highest, God disposes causes in view of certain effects which they are to produce. For spiritual as well as material harvests, He has prepared the seed, without which the harvest will not be obtained.

Prayer is precisely a cause ordained to produce this effect, the obtaining of God's gifts necessary or useful for salvation. All creatures live by the gifts of God, but only intellectual creatures take cognizance of this fact. Stones, plants, and animals receive without knowing that they do so. Man lives by the gifts of God, and he knows it.

Needless to say, we are here dealing with mystery, the mys-tery of human freedom choosing to pray. Garrigou-Lagrange makes his readers face revealed mysteries, which he makes intelligible to the human mind.

SPECIALLY RECOMMENDED

> *Christian Perfection and Contemplation, According to St. Thomas Aquinas and St. John of the Cross*
> *The Three Ways of the Spiritual Life*
> *The Mother of Our Savior and Our Interior Life*

87. Henri Daniel-Rops

The real name of Daniel-Rops was Henri Petiot (1901–1965). He used a pen name to be able to publish while serving as a public-school teacher in the France of his day. His literary output was immense. Besides numerous short stories, essays, and articles, he authored about seventy books, of which twenty were novels. Unlike the writings of Claudel, many of the works of Daniel-Rops have been translated into English.

In 1934 he published his best-known novel, *Death, Where Is Thy Victory?* In this work—which became very popular and was made into a film—he made himself known as a Catholic author. During the difficult days among French Catholics torn between political extremes, Daniel-Rops maintained a balance that relied above all on the Christian values taught by the Church.

His book *The People of the Bible* was confiscated and suppressed by the Gestapo. But it became, as *Sacred History*, the first of twelve volumes on scriptural and ecclesiastical history that were completed only shortly before his death. These works are available in English under the titles *Jesus and His Times* and the *History of the Church of Christ*, which is a number of volumes covering the history of the Church over the centuries.

In the meantime, he became editor of the 150-volume series that appeared in English as the *Twentieth-Century Encyclopedia of Catholicism*. He was elected to the French Academy ten years before his death.

We get some idea of his ability to combine history and theology from his opening chapter of *The Catholic Reformation:*

The series of events which form the history of Catholicism in the mid-sixteenth century are most often depicted as follows. A violent shock causes the very foundations of Christendom to tremble, and whole sections of the Church's ancient edifice are swallowed up in heresy. Her rulers then drag themselves from their lethal indifference; they determine to oppose the Protestant menace, and at last take steps that should have been taken long ago.

Such is the pattern implied by the word "counter-reformation." The term, however, though common, is misleading: it cannot rightly be applied, logically or chronologically, to that sudden awakening as of a startled giant, that wonderful effort of rejuvenation and reorganization, which in a space of thirty years gave to the Church an altogether new appearance. What happened was a true renascence in the fullest etymological sense, more impressive from a Christian point of view than the Renaissance of art and letters upon which contemporary Europe was priding itself. The so-called "counter-reformation" did not begin with the Council of Trent, long after Luther; its origins and initial achievements were much anterior to the fame of Wittenberg. It was undertaken, not by way of answering the "reformers," but in obedience to demands and principles that are part of the unalterable tradition of the Church and proceed from her most fundamental loyalties.

Some critics have said that his historical synthesis was not an original one. This may be granted. But it had the merit of putting at the disposal of a vast reading audience some very readable and thoroughly sound Catholic literature.

SPECIALLY RECOMMENDED

> The Book of Mary
> The Church of the Apostles and Martyrs
> The Church in the Dark Ages
> The Catholic Reformation

88. Karl Adam

In his day, Karl Adam (1876–1966) was regarded as one of the greatest Catholic theologians. He was born in Bavaria, one of a family of ten. After his ordination to the priesthood and two years in parish work and further studies, he spent the rest of his life teaching theology and writing. Not insignificant in the light of later developments is that it was while Karl Adam was teaching dogmatic theology at Tübingen (from 1919) that he delivered his famous lectures on the Church, which brought fame to him. Under the Nazis, his integrity forced him to deliver an outspoken defense of the true faith against the so-called German religion of National Socialism. Forced to flee for his life, he steadfastly refused to compromise.

Many of his books have been translated into other languages. Among his early writings were *Tertullian's Conception of the Church* and *Eucharistic Teaching of St. Augustine.* Later on, he published such well-known books as *Christ Our Brother, The Son of God, The Spirit of Catholicism,* and *One and Holy.*

Among Adam's writings, the one that deserves special attention is *The Spirit of Catholicism.* Within a few years of its publication in 1924, it was translated into ten other languages, including Chinese and Japanese.

The Spirit of Catholicism is not a long book. It was written to provide a calm, clear presentation of the Catholic Church's understanding of herself among world religions but especially within Christianity. Adam's thesis is that true Christianity is more than a system of thought. It is a living stream of divine life flowing out from Christ and bearing His truth and His Life, pure and uncontaminated, down the centuries.

In the chapter "The Church and Peter," Adam describes the special position of Peter among the Twelve. He shows that St. Paul recognized this unique position. In analyzing the crucial dialogue between Jesus and Simon, Adam elaborates on the significance of every detail. Simon's name was changed to Peter to promise him authority that would guarantee the Church doctrinal and corporate stability until the end of time. Through Peter's successors, the Church has become the only guardian of genuine faith in Christ and the only hope of human civilization.

We get some idea of the warmth of the author's language from the book's closing paragraph. The Catholic, it says, affirms the Church first as "it is, for in its actual form, the Church is to him the revelation of the divine Holiness, Justice and Goodness. The Catholic does not desire some ideal Church, a Church of the philosopher or the poet. Though his mother be travel-stained with long journeying, though her countenance be furrowed with care and trouble—yet, she is his mother. In her heart burns the ancient faith. From her hands flow ever the ancient blessings. What would heaven be without God? What would the earth be without this Church? I believe in One, Holy, Catholic and Apostolic Church."

It is worth noting that the University of Tübingen, where Karl Adam gave his famous lectures, later published in book form, had become a Protestant university in Luther's time, and over the centuries, it was a leader in Lutheran theology. Among its faculty were such men as Ferdinand Baur, who denied the authenticity of most of St. Paul's letters. Meanwhile, in 1817, a Catholic faculty was established at Tübingen, and the university soon became an important center of Catholic scholarship.

SPECIALLY RECOMMENDED
The Spirit of Catholicism
The Son of God
Christ Our Brother
The Roots of the Reformation

89. *Evelyn Waugh*

The author of *Brideshead Revisited* wrote his first novel (five hundred words long) at the age of seven! Evelyn Waugh (1903–1966) came of a literary family. His father, Arthur, was a publisher and literary critic. His brother, Alec, was a well-known novelist.

Most of Evelyn Waugh's writing was done after his conversion in 1930. By his own estimate, *Brideshead Revisited* is his best book. This is the story of a great British Catholic family through the decades between the two world wars. When critics found fault with the novel's strong religious atmosphere, Waugh admitted that some people would be outraged "at God being introduced into my story. I believe you can only leave God out by making your characters pure abstractions." Modern novelists "try to represent the whole human mind and soul, and yet omit its determining character—that of being God's creature with a defined purpose. So in my future books there will be two things to make them unpopular, a preoccupation with style and the attempt to represent man more fully, which to me means only one thing, man in his relation to God."

Another of Waugh's popular books is his story of the English martyr Edmund Campion. Considered among the best Catholic biographies of our times, it portrays the young priest who died for his faith as a totally human person, whose deep loyalty to the Vicar of Christ cost him his life. We get some idea of why Evelyn Waugh wrote this short biography from his preface to the American edition. A British life of Campion had been published almost a century before, but its author, Richard Simpson, wrote when there was a lull in the persecution of the Church, at least in England. "We know now," says Waugh, that Simpson's age "was a brief truce" in an unending war. The Church is once again going through a period of opposition, like her Master, except that this one is more virulent than anything that went before:

> We have seen the Church driven underground in one country after another. The martyrdom of Father Pro in Mexico re-enacted Campion's. In fragments and whispers we get news of other saints in the prison camps of Eastern and South Eastern Europe, of cruelty and degradation more frightful than anything in Tudor England and of the same pure light shining in the darkness, uncomprehended. The hunted, trapped, murdered priest is amongst us again, and the voice of Campion comes to us across the centuries as though he were walking at our side.

Evelyn Waugh's writings reveal an author who had a deep sense of history. But he also had keen foresight. His books show every promise of being "relevant" beyond the twentieth century.

SPECIALLY RECOMMENDED

Brideshead Revisited: The Sacred and Profane Memories of Captain Charles Ryder

A Handful of Dust
Edmund Campion

90. *Romano Guardini*

The Verona-born Romano Guardini (1885–1968) grew up in Mainz, Germany, where his father was serving as Italian consul. After ordination, he taught theology at the universities of Berlin, Tübingen, and Munich. From the first years of his teaching, Guardini was regarded as a religious phenomenon of his time. Although he is best known for his writings, his organizational work among youths reveals him as a master of intuitive psychology. He was the leader of the German Catholic Youth Movement, a movement "born, not made," setting the élan vital of young people against the spurious clichés of a culture that produced Nazism and sparked World War II.

We get some idea of the roots of his thinking from his dissertation in 1920 on the Redemption according to St. Bonaventure. It was Bonaventure who emphasized that all human wisdom is folly when compared with the mystical illumination that God sheds on the faithful Christian.

In his writings, Guardini combined the classicism of the South with the philosophical mind of the North. His depth of thought is balanced with an extraordinary clarity of expression. Fully aware of the progress of modern science, he stressed the importance of maintaining the integrity of the Catholic faith in an age when technology was becoming idolized.

Not all of Guardini's books have been translated into English, but many have. Among his best-known are *The Lord; The Way of the Cross; Freedom, Grace, Destiny;* and *The End of the Modern World.*

In *The End of the Modern World,* Guardini was brutally clear in diagnosing the condition of modern thought, which has also penetrated into Catholic circles. It all began, said Guardini, with sowing the seeds of doubt about the truth of Christian revelation. In demonic sequence, the historicity of the Gospel narratives was called into question, the historical fact of Jesus' bodily Resurrection, the actual occurrence of Christ's miracles, the literal truth of Christ's teaching, the reality of his institution of a visible, hierarchical Church—all were so demythologized that nothing was left of the Jesus of history except the Christ of a naive faith that was out of touch with "modern times."

Inevitably the Catholic Church was pushed more and more into the background, and her moral teachings accused of being archaic. The results were predictable.

Not unlike Belloc, Guardini believed that only the principles of Catholic Christianity, founded on the basic principle of the Incarnation, could restore Western society to cultural sanity. Given the virus of doubt in the truth of Christian revelation, a new age has come into existence. It is hostile to everything that historical Christianity has stood for:

> As an absolute standard claiming the right to measure the direction and conduct of human life, Revelation was enduring more and more vigorous attack. The new culture taking shape in Europe bred an outlook which thrust into prominence the increasing opposition to the Church. European man was adopting as self-evident truth the point of view which gave to politics, economics, government, science, art, philosophy and education principles and criteria immanent to themselves. In doing so, men planted the seeds of non-Christian, even anti-Christian ways of life in the soil of Europe. The old insistence that life be ordered by Revelation was taken as an encroachment by the Church, so completely had the new mind seized power over men's imaginations. Even the faithful came to accept this state of affairs, accepting as normal the new order which said that matters of religion belonged in one sphere of life and secular matters in another. The individual man was left adrift to decide to what extent he would live in both of them.

Guardini is indispensable reading for anyone who wants to understand what is going on in the modern world. He is especially necessary for Catholics who want to remain true to their unchangeable faith in an age when change is considered the infallible sign of progress and not to change has become the unforgivable sin.

SPECIALLY RECOMMENDED

The Lord
The Way of the Cross of Our Lord and Our Savior Jesus Christ

Freedom, Grace, Destiny: Three Chapters in the Interpretation of Existence

The End of the Modern World: A Search for Orientation

91. *Katherine Burton*

From associate editor of *McCall's* and *Redbook* magazines Katherine (Kurz) Burton (1884–1969) went on to become one of the most respected Catholic writers in America. In 1910 she married Harry Payne Burton, an editor. Her first book, *The Circus Lady*, was published in 1926.

In 1930, Katherine Burton entered the Church and three years later took up free-lance writing. Her second book did not appear until 1937. Entitled *Sorrow Built a Bridge*, it is the study of Rose Hawthorne, the youngest child of Nathaniel Hawthorne and the founder of a Dominican community of sisters to care for the cancerous poor. In a short time, the book went through ten editions.

Burton published in rapid succession several intensely personal biographies, including *His Dear Persuasion* (Mother Seton), *Celestial Homespun* (Isaac Hecker), and *No Shadow of Turning* (James Kent Stone, later Father Fidelis the Passionist). *In No Strange Land* is a collection of sketches of some outstanding American converts to the Catholic faith. Her own autobiography and reminiscences appeared under the disarming title *The Next Thing*.

Taking her cue from Dante, "How heavy is the great mantle to him who guards it from the mire," Burton's life of St. Pius X is called *The Great Mantle*. It is a masterpiece of spiritual insight into the life of a man whose zeal for orthodoxy was joined with a superhuman charity. (He had not yet been beatified when Burton published the biography.) The Foreword to the book gives some idea of the clear language in which it is written, to bring out the true character of her subject:

Giuseppe Cardinal Sarto had been unwilling to accept the papacy. He finally agreed because he felt that it was the will of God, and he had wanted to do always God's will. During his first months in the Vatican his eyes were often wet with tears, for he did not bend easily to the captive life which a Pope then led, nor to the constraint of political etiquette.

The results justified the sacrifice. During His comparatively short reign he was called on to make many difficult and important decisions. The more than three hundred encyclicals, letters and briefs bearing his signature dealt with every important problem of life, with the state, the family, the individual, the economic order. He had stern decisions to carry out, for the times during which he ruled were full of quick and almost anarchical changes which he met without faltering. His writings showed a brilliant intellect, a balanced personality, and above all they reflected his deep and comprehending love—his desire to restore all things in Christ.

The keynote of his reign was simplicity—the enunciation of a few clear principles, the re-statement, with no compromise and no subtlety, of the basic doctrines of the Church. "He met Modernism and the French situation," said Belloc, "almost it seemed as if a man inspired by sanctity had foreseen the immediate future of Europe."

He never lost the supplementary virtue of unselfish love—a deep humility. Despite the high offices he occupied he remained the humble man he had always been. His heart and soul were to the end those of a holy old country pastor.

One feature of Burton's writing is the accuracy of the facts she narrates, without footnotes but not without painstaking research into important details. Hundreds of testimonies of miraculous cures through the intercession of the Pope were God's way of witnessing to the sanctity of the man on whose tomb is a revealing inscription:

> Born poor and humble of heart,
> Undaunted champion of the Catholic faith,
> Zealous to restore all things in Christ,
> Crowned a holy life with a holy death.

In all her Catholic biographies, Burton makes her characters come to life and inspires her readers to imitate the witness of the persons about whom they read.

SPECIALLY RECOMMENDED

The Great Mantle
Sorrow Built a Bridge
Witness of the Light
The Next Thing: Autobiography and Reminiscences

92. *Christopher Dawson*

The Christian humanist Christopher Dawson (1889–1970) was born at Hay Castle in England. His mother, Mary Bevan, was the daughter of the Anglican archdeacon of Brecknock in Wales. Dawson's early reading of the lives of the Catholic saints and mystics and a visit to Rome led to his conversion to the Catholic faith in 1914. Two years later he married Valery Mills.

Further studies and careful planning prepared Dawson for writing his cultural histories of the world, which established him as the recognized master of cultural history. He begins with the origins of culture in prehistoric Europe and in the ancient East. Then he analyzes how the foundations of Europe were laid on the ruins of the ancient world. Europe, he says, derived its political unity from Rome, its religious unity from the Catholic Church, and its intellectual culture from the classical tradition preserved by the Church, and it embraced the barbarians in its human material. Dawson goes on to show how the fifth to eleventh centuries have been wrongly called the Dark Ages. It was this period that created the groundwork of all future cultural achievements.

Six of his books have received wide circulation: *The Age of the Gods, Religion and World History, The Making of Europe, Enquiries into Religion and Culture, Religion and the Modern State,* and *The Judgement of the Nations.* Among these, the most comprehensive is *The Judgement of the Nations.* Dawson convincingly shows that only a return to the spiritual traditions of Christianity can save modern civilization. Euro-American culture, he believes, is dying for having lost its spiritual roots. What Western people are mainly searching for is their roots. They are wandering in a darkness that can only be overcome by the light of Christ.

However, the Christ that the world needs is the historical Christ. More specifically, it is the Christ whose teachings are faithfully preserved in the Church he founded, which is the Roman Catholic Church, of which the successor of Peter is the unique head. "Today," says Dawson, "she stands as she did under the Roman Empire, as the representative in a changing world of an unchanging spiritual order."

SPECIALLY RECOMMENDED

> *Religion and World History*
> *Progress and Religion*
> *The Crisis of Western Education*
> *Religion and the Rise of Western Culture*

93. *François Mauriac*

When André Gide died in 1951, François Mauriac (1885–1970) logically became the greatest living French novelist. A year later, he received the coveted Nobel Prize for literature and continued producing an astonishing amount of outstanding best-sellers that have been translated into many modern languages.

It seems best to concentrate here on his qualities as a writer and to clarify his position as a Catholic novelist. Literary critics commonly compare him with Gide. No two writers could have been more unlike. Gide was a Protestant who became the typical freethinker, espousing secular morality; Mauriac was a devout Catholic who defended the Church's demanding self-sacrifice in the following of Christ. Gide was an exponent of sexual license; Mauriac never tired proclaiming the hard way of the Cross.

What Mauriac had in common with Gide, however, was a deep awareness of man's inner struggle. Both realized that life is a constant conflict between good and evil. In Mauriac's case, the struggle arose from his naturally sensitive character. Already as a child, he was easily hurt, deeply felt the attitude of others toward him, and had to overcome himself in the smallest things to rise above his tendencies. In this respect, Mauriac was quite unlike most of the authors in the Lifetime Reading Plan. He had amenities from infancy that most Frenchmen did not enjoy and belonged to a well-to-do middle class of landlord farmers and businessmen that were untouched by the hard realities of life commonly experienced by the poor.

Two factors, however, in Mauriac's life qualify him as a spokesman for the Catholic tradition. He was reared from childhood in the best available religious atmosphere. Left fatherless when only twenty months old, Mauriac was brought up by a strictly orthodox Catholic mother, who guided the training of her daughter and four sons according to the Church's faith, and one of her sons, Jean, became an exemplary priest. But from his early years Mauriac was also exposed to literary influences that put his principles to a severe test. What kept him intact was a profound awareness of his need for God.

In reading Mauriac's poetry, but especially his novels, one must not be surprised at his sensual imagination or preoccupation with sin. They should be seen in the larger context of his authentically Catholic faith, even when his language is sometimes abrasive and almost offensive in tone.

Among his better-known works is the *Life of Jesus*. The opening paragraphs of the first edition of this widely read book reveal a great deal about its author:

Of all historians, the biblical scholar is the most deceiving. If he belongs to the category of those who first deny the supernatural and do not see the God in Jesus, we may be certain that he understands nothing of the subject of his studies and all his learning is not worth a farthing. On the other hand, if he be a Christian, we may say that too often his very fervor causes the painter's hand to tremble and obscures his vision; the man named Jesus, whose portrait he draws for us, risks being swallowed up in the lightning power of the second Divine Person.

There is no doubt that the union of learning and mystical understanding in certain writers has given rise in France to admirable works like those of Lagrange, de Grandmaison, Lebreton, Pinard de Laboulaye, Huby. But unfortunately there are others, and we know why reasonable people have come today to deny the historical existence of Christ. The Jesus of the Gospels, at times lowered by historians to the proportions of an ordinary man, at others raised by adoration and love far above the earth where he lived and died, loses, in the eyes of the faithful as in those of the indifferent, all definite outline, and presents none of the features of a real person.

Now it is here that a Catholic writer, even the most ignorant, a novelist—but who knows himself, if I may say so, in heroes of his own invention—has perhaps the right to bring his testimony. No doubt a *Life of Jesus* should be written on one's knees, with a feeling of unworthiness great enough to make the pen drop from the hand. A sinner should blush for his temerity in undertaking such a work.

But such a writer may at least assure the reader that the Jesus of the Gospels is the contrary of an artificial and composite being. Here is the most moving of the great figures of history, and of all the great characters history places before us, the least logical because he is the most living. It is for us to understand him in what is most peculiar and essential to ourselves.

Mauriac then proceeds to delineate a life of Christ that is surely unique. He uses expressions and turns of phrase that Lagrange and de Grandmaison would never have used. But what he says is how he feels, while never wavering in his own convictions that the Jesus of history is the Christ of faith. He had no sympathy with the Modernists, who would divide Jesus Christ. He had no doubt that the Son of Mary—who was human like us in everything except sin—was the Son of God who made heaven and earth.

SPECIALLY RECOMMENDED
> *Life of Jesus*
> *Woman of the Pharisees*
> *St. Margaret of Cortona*
> *The Eucharist*

94. *James Alberione*

The six religious congregations and four aggregated institutes founded by James Alberione (1884–1971) make up what is called the Pauline Family. Their principal apostolate is also one of the most modern in the Catholic Church: it is to use the media of social communication for the spreading of the Gospel.

Shortly before his death in Rome, Alberione was personally visited by Pope Paul VI, who held him in such high esteem that he personally conferred on this "humble and faithful servant" the papal cross of honor *Pro Ecclesia et Pontifice* (For the Church and the Pontiff).

As early as his years as a seminarian in Alba, Italy, Alberione was deeply concerned that so little of the wisdom of Catholicism was being read by the people. Even before his ordination, he decided that, as a priest, he would do all he could to propagate the Gospel through the printed word. What especially disturbed him was to see non-Catholic Christians so familiar with the Bible, which to many Catholics was simply a closed book.

He organized his fellow seminarians into a Bible-distribution group. They bought copies of the New Testament and of the whole Bible, and began what was certainly an innovation in the diocese. First, the seminarians themselves became familiar with the text of the Bible; then they worked out a plan for convincing the people to read the Bible; and, finally, they offered copies of the Scripture, at no cost, to anyone who was interested.

Not long after his ordination, he began planning "an organization of Catholic writers, technicians, book dealers and salesmen" who would teach the faith through the publications apostolate. By 1914 he formed the Little Workers Typographical School, and seven years later the Bishop of Alba blessed the first group of thirteen Pauline priests (headed by Alberione), who pronounced their perpetual vows.

This was the beginning of what came to be called the Pauline Family: the Pious Society of St. Paul, the Disciples of the Divine Master (Brothers), the Daughters of St. Paul, the Sister Disciples of the Divine Master, the Sisters of the Good Shepherd (Pastorelle), and the Sisters of Mary, Queen of the Apostles (Apostolines). Alberione also founded four other institutes. Always Alberione disclaimed that any of this breathtaking achievement was his own doing. In his own words, "From St. Paul it was born by him, it was nourished and raised."

Not surprisingly, Alberione wrote a great deal. But what is less well known is that much of what was later published had originally been spoken by him, recorded, and then printed. It did not take me long to decide to include Alberione in the Reading Plan. He is unqualifiedly Catholic and deeply spiritual. But he is also one whose vision on the use of the media to proclaim Christ has yet to be discovered by millions who may never have heard his name. Two paragraphs from his *Thoughts* illustrate what this means:

The press, motion pictures, radio and television today constitute the most urgent, the most rapid and most efficacious means of the apostolate. It could be that the future reserves other, better means. But for the present, it seems that the heart of the apostle can desire no better instrument for giving God to souls and souls to God.

The apostolate of communications does not aim only at the progress of individual souls. It aims at forming a new mentality in society, giving it a new imprint, a new direction. We often fall into the error of wanting to see fruit in only a particular soul. But the greater fruit is in promoting a mentality in society, a Christian mentality, which will produce Christian sentiments, a Christian life and the fear of God; a mentality that will assure spiritual vitality for souls and a Christian life for society.

No one has improved on Alberione's formula for the sanctification of the mind. The future of mankind in time and eternity begins in the mind. "Sow a thought," he says, "and you will reap an act. Sow an act and you will reap a habit. Sow a habit and you will reap a character. Sow a character, and you will reap a destiny." The implication is clear: use the media to sow the seeds of revealed truth, and you have provided for man's eternal life.

SPECIALLY RECOMMENDED

> *Personality and Configuration with Christ*
> *Thoughts*
> *Glories and Virtues of Mary*
> *Daily Meditations: The Great Prayers, The Great Truths, The Great Virtues*

95. *Jacques Maritain*

The convert from Protestantism, philosopher, and French ambassador to the Vatican Jacques Maritain (1882–1973) was received into the Church in 1906, with his wife, Raïssa, a young Russian Jew. The turning point in Maritain's life came when he discovered in Catholicism something more than the true faith: he also found a philosophy that could direct and regulate all human thought. As a result, he began to study St. Thomas with an apostolic zeal that shaped the rest of his professional life.

In 1917 he was requested by the French hierarchy to begin a manual of philosophy for use in seminaries. As a result, *An Introduction to Philosophy* received worldwide recognition and the Holy See conferred on him an honorary doctorate. Thus began a lifetime of publication that produced a small library.

Typical of his approach to human thought, Maritain held that a philosopher should be free to deal even with the problems of contemporary politics. He refused to associate himself with any political party, either in his native France or elsewhere. When France fell in June 1940, Maritain was in the United States lecturing. He did not return to his native country during the war years, but continued writing and speaking freely in America.

More than a dozen of his books have been published in English. Among the better-known titles are *Art and Scholasticism, Religion and Culture,* and *The Things That Are Not Caesar's.* However, two books are specially noteworthy: *The Degrees of Knowledge* (1932) is considered his greatest philosophical work, and *True Humanism* (1938) deals with the practical problems of our social structure.

The opening chapter of *The Degrees of Knowledge* illustrates Maritain's approach and his unique vocabulary:

The pressing interest of the present crisis arises from the fact that, being more universal than any other, it forces us all to make decisive choices. Here we have come to the parting of the ways. In virtue of the West's failures (for it has abused Divine graces and allowed the gifts it had to render fruitful for God to be lost) it discovers that, being no longer supported by the order of charity, the order of reason is corrupted through and through and is no longer good for anything. The evil wrought by the rationalist has produced a tension between nature and the *form of reason.* Thenceforth, it has become very difficult to cling to what is human. Its stake must either be set above reason and still on its side, or below reason and against it. Now the theological virtues and the supernatural gifts are the only things that are above reason. On all sides—even in the ranks of the new humanists or the partisans of dialectical materialism— . . . the cry is heard: spirit, spirituality! But upon what spirit are you calling? If it is not the Holy Spirit, you might just as well call upon the spirit of wood alcohol or the spirit of wine. The whole so-called spiritual, all the self-styled suprarational which does not exist in charity only serves animality in the final reckoning. Hatred for reason will never be anything but a revolt of the genus against its specific difference. Dreaming is quite the contrary to contemplation. If purity consists in a perfect releasing of life in accordance with the trends of its own mechanisms, it exists more truly in the brute than in the saint.

Maritain is not easy reading, but he is most satisfying to those who take the trouble to understand what he is saying. His great contribution to Catholic literature has been the opening of the mind to understanding something of the mysteries revealed to the human race by God.

SPECIALLY RECOMMENDED
> *An Introduction to Philosophy*
> *Prayer and Intelligence*
> *The Degrees of Knowledge*
> *Art and Scholasticism*

96. *Arnold Lunn*

The writings of Arnold Lunn (1888–1974) are the story of a deeply perceptive mind, first, in search of the truth and, then, possessed of a great love for the truth that he discovered on his conversion to the Catholic faith in 1933.

His father, Sir Henry Lunn, was a Methodist minister who in 1887 went with his family to India, where Arnold was born at Madras. After a year in India, the family returned to England. Controversy over mission policy prompted the father to leave the ministry, though he remained a lay preacher. In 1892, Henry Lunn sponsored a reunion conference at Grindelwald, Switzerland, which changed his young son's life. The controversial subject of Christian unity, along with the experience of the Alps, shaped Arnold's whole future.

From 1892, Arnold Lunn spent most of his summers, and after the age of eight practically every winter, in the Alps. As a result, he developed the two great hobbies of his life, mountain climbing and skiing. He played an important part in the development of ski racing, and his book *Alpine Skiing at All Heights and Seasons* is a recognized classic study of snow and avalanche craft.

A polemicist by temperament, he wrote several books of controversy. He collaborated in the writing of *Difficulties* (with Ronald A. Knox), *Is Christianity True?* (with C. E. M. Joad), and *Science and the Supernatural* (with J. B. S. Haldane). All were published before his conversion.

In 1924 he wrote the anti-Catholic *Roman Catholicism*. Immediately his friends "began to prophesy my conversion." Annoyed by the forecast, he said he would just as likely become a Buddhist as a Catholic.

After entering the Church, Lunn wrote two books about his conversion, *Now I See* and *Within That City*. The first is a fusion of human experience and sound logic. It is a masterpiece of defense of the Catholic Church, not only as the only true form of Christianity but as the standard and norm for world religion and, indeed, for all rational philosophy.

Statements from *Now I See* illustrate its whole contents:

Churches are vital in exact proportion to the number of Catholic doctrines they contain.

Churches regain lost vigor when they approach, and lose in evangelical power as they retreat from, Rome.

If Rome dies, other Churches may order their coffins.

The pleasure with which the mind follows the sequence of reasoning which establishes a mathematical theorem, has its counterpart in the melancholy satisfaction with which the Catholic studies the consequences which inevitably follow on the surrender of the Catholic philosophy.

It is certainly stuffy of the clergy to object to "shameless pleasure." "Birth control," adds Mr. Joad triumphantly, "in enabling the pleasures of sex to be tasted without its penalties has removed the most formidable deterrent, not only to regular but to irregular sexual intercourse." I thanked Mr. Joad for making the issue so clear.

The Catholic looks out from the walls of his citadel and sees a world relapsing into that paganism from which Christianity emerged. Once more the Hun is knocking at the gate. It is not only the traditional creed of Europe which is threatened. The new pagans attack with even greater enmity the traditional morality and culture of our race.

Lunn's awareness of the depth of the struggle enables him to pinpoint the main target of godless secularism in modern times:

The Catholic knows that the enemy has long ceased to concern himself with . . . dispersed and uncoordinated forces, but is concentrating all his attack on the central citadel. . . .

The contempt with which the Victorian rationalist regarded the Church is giving way to hatred and respect for the one fortress which will never fail, and the one army which will never surrender.

Few writers have expressed more clearly why the Catholic Church believes in the infallibility of the Pope:

There are two, and only two, intelligent lines of attack on the dogma of papal infallibility. You can attack the infallibility of Jesus Christ or you can attack the belief that Jesus founded an infallible church with authority to teach in His name. We accept the infallibility of the Pope on the authority of the infallibility of the Church on the authority of the infallible Christ.

Even Lunn's severest critics admitted the firmness of his logic, and the soundness of his thinking.

His most personal book is his autobiographical *Come What May*. Yet, the closing words of *Now I See* best reveal Arnold Lunn's true spirit. Identifying himself with Ronald Knox, he wrote, "One thing in this world is different from all others. It has personality and a force. It is recognized and (when recognized) most violently loved or hated. It is the Catholic Church. Within that household the human spirit has roof and hearth. Outside it is the Night."

SPECIALLY RECOMMENDED
Now I See: Autobiography
The Revolt Against Reason
Switzerland, Its Literary, Historical and Topographical Landmarks
A Saint in the Slave Trade: Peter Claver, 1581–1654

97. *Charles Journet*

The Swiss theologian Charles Journet (1891–1975) was over sixty when his first book was published in English. But by that time he had established a reputation for scholarly orthodoxy, one that stands out more clearly today than ever before. Most of his professional life was spent as professor of theology at the Grand Séminaire in Fribourg, Switzerland, where he specialized in ecclesiology, or the science of the Church.

Published over a period of forty years, his books justify what the future Pope Paul VI wrote to him in the name of Pope Pius XII. Your work, he said, "will help many of our contemporaries to get a firmer grasp on this mystery of the Church, which perpetuates through the centuries and the vicissitudes of history the very mystery of the Word Incarnate."

Six of Journet's publications are specifically to be commended. And some of them have the quality of classics. After Journet's tireless work as theologian to the Swiss bishops during the Second Vatican Council, Pope Paul VI made him a cardinal archbishop in 1965.

Journet was a powerful witness to the granite soundness of the Second Vatican Council's orthodoxy, as witnessed by the great extent to which he influenced the council's teaching, notably in the area of ecclesiology. What Journet brought out is the valid development of doctrine—especially on the nature of the Church—that had taken place in Catholic thinking since the sixteenth century.

Anyone who wishes to understand the mind of the last general council must become familiar with the writings of Journet. The key to his thought is the distinction he makes between Christ's action in our favor "from a distance" and His action "by immediate contact." Journet then wrote:

Jesus has been "taken up into heaven." He sits on the right hand of God, and is fully associated with His Father's power. Is His action to be restricted from now onwards to action from a distance? Is this the end of His action by contact? No, for before He left us He willed that there should always be among us certain men invested with divine powers, by whom the action that He initiates from heaven may be sensibly conveyed to each of us and may continue to reach us in the only way connatural to us—through direct contact. They are the hierarchic powers.

These powers are essentially ministerial, that is to say, transmitters. They would be without effect if the divine power, passing into the heart of Christ, did not perpetually come to touch them into life. They comprise two kinds of powers: the jurisdictional powers, transmitting truth, and the sacramental powers, transmitting grace. Our Lord Himself announced, prepared and instituted them, while he was still visible in our midst.

It appears in this that the highest of these powers, the power of order, is to give us His very presence itself, real and corporeal, under the sacramental veils.

If this is the central theme of *The Church of the Word Incarnate*, it is the underlying premise of everything that Journet wrote about the Mystical Body, which is the Catholic Church on earth.

Always basic to his views is the fact that God became man in order that by the sacrifice of His humanity on Calvary we might be redeemed. But a second fact is also true: it is through His humanity present in the Holy Eucharist and active through the bishops and priests, whom He ordained, that Christ now communicates the graces He merited for us on the Cross.

Journet's first book to appear in English was *The Wisdom of Faith*, followed by *The Dark Knowledge of God*, *The Primacy of Peter*, *The Meaning of Grace*, and *The Meaning of Evil*. They are all valuable sources of clear thinking about the cardinal mysteries of Christianity. They provide background and deeper insight into the meaning of the Church as the visible institution that now carries on the work of the Incarnation.

SPECIALLY RECOMMENDED
> *The Church of the Word Incarnate*
> *The Primacy of Peter*
> *The Meaning of Grace*
> *The Wisdom of Faith: An Introduction to Theology*

98. *Dietrich von Hildebrand*

The philosopher and author Dietrich Adolph von Hildebrand (1889–1977) was born in Florence, Italy, and died in New Rochelle, New York. His conversion to the Catholic faith in 1914 was also the beginning of a zealous proclamation of what he believed. His more than thirty books witness to the depth of his religious convictions. They also reveal a personality that was deeply in love with Christ and fearless in defending the Church against any compromise with the world.

All his books are worth reading. But perhaps his most lasting work will be *Transformation in Christ*, first published in 1948. The central theme of this book is the cooperative role man must play in the drama of the supernatural life. God provides the soul of this life in the sanctifying grace we receive at Baptism. He also provides the faculties of this life, which are the infused virtues of faith, hope, and charity. He further provides the actual graces we constantly need to enlighten our minds and inspire our wills on the way to heaven. But we must do our part. Our part is to be constantly ready to change, which means to change our natural desires and inclinations in conformity with the directions offered us by the grace of God:

A strong desire must fill us to become different beings, to mortify our old selves and re-arise as new men in Christ. This desire, this readiness to "decrease" so that "He may grow in us," is the first elementary precondition for the transformation in Christ. It is the primal gesture by which man reacts to the "light of Christ," that has reached his eyes: the original gesture directed to God. It is, in other words, the adequate consequence of our being in need of redemption on the one hand, and our comprehension of being called by Christ on the other. Our surrender to Christ implies a readiness to let Him fully transform us without setting any limit to the modification of our nature under His influence.

Having set the groundwork for his study of our surrender to God's grace, von Hildebrand explores some fifteen demands that this places on our selfish human nature. The bedrock on our part is the honest admission of our sinfulness. We are sinners by inheritance through original sin. We are sinners by environment because of the sin-laden world in which we live. And we are actual sinners by the personal and deliberate offenses we have committed against the Divine Majesty. On all three counts, but especially on the third, we need to be converted. Basic to conversion is contrition. "The true Christian says, with David, 'A sacrifice to God is an afflicted spirit; a contrite and humbled heart, O God, thou wilt not despise.' From contrition thus experienced there will arise in him the genuine and heroic determination to become 'a new man.' That kind of contrition alone enables him to anchor himself in God." This means a lifelong process of conversion, anointed by contrition and inspired by faith conviction. Only in this way can we hope to be gradually transformed in Christ, which means by His grace, in His image, and according to His divine will.

Von Hildebrand is unique among Catholic authors in publishing no less than four books on chastity. *In Defense of Purity* was published in the year (1933) he was forced to flee from Germany because of his opposition to the Nazis. Nine years later appeared *Marriage,* by which the author meant especially the sacrament of marriage instituted by the Church.

His *Encyclical Humanae Vitae* and *Celibacy and the Crisis of Faith* are masterpieces of Catholic apologetics. They also reveal his keen awareness of the eye of the tornado that struck the Catholic world after the Second Vatican Council. It was the Church's uncompromising stand on the two moral issues that affected the clergy and the laity—celibacy and contraception.

His critics have charged he was out of sympathy with the changes of the Church produced by the Second Vatican Council. More accurately, however, he was out of sympathy with the unwarranted changes that some had introduced in the name of the Council.

SPECIALLY RECOMMENDED

> *Transformation in Christ: On the Christian Attitude of Mind*
> *Marriage: the Mystery of Faithful Love*
> *Celibacy and the Crisis of Faith*
> *The Sacred Heart: An Analysis of Human and Divine Affection*

99. *Étienne Gilson*

The outstanding modern theologian of medieval philosophy, Étienne Gilson (1884–1978), was born in Paris and was a dedicated Catholic from childhood. Building on his early Catholic education, Gilson discovered his love of philosophy in secular institutions, culminating in his years at the Sorbonne.

Gilson's lifework was to go back to the original writings of the philosophers, beginning with Descartes, on whom he wrote his doctoral dissertation. As teacher at the universities of Lille, Strasbourg, and Paris, he introduced the regular study of such men as Thomas Aquinas, Augustine, and Bonaventure. His published books on the medieval philosopher-theologians became the standard sources, first in Europe and then in the Americas. In 1929 he founded the Pontifical Institute of Mediaeval Studies at Toronto, and in 1949 published his classic *History of Christian Philosophy in the Middle Ages.*

Basic to Gilson's thinking are two principles that dominate all of his writing: (1) There is a distinctive and identifiable Christian philosophy; it consists in the reflection of believing theologians as they speculate about questions that are accessible, on principle, to man's natural reason. (2) St. Thomas Aquinas himself, not his interpreters, is the best model of a true Christian philosopher. Thomism, therefore, is the philosophy of a theologian who grounds his explanation of revealed truth on a metaphysics which holds that an actual reality exists and that the human mind can know objective truth.

Among the other principal works of Gilson available in English are *The Spirit of Medieval Philosophy* and *The Christian Philosophy of St. Thomas Aquinas.* An excellent collection of lengthy passages from his writings was published as *A Gilson Reader* (1957). It is organized in seven sections, coordinated by an analytical index.

Central to Gilson's writing is the realization that Catholics today, more than ever before, need not only to believe but to know why and how they believe. In *Wisdom and Time,* Gilson explains how this grave need is expressed by a strong desire to learn:

One of the most noteworthy characteristics of present-day Catholicism is the desire of Catholic believers to be better instructed in their faith. The fact is not absolutely new. In a sense it is as old as the Church.

Before the time of the Gospel, the truth concerning man and the world had remained the privilege of a single social class, and even of the intellectual elite of a chosen people, the Greek people.

Contrariwise, from the time of the preaching of Christ and the teaching of St. Paul, it became clear that all men, learned or ignorant, Greeks or barbarians, rich or poor, free or slave, were called by God to know the very same truth concerning the universe, man and his destiny.

What has happened in our day is the rise of a global sense of equality among people. Everyone on every level of society wants an equal opportunity to learn. The education of millions has reached a scale never seen before in human history. And the desire to know, simply to understand, includes the desire of

Catholics to understand their faith. It is a hunger that is born of grace, but that builds on nature. The Church of today, even more than the Christendom of the past, "believes and knows what it believes, but it has never experienced so strong a desire to know why and how it believes."

It was Gilson's lifetime ambition to help satisfy this hunger among the faithful. His books on medieval philosophy have as their common denominator the effort to make us understand what we believe. It was characteristic of the medieval mind in the thirteenth century; it is a characteristic that is sweeping the Catholic Church in our own day.

The growing literature on Gilson himself, but especially on the insights he published, shows that he has restored medieval thought to a place of honor. His influence has been felt not only among scholars but among Christian believers in the whole literate world.

SPECIALLY RECOMMENDED

History of Christian Philosophy in the Middle Ages
A Gilson Reader: Selected Writings
Modern Philosophy: Descartes to Kant
Recent Philosophy: Hegel to the Present

100. *Fulton J. Sheen*

No Catholic author in Catholic American history had a more eventful life than Fulton John Sheen (1895–1979). A few months before his death, he was embraced by Pope John Paul II in St. Patrick's Cathedral in New York. The meeting was the crowning experience of Sheen's life; the Pope told him, "You have written and spoken well of the Lord Jesus. You are a loyal son of the Church."

The papal statement synthesizes an extraordinary life. Born in El Paso, Illinois, Sheen was director of the Society for the Propagation of the Faith in the United States; Bishop of Rochester, New York; a popular radio and television personality; and a voluminous writer. At the peak of his apostolic work, I was asked to write a piece on Fulton Sheen for *La civiltà cattolica* in Rome. He wrote back a gracious acknowledgment of my summary of his career. "I only hope," he told me, "that the Lord has as favorable a judgment of me when I meet Him in eternity as you have in your article." The last time I saw him at his residence in Manhattan, we first spent about a half-hour together before the Blessed Sacrament in his private chapel. "It is before Our Lord in the Eucharist," he confided, "that I think out most of my talks and publications."

Fulton Sheen's bibliography reads like a library catalog. Shortly after his death, his autobiography, *Treasure in Clay*, was published. I recommend that anyone who wants to read Sheen's writings in depth begin with this, his last book. "Carlyle was wrong," he begins, "in saying that there is no life of a man faithfully recorded. Mine was! The ink used was blood, the parchment was skin, the pen was a spear. Over eighty chapters make up the book, each for a year of my life." Then he goes on:

That autobiography is the crucifix, the inside story of my life, not in the way it walks the stage of time, but how it was recorded, taped and written in the Book of Life. It is not the autobiography that I tell you but the autobiography *I read to myself.* In the crown of thorns, I see my pride, my grasping for earthly toys in the pierced Hands, my flight from shepherding care in the pierced Feet, my wasted love in the wounded Heart, and my prurient desires in the flesh hanging from Him like purple rags. Almost every time I turn a page of that book, my heart weeps at what *eros* has done to *agape*, what the "I" has done to the "Thou," what the professed friend has done to the Beloved.

The more familiar a reader becomes with Sheen's writings, the more they reveal the author behind the page. It is an author who, with all his admitted human failings, had a great intellect that he placed at the disposal of Providence and who allowed God to wear him out in the service of souls.

From his first book, *God and Intelligence in Modern Philosophy* (1925), to the one-volume edition of *Life Is Worth Living* (1978), Sheen averaged more than one book a year. It is noteworthy that much of his published writing had originally been lectures or conference papers. One result is that his books are like conversations with the reader, but with one important difference: his language is always clear, even crystal clear. And his ideas are never abstract in a pedantic sense but are constantly illustrated with stories from real life and explained in concrete terms that remind one of Christ's own teaching by telling parables.

One of the less-familiar aspects of Fulton Sheen's writing career is the zeal that motivated everything he wrote. His driving purpose was not to inform or inspire, except as a means to an end. That end was to make Christ better known and loved by the millions who heard him speak or read his books.

The closing chapter of his autobiography is a perfect synthesis of how he exercised his apostolic zeal up to the last hours of his life. Fellow patients at the hospital were taught about Christ's mercy to sinners and stray sheep were persuaded to return to the fold, and with unbelievers he shared the treasures of his own deep Catholic faith.

But Sheen made one thing especially clear in the several million words of print that he published: there is no true peace on earth, and no promise of happiness in the life to come except at the price of the Cross. Paganism, he would say, is Christianity without the Cross. It is this simple truth that readers of Fulton Sheen will learn, above all, from his voluminous writings.

SPECIALLY RECOMMENDED
> *Treasure in Clay: the Autobiography of Fulton Sheen*
> *Peace of Soul*
> *These Are the Sacraments*
> *Three to Get Married*

101. *Igino Giordani*

There are few Catholic writers in modern times who have a thorough grasp of the social dimension of Christianity. Igino Giordani (1894–1980) is one author who did. Quite unknown in the English-speaking world, Giordani had a long and successful career in Italy as teacher and writer. He received the Premio

Savoia-Brabante award for his books *The Social Message of Jesus* and *The Social Message of the Apostles.* On that occasion, in February 1939, the Vatican made the following announcement: "These two works, which complement each other, together evidence the loftiness of the theme and the author's skill in overcoming its inherent difficulties. They represent a major contribution to social and historical research on early Christianity. They are based on a wide knowledge and understanding of the field. They are the fruit of long years of study by one who has completely dedicated himself to this task." A third volume, *The Social Message of the Early Church Fathers,* completes Giordani's trilogy. Together, these books are unique in covering a field of Catholic thought for which there is no equivalent in the English language.

The author did what no one else has done and in such plain words and with such complete commitment to Catholic social principles. He placed these principles into the historical framework of our own times. His work shows how the social teachings of Christ elevated those of pre-Christian Judaism. It compares the Catholic Church's understanding of these teachings with those of Protestantism and relates these doctrines to those of Marxism in today's Communist societies.

Every major social issue that is shaking the modern world to its foundations is covered calmly and clearly from the perspective of the Catholic faith. And each of these issues is placed within its original setting: in the Gospels, in the Apostolic Age, and in the writings of the Church Fathers, who were the earliest witnesses to the Church's authoritative tradition.

What bears emphasis is that Giordani did not give a mere outline or historical summary. He was specific and relevant to the conditions of our day. In *The Social Message of Jesus,* his comments on "The Christian Woman" are typical:

Woman enters Christian society endowed with equal rights with man because she enters it with a soul, and among souls there is no distinction of sex or class. But she enters it also with the distinctive nature of woman and so, dictates are imposed on her which are most suited to that nature.

In the cycle of Redemption, the highest human creature after Christ is a woman, Mary, in whom humanity has collaborated in the highest degree with the work of God.

Thus a new dignity and a new office in the life of society are given or restored to woman, and society will feel much more than in antiquity the influence of her feminine nature.

Through pages of historical data, the author shows that authentic women's liberation began with Christianity. And the only true freedom for women today depends on the teachings of Christ.

Of the three books by Giordani, *The Social Message of Jesus* is basic to the other two. All three should be read, however, to grasp the central message that this Vatican authority so ably conveyed—that Christianity is "the one religion most richly charged with social efficacy, a religion that is of its very essence social."

SPECIALLY RECOMMENDED
> *The Social Message of Jesus*
> *The Social Message of the Early Church Fathers*
> *Mary of Nazareth*

102. *Frank Sheed*

There are not many authors who are also successful publishers. Francis Joseph Sheed (1897–1981) was both. Born in Sydney, Australia, of Irish ancestry, Sheed went to England to practice law. There he developed extraordinary skill as master of the Catholic Evidence Guild. As Guild speaker, he addressed over three thousand street-corner and indoor meetings.

In 1926, he married Mary Josephine ("Maisie") Ward and together they founded the Catholic publishing house of Sheed and Ward in London. Six years later, they established an office in New York. They had two children, Rosemary and Wilfrid, the well-known novelist and critic.

Sheed wrote some twenty books, of which the best-known

are *Theology and Sanity* and *To Know Christ Jesus,* as well as a translation of St. Augustine's *Confessions* that many consider the best English translation of that classic autobiography.

Theology and Sanity has been a best-seller for decades, but it is much more. It is the fruit of years of experience in presenting the Catholic faith to thousands of curious and often hostile listeners, who had one thing in common—a hunger for the truth. Sheed goes to the heart of the matter in his opening paragraphs:

> My concern in this book is not with the Will but with the Intellect, not with sanctity but with sanity. The difference is too often overlooked in the practice of religion. The soul has two faculties and they should be clearly distinguished. There is the Will: its work is to love—and so to choose, to decide, to act. There is the intellect: its work is to know, to understand, to see: to see what? to see what's there.
>
> I have said that my concern is with the intellect rather than with the will: this not because the intellect matters more in religion than the will, but because it does matter and tends to be neglected, and the neglect is bad. I realize that salvation depends directly upon the will. We are saved or damned according to what we love. If we love God, we shall ultimately get God: we shall be saved. If we love self in preference to God then we shall get self apart from God: we shall be damned. But though in our relation to God the intellect does not matter as much as the will (and indeed depends for its health upon the will), it does matter, and as I have said, it is too much neglected—to the great misfortune of the will, for we can never attain a maximum love of God with only a minimum knowledge of God.
>
> For the soul's full functioning, we need a Catholic intellect as well as a Catholic will. We have a Catholic will when we love God and obey God, love the Church and obey the Church. We have a Catholic intellect when we live consciously in the presence of the realities that God through his Church has revealed. A good working test of a Catholic will is that we should do what the Church says. But for a Catholic intellect, we must also see what the Church sees. This means that when we look out upon the Universe we see the same Universe that the Church sees; and the enormous advantage of this is that the Universe the Church sees is the real Universe, because She is the Church of God. Seeing what She sees means seeing what is there. And just as loving what is good is sanctity, or the health of the will, so seeing what is there is sanity or the health of the intellect.

Throughout his writing, Sheed insists on the absolute need of our minds to *know* our faith, to *think* through what we believe, to try to *understand* God's revealed truth, and mentally *grasp* something of the meaning of divine mysteries. Sheed had no doubt that Christ meant to be taken literally when He promised, "You shall *know* the truth, and the truth shall make you free" (John 8:32).

SPECIALLY RECOMMENDED
Theology and Sanity
Communism and Man
The Church and I
Marriage and the Family

103. *Hubert van Zeller*

Born in 1905 in Suez, Egypt, Hubert van Zeller would say that "the dry land of the desert reaches my nostrils still." Studies at Downside Abbey in England led to his entering the Benedictines there, where he was also ordained a priest in 1930. He died in 1984.

Interest in the Bible from childhood led to his early publications. His first books, *Prophets and Princes* and *Watch and Pray*, appeared in 1935 and were followed by *Sackcloth and Ashes*. While ill in bed, he wrote *Isaias: Man of Ideas* to see "if the public was ready to take full-length biographies instead of, as hitherto, snapshot impressions of people and periods." Because of the favorable reception accorded this new venture, Zeller wrote a series of books on the major prophets, including *Daniel: Man of Desires, Jeremias: Man of Tears*, and *Ezechiel: Man of Signs*. Under the pseudonym Hugh Venning, he wrote the novel *The End* and a series of plays, including *Kaleidoscope, Portmanteau, Up the Garden Path* and *The King with Half a Crown*. His short story "A Quiet Afternoon" is about the philosopher Plato. The titles of most of his other books are consciously eye-catching: *We Live with Our Eyes Open, Famine of the Spirit, We Work While the Light Lasts, We Sing While There's Voice Left*, and *Praying While You Work*.

We get some idea of van Zeller's approach to the great truths of life and of his light touch in writing from *We Die Standing Up*. It is almost autobiographical and eminently practical in applying the mysteries of faith to the art—and trial—of daily living:

Nature craves for rest—a rest which fallen nature is obliged to forego. Or at all events to defer. We pray that eternal rest be granted to the dead. It is the best thing we can think of. Eternal rest and perpetual light. These are the things we know we can never fully enjoy in this life, so we pray that our friends may enjoy them fully in the next. In the meantime, there is the business of taking off coats and spitting on hands. There are some—not so many as there used to be but some—who for one reason or another do not work. They rest. Even in this life they rest. But such is the strangely unpractical joke of nature that their leisure, their envied ease, is almost as great a burden to them as work would have been. Indeed, labour is seldom so exhausting as leisure.

Though work is meant to be an effort it is not meant to be an agony. In fact, it can sometimes be an anodyne. "I must have something to do . . . anything to take my mind off it." In sorrow, idleness is fatal; occupation is essential. It seems, then, that we cannot escape the "truth" that struggle, and even to a certain point, strain, is necessary to the general well-being of man. It is part of God's scheme. And if we look upon labour *only* as a punishment, we miss at least half the point of it.

"Work out your salvation," says the Bible, not let it come to you as the result of a single act of faith made from the depths of an armchair. Life is intended to be a battle—with a battle's uncertainties, bloodshed, strain, breaking points, and above all with a battle's joys. Long before the final victory we are meant to taste the satisfaction of fighting. It is this satisfaction, it is these joys, that the world wants to experience without the disgusting necessity of having to fight for them.

When we begin to wallow in our rest or in our pleasure we begin also to tire. The battle of life, if we give up fighting, becomes the most awful bore. Never before has there been such universal complaint against the dullness of existence, and yet never before has there been such a universal attempt to lift the burden of toil from the shoulders of man.

Van Zeller is an extraordinary writer. All his books are worth reading. Some require rereading to get to the central message he wants to convey. Always practical and down-to-earth, he manages to combine a deep understanding of the Christian faith, with a clear application to the everyday needs of life.

One thing he never leaves in doubt, no matter what subject he is treating: the members of Christ's Mystical Body on earth belong to the Church Militant. Only those who have won the victory over the world, the flesh, and the devil will have a title to the Church Triumphant that awaits us in eternity.

   We Die Standing Up
   Approach to Christian Sculpture
   The End: A Projection Not a Prophecy
   *Praying While You Work: Devotions for the Use of Martha Rather
      than Mary*

104. *John C. H. Wu*

Wu Ching-hsiung, known in the West as John C. H. Wu (1899–
1986), is the most prominent Chinese Catholic author of modern times. Lawyer, political philosopher, educator, and theologian of spirituality, Wu was president of the Special High Court
at Shanghai, founder of *J'ien Hsia Monthly*, translator of the
Psalms and the New Testament, and Chinese minister to the
Holy See.

In 1937, during the war between China and Japan, Wu became a Catholic. He attributed his conversion to a chance reading of the autobiography of St. Thérèse of Lisieux. What especially struck him was the Little Flower's message of God's love
for us and of our unbounded faith in God's mercy. He had
found his Protestant religion cold and looked into Confucianism, Buddhism, and Taoism. But they did not satisfy his hunger
for union with God. What attracted Wu to Catholicism was not
its intellectual integrity but the simplicity of the Catholic religion, its recognition that God's love is an unfathomable mystery, and its demand for a childlike trust in the Almighty.

He was commissioned by Chiang Kai-shek to translate the
Psalms, and during his mission to the Vatican he completed the
translation of the New Testament into classic Chinese. While a
visiting professor of Chinese philosophy in Honolulu, he wrote
the autobiographical volume *Beyond East and West*. The book drew
wide attention for its synthesis of the author's thirty-year spiritual odyssey and his search for unchangeable moral principles
that all human beings could follow. Another book, *The Interior*

Carmel, also written in English, was a study of the Christian path to holiness.

Wu spent most of his later years as a Catholic writer in the United States. Legal philosophy had been his first love. He therefore returned to this subject like one who was fulfilling a debt of honor. In Wu's understanding, the author of the natural law was God, who either promulgated this law through a special revelation, as to Moses in the Decalogue, or imprinted the essentials of this law in the heart of every human being. Although these ideas were basic Catholic teaching, Wu expressed them with the authority of an academically trained scholar. As a result, he had a profound influence in circles that would otherwise have been untouched by Christian principles. Two of his books, the *Fountain of Justice* and *Cases and Materials on Jurisprudence,* represented Wu's mature thinking in this field.

There is no easy way of summarizing John Wu's influence as an author. Perhaps the simplest is to quote at some length from his *Interior Carmel,* whose subtitle is *The Threefold Way of Love:*

The idea that our interior life must grow, and that in its growth it usually passes through certain stages or phases, is not peculiar to Christianity. We find the same idea, for instance, in Buddhism, which asserts that one begins with abstention from evil, passes through the period of confirmation in the virtues, and finally arrives at the state of wisdom. In Confucianism, one speaks of "entering the door," "ascending to the hall," and "being admitted into the secret chamber." There is no question that Confucius conceived of the way of wisdom and goodness as a growing process consisting of three progressive phases. "To know about it," he said, "is not so good as to take interest in it; to take interest in it is not so good as to rejoice in it." Using a homely analogy drawn from his agricultural environment, he said, "There are cases in which the blade springs, but the plant does not go on to flower! There are cases where it flowers but produces no fruit."

It should, of course, be noted that both Confucius and Buddha moved in the same sphere of nature, while His is the sphere of grace. He comes from heaven and bears witness of what He has seen and heard, while they are of earth, and from the earth they speak. But the point is that even grace is sown upon the earth, that is, human nature; and, therefore, the life of grace has to grow according to the gradual steps followed in the normal development of human nature, and is subject to the rhythms of life as symbolized by "night and day."

In the life of grace, as in the life of natural morality and wisdom, ripeness is all. In one as in the other, one must continuously grow toward ripeness; for not to advance is to fall back. The reason why so many Christians are frustrated and stunted is that they do not realize the vital importance of continual progress in the spiritual life, and pay but scant attention to the laws of interior growth. They are so fascinated by the progress of the physical sciences and material civilization that they seem to have no time for, nor attraction to the things of the spirit.

Throughout his writings, Wu constantly draws on the basic wisdom of the Orient. He sees in Christianity the fulfillment of the best in non-Christian thought. It is not too much to see in this Chinese sage the promise of a glorious future for the Gospel in the East.

SPECIALLY RECOMMENDED

>*The Science of Love: A Study in the Teachings of Thérèse of Lisieux*
>*Beyond East and West*
>*Fountain of Justice: A Study in the Natural Law*
>*The Interior Carmel: The Threefold Way of Love*

BIBLIOGRAPHY

Bibliographic
Introduction

In order that this bibliography may be of maximum use to the readers in helping them to find the titles, it is organized in the following way:

1. The most comprehensive category of works is listed first.

2. After collections of works and writings, the other titles are listed in roughly chronological order according to the sequence in which they were published. The purpose of this procedure is to reveal to the reader the development in the thought of the writers as they grew in their respective relationships to God. In some cases the earlier works of the writers were written before the writer's conversion to Catholicism.

3. Over 98 percent of the titles are given along with their publishers. After months of research, it was decided to include also some titles without a publisher, especially of foreign writers. This was done where it is morally certain that a writing was either translated or at some time has been available in English.

1. St. Ignatius of Antioch

The Epistles of St. Ignatius, Bishop of Antioch, S.P.C.K.; Pontificum Institutum Orientatium Studiorum.

The Epistles of Clement of Rome and Ignatius of Antioch, in Ancient Christian Writers (Vol. 1), Newman Press.

"Letters of St. Ignatius of Antioch," from *The Apostolic Fathers* in The Fathers of the Church (Vol. 1), Catholic University of America Press; and in *The Apostolic Fathers*, W. Heinemann; Macmillan.

2. St. Justin Martyr

Writings of Saint Justin Martyr, in The Fathers of the Church (Vol. 6), Catholic University of America Press.

The Apologies, American Book Co. contains the first and second *Apologies*.

Saint Justin Martyr:
  The First Apology,
  The Second Apology,
  Dialogue with Trypho,
  Exhortation to the Greeks,
  Discourse to the Greeks,
  The Monarchy, or The Rule of God, Christian Heritage, Inc.
Letters, in The Fathers of the Church (Vol. 51), Catholic University of America Press.
Treatises, in The Fathers of the Church (Vol. 36), Catholic University of America Press.
Letters of St. Cyprian of Carthage in Ancient Christian Writers (Vol. 43–44), Newman Press.
The Lord's Prayer, Christian Classics; S.P.C.K.

3. St. Irenaeus

Adversus Haereses (Unmasking and Refutations of the False Gnosis), also known as *The Treatise of Irenaeus of Lugdunum Against the Heretics* (2 vols.), S.P.C.K. Also in A Library of Fathers of the Holy Catholic Church (Vol. 42), Parker of Oxford; in The Ante-Nicene Christian Library (Vols. 5 and 9), Edinburgh; and in Ante-Nicene Fathers (Vol. 1), Scribner.
Presentation of the Apostolic Preaching, in Ancient Christian Writers (Vol. 16), Newman Press; S.P.C.K.; also published as *The Demonstration of the Apostolic Preaching,* Macmillan.

4. Tertullian

Apologetical Works (Vol. 1), in The Fathers of the Church (Vol. 10), Catholic University of America Press.
Disciplinary, Moral and Ascetical Works, in The Fathers of the Church (Vol. 40), Catholic University of America Press.
Treatise on the Incarnation, S.P.C.K.
Adversus Marcionem, Clarendon Press, Oxford.
Apologeticus, Cambridge University Press.
De Baptismo Liber: Homily on Baptism, S.P.C.K.
Treatise on Marriage and Remarriage: To His Wife; An Exhortation to Chastity; Monogamy, in Ancient Christian Writers (Vol. 13), Newman Press.
The Treatise Against Hermogenes, in Ancient Christian Writers (Vol. 24), Newman Press.
Treatise on Penance: On Penitence and Purity, in Ancient Christian Writers (Vol. 28), Newman Press.
To the Nations, in Ante-Nicene Christian Library (Vol. 11), Edinburgh.
Against the Jews, in Ante-Nicene Christian Library (Vol. 18), Edinburgh.
Against Marcion, in Ante-Nicene Christian Library (Vol. 7), Edinburgh.
Tertullian's Treatise Against Praxeas, S.P.C.K.
Against Valentinian, in Ante-Nicene Christian Library (Vol. 15), Edinburgh.
Treatise on the Resurrection: Concerning the Resurrection of the Flesh, S.P.C.K.

Tract on Prayer, S.P.C.K.
To the Martyrs.
Prescription on the Heretics.

5. St. Cyprian

Complete Works, in A Library of the Fathers of the Holy Catholic Church, Parker of Oxford.

Complete Works, in Ante-Nicene Fathers, The Christian Literature. See also the supplementary edition by A. Menzies. (10 vols.), Scribner.

St. Cyprian on the Lord's Prayer, S.P.C.K.

The Lapsed, the Unity of the Catholic Church, in The Ancient Christian Writers (Vol. 25), Newman Press; B. Herder.

6. Lactantius

The Minor Works: The Workmanship of God; The Wrath of God; The Deaths of the Persecutors; The Phoenix, in The Fathers of the Church (Vol. 54), Catholic University of America Press.

The Divine Institutes (Books 1–7), in The Fathers of the Church (Vol. 49), Catholic University of America Press.

7. Eusebius

Ecclesiastical History (10 books), in The Fathers of the Church (Vols. 19 and 29), Catholic University of America Press.

Ecclesiastical History, Loeb Classical Library, Harvard University Press; Penguin; S. Bagster; Stanford and Swords; G. Bell.

The Essential Eusebius, New American Library.

Life of the Blessed Emperor Constantine from 306 to 337 A.D., S. Bagster.

Preparation for the Gospel (2 vols.), Baker Book House, Clarendon Press, Oxford.

Treatise of Eusebius Against the Life of Apollonius of Tyana, W. Heinemann; Macmillan.

In Praise of Constantine, a historical study and new translation of Eusebius' *Tricennial Orations,* University of California Press.

8. St. Athanasius

The Incarnation of the Word of God, University of Pennsylvania Press; Macmillan.

On the Incarnation; Letters of St. Athanasius on the Interpretation of the Psalms, St. Vladimir's Orthodox Theological Seminary.

The Letters of St. Athanasius Concerning the Holy Spirit, Epworth Press.

The Life of Saint Anthony, in Ancient Christian Writers (Vol. 10), Newman Press; Burns and Oates.

Contra Gentes and De Incarnatione, Clarendon Press, Oxford.

Selected Treatises of St. Athanasius in Controversy with the Arians (2 vols.), Longman, Green.

Life of St. Anthony by St. Athanasius, from *Early Christian Biographies* in The Fathers of
the Church (Vol. 15), Catholic University of America Press; Benzinger.
St. Athanasius on the Psalms, A. R. Mowbray.

9. Prudentius

Poems (2 vols.), Catholic University of America Press.
Complete Works (2 vols.), Harvard University Press.
The Last Poets of Imperial Rome, Penguin Classics.
Hymns of Aurelius Prudentius, Macmillan and Bowes; J. Lane; J. M. Dent-Temple
Classics.

10. St. John Chrysostom

Homilies on the Gospel of St. John in A Library of the Fathers (Vols. 4, 7, 9, 11, 12,
14, 15, 17, 28), Oxford; and in Nicene and Post-Nicene Fathers (28 vols.),
Scribner.
On the Priesthood, Benzinger; S.P.C.K.; Newman Press; Macmillan; M. H. Gill.
Leaves from Chrysostom (selections), Burns and Oates.
St. John Chrysostom, Baptismal Instructions, in Ancient Christian Writers (Vol. 31),
Newman Press.
St. John Chrysostom, Commentary on St. John The Apostle and Evangelist, in The Fathers
of the Church (Vol. 33), Catholic University of America Press.
Address on Vainglory and the Right Way for Parents to Bring Up Their Children, in
Laistner, *Christianity and Pagan Culture in the Later Roman Empire,* Cornell Univer-
sity Press.

11. St. Augustine

The Complete Works: Post Nicene Fathers, T. & T. Clark.
The Works of Aurelius Augustinus (15 vols.), T. & T. Clark.
Basic Writings of St. Augustine (2 vols.), Random House.
Writings of Saint Augustine, In The Fathers of the Church: A New Translation,
Catholic University of America Press:
    On Music (Vol. 2).
    Against Lying (Vol. 16).
    The Trinity (Vol. 18).
    Against Julian (Vol. 35).
    The Retractions (Vol. 60).
Ancient Christian Writers, No. 9 et al., Newman Press.
The City of God, J. M. Dent; E. P. Dutton; Modern Library; Doubleday-Image.
The City of God Against the Pagans, Penguin; Harvard University Press (Loeb Clas-
sics).
Concerning the Teacher, in *The Basic Writings of Saint Augustine,* Random House.
Confessions, Sheed and Ward; New American Library; Penguin; Harvard Univer-
sity Press (Loeb Classics); Burns and Oates; Chatto and Windus; J. M. Dent;
E. P. Dutton.

Selected Letters, Harvard University (Loeb Classics).
On Free Choice of the Will, Bobbs-Merrill; Peter Reilly.
The Political Writings of St. Augustine, Regnery Gateway.
Of True Religion, Regnery.
On Christian Doctrine, Bobbs-Merrill; Liberal Arts.
A Library of Fathers of the Holy Catholic Church (15 vols.: 1, 16, 20, 22, 24, 25, 26, 29, 30, 32, 37), Parker of Oxford.
A Select Library of the Nicene and Post-Nicene Fathers (4 vols.), Christian Literature.
Against the Academics (also known as *Answer to Skeptics*), Newman Press; Marquette University Press; Cosmopolitan Science and Art Service.
The Augustine Synthesis, Sheed and Ward.
An Augustine Reader, Doubleday.
The Catholic and Manichean Ways of Life, Catholic University of America Press.
The Christian Life: Compiled Composite, F. Pustet.
De Beata Vita: Happiness, Peter Reilly; Catholic University of America Press; B. Herder.
De Dono Perseverantiae: On the Gift of Perseverance (translated), Catholic University of America Press.
Eighty-three Different Questions, Catholic University of America Press.
Enchiridion: On Faith, Hope, and Charity, S.P.C.K.; Westminster Press; Newman Bookshop; New American Library; Regnery Gateway.
The Essential Augustine, New American Library; Hackett.
Later Works, Westminster Press.
Leaves from St. Augustine, Washbourne.
The Lord's Sermon on the Mount, Newman Press; Fortress Press.
Nine Sermons on the Psalms, Longman.
On the Psalms, in Ancient Christian Writers (Vol. 29), Newman Press.
Readings from St. Augustine on the Psalms, Burns and Oates.
The Spirit and the Letter, S.P.C.K.
The Philosophy of Teaching: De Magistro, Villanova.
The Political Writings, Regnery.
The Rule of St. Augustine, Darton, Longman, and Todd; Doubleday-Image.
The Retractions, Catholic University of America Press.
Select Letters, W. Heinemann; G. P. Putnam; Loeb Classical Library.
Select Sermons, B. Herder; Holt, Rinehart & Winston; Newman Press.
The Soliloquies, Cosmopolitan; Sands.
The Trinity, Catholic University of America Press.
On the Nature of the Good, Against the Manichees, Dobs.

12. St. Jerome

The Homilies of Saint Jerome, in The Fathers of the Church (Vols. 48 and 57), Catholic University of America Press.
Saint Jerome: Dogmatic and Polemical Works, including *On the Perpetual Virginity of the Blessed Mary Against Helvidius; The Apology Against the Books of Rufinus;* and *The Dialogue Against the Pelagians* in The Fathers of the Church (Vol. 53), Catholic University of America Press.

Letters of St. Jerome, Newman Press; Harvard University Press (Loeb Classics);
  Browne and Nolan; Richview Press; G. P. Putnam.
The First Desert Hero: St. Jerome's "Vita Pauli," King.
The Middle English Bible: Prefatory Epistles of St. Jerome, Columbia University Press.
On Illustrious (Famous) Men, Catholic Traditions, Consortium Books.

13. St. Vincent of Lérins

Commonitorium, in The Fathers of the Church (Vol. 7), Catholic University of
  America Press.
Against Heresy, Parker.

14. Boethius

The Theological Tractates, Harvard University Press; W. Heinemann; G. P. Putnam.
The Consolation of Philosophy, Harvard University Press; Penguin; Library of Liberal Arts.

15. St. Benedict

Saint Benedict's Rule, Sands; Herder.
The Rule of Saint Benedict, Oxford; Newman Press; Doubleday-Image.
St. Benedict's Rule for Monasteries, The Liturgical Press. (Latin and English); Cister-
  cian Publications (No. 99).
The Holy Rule of Our Most Holy Father Saint Benedict, Belmont.
Households of God: the Rule of St. Benedict with Explanations for Monks and Laypeople Today,
  Cistercian Publications.

16. The Venerable Bede

A History of the English Church and People, Penguin; G. Bell.
Life of Cuthbert, in *The Lives of the Saints,* Penguin.
Historical Works: Latin, Oxford University Press.
Two Lives of Saint Cuthbert (Including Bede's Prose Life—Latin and English), Oxford Uni-
  versity Press; Greenwood Press.
Bede's Ecclesiastical History of the English People, Clarendon Press, Oxford.
*The Ecclesiastical History of the English People and Other Selections from the Writings of the
  Venerable Bede,* Washington Square Press.
The Commentary on the Seven Catholic Epistles of Bede the Venerable, Cistercian Publica-
  tions.
The Complete Works: Latin-English, Whittaker.
Baedae Opera Historica (with an English Translation), G. P. Putnam.

17. St. Anselm

Anselm of Canterbury: Works (3 vols.), E. Mellen.

St. Anselm's Basic Writings: Proslogium; Monologium; Gaunilon's On Behalf of the Fool; and Cur Deus Homo, Open Court.

Prayers and Meditations of St. Anselm, Penguin; Parker; Burns and Oates; Methuen; A. R. Mowbray; Morehouse-Gorham.

St. Anselm's Proslogium, Clarendon Press, Oxford.

Anselm of Canterbury: Trinity, Incarnation, and Redemption; Theological Treatises, Harper & Row; E. Mellen; Harvard Divinity School (3 vols.).

Why God Became Man and the Virgin Conception, Magi Books.

Truth, Freedom and Evil: Three Philosophical Dialogues, E. Mellen.

The De Grammatico of St. Anselm, The Theory of Paronomy, University of Notre Dame Press.

18. St. Bernard of Clairvaux

The Works of St. Bernard of Clairvaux (Cistercian Publications):

Treatises I: Apologia to Abbot William; On Precept and Dispensation.

Treatises II: The Steps of Humility; On Loving God.

Treatises III: On Grace and Free Will; In Praise of the New Knighthood.

Sermons on the Song of Songs (4 vols.).

Five Books on Consideration: Advice to a Pope.

The Life and Death of Saint Malachy the Irishman.

Magnificat: Homilies in Praise of the Blessed Virgin Mary.

Sermons on Conversion: A Sermon to Clerics, Lenten Sermons on Psalm 91.

Prologue to the Cistercian Antiphonary: On Monastic Chant.

Letters (2 vols.).

Sermons on the Liturgical Year (4 vols.).

Occasional Sermons (2 vols.).

Sentences.

St. Bernard's Sermons on the Nativity.

On the Life and Duties of a Bishop.

Against the Errors of Abelard.

Life and Works of St. Bernard (4 vols.), John Hodges.

De Diligendo Deo (On Loving God), E. P. Dutton.

Sermons on the Canticle of Canticles (2 vols.), Browne and Nolan.

The Letters of St. Bernard of Clairvaux, Burns and Oates; Regnery.

St. Bernard on the Christian Year: Selections from His Sermons.

19. St. Francis of Assisi

Francis and Clare: The Complete Works, Paulist Press.

St. Francis of Assisi Writings: English Omnibus of the Sources for the Life of St. Francis, Franciscan Herald Press; Burns and Oates.

The Writings of St. Francis of Assisi, Franciscan Herald Press.

Memorable Words of Saint Francis, Franciscan Herald Press.
The Canticle of Creatures, Franciscan Herald Press.
St. Francis of Assisi: His Life and Writings as Recorded by His Contemporaries, A. R. Mowbray.
The Words of St. Francis: An Anthology, Franciscan Herald Press.
Fioretti: The Little Flowers of St. Francis, Doubleday-Image; Peter Paupers; J. M. Dent; E. P. Dutton; St. Anthony Guild Press.

20. St. Thomas Aquinas

Basic Writings (2 vols.), Random House.
Summa Contra Gentiles (4 books), University of Notre Dame Press.
On the Truth of the Catholic Faith (5 vols.), Doubleday.
Summa Theologiae (22 vols.), Burns, Oates, and Washbourne; Christian Classics; bilingual edition (60 vols.), Benzinger; bilingual edition, McGraw-Hill.
De Veritate: On Truth (3 vols.), Regnery.
De Potentia Dei: On the Power of God (3 vols.), Burns, Oates & Washbourne.
On the Power of God (3 vols. in 1), Newman Press.
Disputed Questions on Evil: De Malo, University of Notre Dame Press.
De Spiritualibus Creaturis; On Spiritual Creatures, Marquette University Press.
De Anima: On the Soul, St. Louis University Press.
On the Virtues in General, Prentice Hall; Providence College Press.
On Charity, Marquette University Press.
Catena Aurea: Commentary on the Four Gospels (4 vols.), Oxford University Press.
Commentary on the Gospel of St. John (Part I), Magi Books.
Commentary on St. Paul's Epistle to the Galatians, Magi Books.
Commentary on St. Paul's Epistle to the Ephesians, Magi Books.
Commentary on St. Paul's First Letter to the Thessalonians and the Letter to the Philippians, Magi Books.
Aristotle on Interpretation: Commentary by St. Thomas and Cajetan, Marquette University Press.
Commentary on the Posterior Analytics of Aristotle, Magi Books.
Commentary on Aristotle's Physics, Yale University Press.
Exposition of Aristotle's Treatise On the Heavens, College of St. Mary of the Springs.
Aristotle's De Anima with the Commentary of St. Thomas Aquinas, Yale University Press.
Commentary on the Metaphysics of Aristotle (2 vols.), Regnery.
Commentary on the Nichomachean Ethics (2 vols.), Regnery.
The Trinity and the Unicity of the Intellect, B. Herder.
On Searching into God, Blackfriars.
Divisions and Methods of the Sciences, Toronto Pontifical Institute of Medieval Studies.
An Apology for the Religious Orders, Newman Press; Sands.
On the Unity of the Intellect Against the Averroists, Marquette University Press.
On Being and Essence, Toronto Pontifical Institute of Medieval Studies; Notre Dame University Press.
On the Principles of Nature (to Brother Sylvester), St. Louis University Press; North Central.
Compendium of Theology, St. Louis University.

Treatise on Separate Substances, West Hartford, Conn.

On Kingship, Toronto Pontifical Institute of Medieval Studies.

On the Eternity of the World (by St. Thomas Aquinas, Siger of Brabant, St. Bonaventure), Marquette University Press.

"St. Thomas on the Movement of the Heart: De Motu Cordis," *Journal of the History of Medicine* 15 (1960).

"Saint Thomas: On Combining of the Elements: De mixtione elemetorum," *Isis* 51 (1960).

"The Commentary of St. Thomas on the *De Caelo* of Aristotle," *Sapientia* 29 (1974).

"On the Buying and Selling on Credit: De Emptione et Venditione ad Tempus," *Irish Ecclesiastical Record* 31 (1928).

"On the Government of the Jews: De Regime Judaeorum," in *Selected Political Writings*, Blackwell.

The Letters of St. Thomas Aquinas: De Occultis Naturae, Catholic University of America Press.

The Three Greatest Prayers: Apostle's Creed, Our Father, Hail Mary, Burns, Oates & Washbourne.

The Catechetical Instructions of St. Thomas Aquinas: On the Apostles' Creed; Explanation of the Ten Commandments; Explanation of the Sacraments; Explanation of the Lord's Prayer; The Hail Mary, Joseph F. Wagner; B. Herder.

The Commandments of God, Burns and Oates.

Selected Writings, Everyman; J. M. Dent; E. P. Dutton; Bobbs-Merrill.

Meditations, Long's College Book Co.

21. St. Bonaventure

The Works of Bonaventure (5 vols.), St. Anthony Guild Press:

Vol. I, *Mystical Opuscula: The Journey of the Mind to God; The Triple Way, or Love Enkindled; The Tree of Life; The Mystical Vine; On the Perfection of Life, Addressed to Sisters; Non-Scriptural References.*

Vol. II, *The Breviloquium.*

Vol. III, *Opuscula Second Series: Praise of the Holy Cross; On Retracing the Arts to Theology; Soliloquy on the Four Spiritual Exercises; The Six Wings of the Seraph; The Five Feasts of the Child Jesus; On How to Prepare for the Celebration of Mass; On the Government of Soul; Letter Containing Twenty-five Points to Remember; Non-Scriptural References.*

Vol. IV, *Defense of the Mendicants.*

Vol. V, *Collations on the Six Days.*

Bonaventure: The Soul's Journey to God; The Tree of Life, The Life of St. Francis, Paulist Press.

Breviloquium, B. Herder.

St. Bonaventure's "De Reductione Artium ad Theologiam," St. Bonaventure College/ University.

St. Bonaventure's "Disputed Questions on the Mystery of the Trinity," Franciscan Institute of St. Bonaventure's University.

Holiness of Life, B. Herder.

The Mind's Road to God, Liberal Arts Press.

Itinerarium Mentis in Deum, Franciscan Institute, St. Bonaventure's University.
The Mirror of the Blessed Virgin Mary; and The Psalter of Our Lady, B. Herder.
The Mystical Vine: A Treatise on the Passion of Our Lord, A. R. Mowbray.

22. Bl. Jacobus de Voragine

The Golden Legend of Jacobus de Voragine, Longman, Green (2 vols.); Arno Press (one-vol. edition); Kelmscott Press (3 vols.); J. M. Dent-Temple Classics (7 vols.).

23. Dante

Complete Works (6 vols.): *Vita Nuova* and *Canzoniere* (Italian and English); *Convivio* (English only); *Latin Works* (English only: includes *De Vulgari Eloquentia, De Monarchia, Epistles, and Eclogues, and Quaestio de Aqua et Terra); Inferno* (Italian and English); *Purgatorio* (Italian and English); *Paradiso* (Italian and English), J. M. Dent-Temple Classics.
The Divine Comedy, Princeton University Press; Oxford University Press; Harvard University Press; J. M. Dent-Temple Classics; Penguin; Rinehart; Norton; Modern Library.
  Inferno, Mentor; Duke University Press; Harper; Rutgers University Press; Indiana University Press;
  Purgatorio, Mentor; New American Library.
  Paradiso, New American Library.
Dante's Lyric Poetry, Clarendon Press, Oxford.
Dante's "Vita nuova," Indiana University Press; Thomas Y. Crowell; Heath.
Literary Criticism of Dante Alighieri, University of Nebraska Press.
On World Government, Library of the Liberal Arts.
Monarchy and Three Political Letters, Hyperion.
Epistolae: The Letters of Dante, Clarendon Press, Oxford; Houghton, Mifflin.
The Portable Dante, Penguin.

24. St. Catherine of Siena

The Dialogue of the Seraphic Virgin, Catherine of Siena, Christian Classics; Paulist Press; Burns and Oates; Tan Books.
Saint Catherine of Siena as Seen in Her Letters, J. M. Dent.
The Prayers of Catherine of Siena, Paulist Press.
The Little Flowers of St. Catherine of Siena, E. M. Lohman.
Prologues, Kegan Paul, Trench, Tribner.

25. Geoffrey Chaucer

Complete Works, Houghton Mifflin; Holt, Rinehart & Winston; Everyman's Library.
Troilus and Criseyde, Princeton University Press.
The Canterbury Tales, E. P. Dutton; Penguin (modern translation); Rinehart.
Troilus and Criseyde (modern translation), Penguin; Vintage-Random House.

26. Thomas à Kempis

The Works, Kegan Paul.
The Imitation of Christ, Doubleday-Image (based on Richard Whitford transla-
tion); Penguin; Sheed and Ward; Anthony Clarke; Bruce; Newman Press.
The Imitation of Mary, Newman Press.
Alphabet of a Scholar in the School of Christ, J. Murphy.
The Little Garden of Roses and Valley of Lillies, J. Murphy.
Golden Words, Benzinger.
The Little Follower of Jesus, P. J. Kenedy.
Lesser Imitation, Benzinger.
Meditations on the Incarnation of Christ, B. Herder; Kegan Paul.
Meditations on the Life of Christ, E. P. Dutton; Parker.
Meditations on the Passion and Resurrection of Our Lord, Benzinger.
The Three Tabernacles: A Golden Treatise, M. H. Gill.
Prayers and Meditations on the Life of Christ, B. Herder; Kegan Paul.
Sermons to the Novices Regular, B. Herder; Kegan Paul.
True Wisdom, Benzinger; R. and T. Washbourne.
Acceptable Time, Paulist Press.
Babes of Bethlehem, Paulist Press.
Daily Readings for Lent, Paulist Press.
Thought on Holy Week, Paulist Press.
St. Lydwine of Schiedam, Benzinger; Burns and Oates.
Founders of the New Devotion: Lives of G. Groote, F. Radewyns, and Their Followers, B.
Herder; Kegan Paul.
Chronicle of the Canons Regular of Mt. St. Agnes, B. Herder; Kegan Paul.
In Praise of the Blessed Virgin Mary, Bruce.
Meditations of Our Lady, St. Dominic's Press of Sitchling, Sussex.

27. St. Catherine of Genoa

Saint Catherine of Genoa: Treatise on Purgatory; The Dialogue, Sheed and Ward.
*Life and Doctrine of Saint Catherine of Genoa: A Dialogue Between the Soul and Body; Self-
Love; The Mind and Humanity of Our Lord; A Treatise on Purgatory*, The Catholic
Publication Society.
The Life and Sayings of Saint Catherine of Genoa, Alba House.
Treatise on Purgatory, Burns and Oates; Benzinger.
Life and Doctrine of Saint Catherine of Genoa, Christian Press Association.
Life of Madam Catharina Adorna, Harper.

28. St. Thomas More

English Works (Selections), Clarendon Press, Oxford.
The Tower Works: Devotional Writings, Yale University Press.
The Complete Works, Yale University Press.
The History of King Richard III, Yale University Press.

Translations of Lucian, Yale University Press.

Responsio ad Lutherum (2 vols.), Yale University Press; Catholic University of America Press.

The Confutation of Tyndale's Answer (3 vols.), Yale University Press.

A Dialogue of Comfort Against Tribulation, Yale University Press; Indiana University Press; Sheed and Ward.

The Supplication of Souls, Newman Press; De Capo Press.

Latin Epigrams (translated), University of Chicago Press.

The Last Letters of Blessed Thomas More, Manresa Press.

The Dialogue Concerning Tyndale, Eyre and Spottiswoode.

A Dialogue Concerning Heresies (2 vols.), Yale University Press.

The Apologye of Syr T. More, Knight, Da Capo Press.

The Answer to a Poisoned Book, Yale University Press.

Treatise on the Passion; Treatise on the Blessed Body, Yale University Press.

Treatise on the Passion, Yale University Press.

Crumbs of Comfort, Burns and Oates.

De Tristitia Christi (2 vols.), Yale University Press.

Thomas More's Prayerbook, Yale University Press.

St. Thomas More: Selected Letters, Yale University Press.

Utopia, Oxford University Press; Yale University Press; W. Scot; J. M. Dent.

The History of King Richard III and Selections from the English and Latin Poems, Yale University Press.

The Correspondence of Sir Thomas More, Princeton University Press.

The Wit and Wisdom of Blessed Thomas More, Burns and Oates.

The Essential Thomas More, New American Library (Mentor-Omega).

English Prayers and Treatise on the Holy Eucharist.

St. Thomas More, Burns and Oates.

29. St. Ignatius Loyola

The Constitutions of the Society of Jesus, The Institute of Jesuit Sources.

Letters of Saint Ignatius of Loyola, B. Herder.

Spiritual Exercises of St. Ignatius, B. Herder; M. H. Gill; Doubleday-Image; Newman Press; P. J. Kenedy; J. Murphy; University Press of America; Anthony Clarke; Wagner; Burns and Oates.

Translation and Commentary on Spiritual Exercises, Burns and Oates.

Letters and Instructions of St. Ignatius Loyola, The Catholic Library.

Letters to Women, Herder and Herder.

The Autobiography of St. Ignatius, Benzinger; Harper Torchbooks.

Counsels for Jesuits: Selected Letters and Instructions, Loyola University Press of Chicago.

Manresa: The Spiritual Exercises of St. Ignatius for General Use, F. Pustet.

Ignatius de Loyola, Power of Imaging: A Philosophical Hermeneutic of Imagining Through the Collected Works of St. Ignatius, with a Translation of These Works, State University of New York Press of Albany.

Letters and Instructions, Vol. 1 (1524–47), B. Herder.

Letters of St. Ignatius of Loyola, Selected, Loyola University Press of Chicago.

St. Ignatius' Own Story, as Told to Luis Gonsealez de Camara; with a Sampling of His Letters, Regnery.
The Spiritual Journal of St. Ignatius Loyola, 1544–1545, Woodstock College Press.
Thoughts of St. Ignatius Loyola for Every Day of the Year, Benzinger.

30. St. Teresa of Ávila

The Complete Works of Saint Teresa of Jesus (3 vols.), Sheed and Ward; Institute of Carmelite Studies.
The Life of St. Teresa of Jesus, T. Baker; Newman Press; P. J. Kenedy; Burns and Oates.
The Way of Perfection, T. Baker; Newman Bookshop.
The Book of the Foundations, T. Baker; T. Jones.
The Interior Castle; or the Mansions and Exclamations of the Soul to God, Sands; Doubleday-Image; Paulist Press; T. Baker.
The Letters of St. Teresa, T. Baker; Burns and Oates; Benzinger.
St. Teresa's Pater Noster: Treatise on Prayer, Burns and Oates.

31. St. John of the Cross

The Complete Works of St. John of the Cross (3 vols.), Burns and Oates; T. Baker.
The Mystical Doctrine of St. John of The Cross (an abridgement), Sheed and Ward; Newman Press; Institute of Carmelite Studies; Doubleday.
Ascent of Mount Carmel, Doubleday-Image; T. Baker.
Dark Night of the Soul: A Classic in the Literature of Mysticism, Doubleday-Image; T. Baker.
Poems of St. John of the Cross, Pantheon; S.P.C.K.; New Directions; University of Chicago Press.
Instructions and Precautions: Some Spiritual Letters to the Nuns of His Order, Wheeling, West Virginia, Monastery of St. Teresa and St. John of the Cross.
The Living Flame of Love, with Letters, Poems, and Minor Writings, T. Baker.
St. John of the Cross: His Life and Poetry (translated), Cambridge University Press.
A Spiritual Canticle of the Soul and the Bridegroom Christ, T. Baker.

32. Miguel de Cervantes Saavedra

The Selected Works, Chatto and Windus.
Don Quixote, Signet Classics; New American Library; Modern Library.
The Adventures of Don Quixote, Penguin Classics.
Don Quixote, W. W. Norton (critical edition); Viking Press.
The Exemplary Novels, Cassell; Doubleday.
Six Exemplary Novels, Barron's Educational Series.
The "Interludes" of Cervantes, Princeton University Press.
The Portable Cervantes, Viking Press.
Cervantes: His Life, His Times, His Work, American Heritage Press.

33. St. Robert Bellarmine

De Laicis: or the Treatise on Civil Government, Fordham University Press.
Commentary on the Book of Psalms, James Duffy.
The Seven Words Spoken by Christ on the Cross, Burns and Oates; Spiritual Book Associates; Carroll Press.
The Mind's Ascent to God, or The Ascent of the Mind to God, Morehouse; Benzinger; Burns and Oates.
Extracts in Politics and Government From The Supreme Pontiff From the Third Controversy, Country Dollar Press.
An Ample Declaration of the Christian Doctrine, Scholar Press.
The Ascent of the Mind to God by a Ladder of Things Created, Burns and Oates; Scholar Press.
The Art of Dying Well, Scholar Press; T. Richardson.
The Autobiography of St. Robert Bellarmine, Woodstock College Press.
A Catechism of Christian Doctrine, P. Donahue.
The Felicity of the Saints, Fielding Lucas.
The Mourning of the Dove, or, Of the Great Benefit and Good of Teares.
How True Christian Libertie Consisteth in the True Service of God and Not to Doe What Each One Listeth as Our CARNALL GOSPELLERS WOLD HAVE IT TO BE; and Of the Seven Words Spoken by Christ Upon the Cross, English Recusant Literature 207, Scholar Press.
Power of the Pope in Temporal Affairs, Against William Barclay, Country Dollar Press.
Reply to the Principal Points of the Arguement, Which is Falsely Entitled Catholic, for the Succession of Henry of Navarre to the Kingdom of France, The Moore Series of English Translations of Source Books, Country Dollar Press.
A Shorte Catechism of Cardinal Bellarmine Illustrated with the Images, English Recusant Literature 126, Scholar Press.

34. St. Francis de Sales

Library of St. Francis de Sales: Works of This Doctor Translated into English, Benzinger.
The Devout Life of Saint Francis de Sales, F. Pustet; Newman Press; Burns and Oates.
Treatise on the Love of God, Sands; Newman Press; Tan Books (3 vols.); Greenwood Press.
The Spiritual Directory of Saint Francis de Sales for People Living in the World, Newman Press.
The Spiritual Guide for Priests: The Spiritual Directory of St. Francis de Sales Adapted to the Use of Priests, Newman Press.
St. Francis de Sales: Selected Letters, Sands; Faber & Faber & Faber.
The Sermons of St. Francis de Sales on Prayer, Tan Books.
St. Francis de Sales in His Letters, Sands.
Spiritual Conferences, Newman Press; D. & J. Sadlier.
On the Preacher and Preaching, Regnery.
A Diary of Meditations, or a Year with St. Francis of Sales, Regnery.
Spiritual Maxims of St. Francis de Sales, Harper; Longman, Green.
A Year with St. Francis de Sales: Short Passages from his Writings, Regnery.

Letter to Persons in the World, Benzinger.
Letters to Persons in Religion, Newman Press.
Introduction to the Devout Life, Newman Press; F. Pustet; Burns and Oates.
The Catholic Controversy, Burns and Oates.
Golden Counsels of St. Francis de Sales, St. Louis Visitation Convent.
Consoling Thoughts of St. Francis de Sales: Gathered and Arranged, F. Pustet.
The Mystical Explanation of the Canticle of Canticles by St. Francis de Sales, Burns and Oates.
The Way to God: Collected Sayings About the Religious Life, Ars Sacra of Munich.

35. Richard Crashaw

Complete Works (2 vols.), A.M.S. Press.
Complete Poetry, Doubleday; Doubleday-Anchor.
Poems English, Latin, and Greek (2 vols. and Supplement, 2nd ed.), Clarendon Press, Oxford.
The Religious Poems of Richard Crashaw, Including "An Apologie," B. Herder; Manresa Press.

36. St. Margaret Mary Alacoque

The Autobiography of St. Margaret Mary, Newman Press; Darton, Longman, and Todd.
Life of Saint Margaret Mary Alacoque, Visitation Library.
The Letters of Saint Margaret Mary Alacoque, Regnery.

37. St. Louis Grignion de Montfort

The Love of Eternal Wisdom, Montfort Publications.
Preparation for a Happy Death, Montfort Publications.
Friends of the Cross, Montfort Publications.
Prayer for Missionaries, Montfort Publications.
The Secret of the Rosary, Montfort Publications; Tan Books.
The Secret of Mary, Montfort Publications.
True Devotion to Mary, Montfort Publications; St. Paul Books and Media.

38. Alban Butler

Butler's Lives of the Saints (2 vols.), Eugene Community; Burns and Oates; edited, revised, supplemented, P. J. Kenedy (4 vols.).
Meditations and Discourses on the Sublime Truths and Important Duties of Christianity, J. P. Coghlan. Posthumous.
The Moveable Feasts, Fasts, and Other Annual Observances of the Catholic Church, John Doyle; E. Dunigan. Posthumous.

39. St. Alphonsus de Liguori

Preparation for Death, Redemptorist Fathers.
Way of Salvation and of Perfection, Redemptorist Fathers.
Great Means of Salvation and of Perfection, Redemptorist Fathers.
The Incarnation, Birth, and Infancy of Jesus Christ, Redemptorist Fathers.
The Passion and Death of Jesus Christ, Redemptorist Fathers.
The Holy Eucharist, Redemptorist Fathers.
The Glories of Mary, Redemptorist Fathers; Tan Books.
Victories of the Martyrs, Redemptorist Fathers.
The True Spouse of Jesus Christ, Redemptorist Fathers.
Dignities and Duties of the Priest, Redemptorist Fathers.
The Holy Mass, Redemptorist Fathers.
The Divine Office, Redemptorist Fathers.
Preaching, Redemptorist Fathers.
Sermons for Sundays, Redemptorist Fathers.
Miscellany, Redemptorist Fathers.
Letters (4 vols.), Redemptorist Fathers.
Uniformity with God's Will, Tan Books.
The Twelve Steps to Holiness and Salvation (or, The School of Christian Prefection), Tan Books.

40. Anne Catherine Emmerich

The Dolorous Passion of Our Lord Jesus Christ, from the Meditations of Anne Catherine Emmerich, Burns and Oates; Gordon Press; Tan Books.
The Lowly Life and Bitter Passion of Our Lord Jesus Christ and His Blessed Mother (4 vols.), Desclee; Sentinel Press; Tan Books.
The Life of the Blessed Virgin, Tan Books.

41. Frederick William Faber

The Cherwell Water-Lily and Other Poems, J. G. F. & J. Rivington; Parker.
The Styrian Lake and other Poems, J. G. F. & J. Rivington.
Sights and Thoughts in Foreign Churches and Among Foreign Peoples, J. G. F. & J. Rivington.
Examination of Conscience: A Tract, translation of the Seven Books of St. Optatus, Bishop of Milevis, on the Schism of the Donatists. In The Library of the Fathers, Parker of Oxford.
Sir Lancelot: A Legend of the Middle Ages, in The Series of Lives of the English Saints, T. Richardson.
Lives of Saints Paulinus, Edwin, Ethulburga, Oswald, Oswin, Abba, Adammair, Bega, Wilfred, in The Series of Lives of the English Saints, L. Toovey.
The Rosary and Other Poems, L. Toovey.
The Spirit and Genius of St. Philip Neri, Burns and Lambert Scruples; J. Murphy.
The Life of St. Rose of Lima, P. J. Kenedy.

All for Jesus, Newman Press.
Growth in Holiness, or the Progress of the Spiritual Life, J. Murphy.
The Blessed Sacrament, or the Works and Ways of God, P. Reilly; J. Murphy; G.
  Quigley; Tan Books.
An Explanation of the Doctrine and Definition of the Immaculate Conception.
Poems, J. Murphy; T. Richardson.
The Creator and the Creature, or the Wonders of Divine Love, Newman Press; Tan Books.
Ethel's Book, or Tales of the Angels, J. Murphy.
The Foot of the Cross, or The Sorrows of Mary, Burns and Oates; Peter Reilly; Tan
  Books.
Spiritual Conferences, Peter Reilly; J. Murphy.
The Precious Blood, or the Price of Our Salvation, J. Murphy.
Bethlehem, J. Murphy.
Devotion to the Pope, J. Murphy.
Devotion to the Church, J. Murphy.
Notes on Doctrinal and Spiritual Subjects, Burns and Oates.
Notes on Community Life in the Oratory, Bowden.
Hymns, E. P. Dutton; R. West.
Faber, Poet and Priest: Selected Letters, D. Brown.
A Father Faber Heritage, Newman Press.
Consoling Thoughts from Father Faber (Selected and Arranged), R. and T. Washbourne;
  Benzinger.
An Essay on Beatification, Canonization, and the Process of the Congregation of Rites, T.
  Richardson.
Characteristics from the Writings of Father Faber (Arranged), R. and T. Washbourne.

42. St. Peter Julian Eymard

The Divine Eucharist: Extracts from the Writings and Sermons (4 vols.), Fathers of the
  Blessed Sacrament.
The Real Presence, Eymard League; Sentinel Press.
Holy Communion, Eymard League; Sentinel Press.
Eucharistic Retreats, Eymard League; Sentinel Press.
The Eucharist and Christian Perfection I, Eymard League; Sentinel Press.
The Eucharist and Christian Perfection II, Eymard League; Sentinel Press.
A Eucharistic Handbook, Eymard League; Sentinel Press.
Our Lady of the Blessed Sacrament, Eucharistic League; Sentinel Press.
Month of St. Joseph, Eymard League; Sentinel Press.
In the Light of the Monstrance, Eymard League; Sentinel Press.

43. Alessandro Manzoni

The Betrothed, Macmillan; E. P. Dutton; Penguin.
The Betrothed Lovers with *The Column of Infamy: 19th Century Edition.*
On the Historical Novel, University of Nebraska Press.
Translations of Poems Ancient and Modern.
Modern Italian Poets, Essays and Versions.
The Sacred Hymns and Napoleonic Ode of Manzoni.

A Vindication of Catholic Morality or Refutation of the Charges Brought Against It by Sismondi in His History.
The Column of Infamy.
A Dialogue of the Artist's Idea.

44. Prosper Guéranger

The Liturgical Year (15 vols.): *Advent to the Last Sunday of Pentecost,* Newman Press; Duffy; Burns and Oates.
Life of Saint Cecilia, Virgin and Martyr, P. F. Cunningham; P. J. Kenedy.
Advent: Its Meaning and Purpose, Paulist Press.
Digest of the Liturgical Seasons, St. Meinrad Abbey Grail Press.
Explanation of the Prayers and the Ceremonies of the Mass, Duffy; Carroll Press.
Lent: Its Meaning and Purpose, Paulist Press.
The Medal or Cross of St. Benedict, Burns and Oates.
Our Faith by Our Prayers, Stanbrook.
Religious and Monastic Life Explained, B. Herder; Sands.

45. Orestes Brownson

The American Republic: Its Constitution, Tendencies, and Destiny, Kelly; College and University Press.
Essays and Reviews Chiefly on Theology, Politics, and Socialism, Ayer; Arno Press.
The Laboring Classes, School Facsimiles.
Works of Orestes Brownson (20 vols.), A.M.S. Press; T. Nourse of Detroit.
The Brownson Reader, P. J. Kenedy; Ayer.
Saint Worship, the Worship of Mary, St. Anthony Guild Press.
Brownson's Views, Benzinger.
The Brownson-Hecker Correspondence, University of Notre Dame Press.
Conversations on Liberalism and the Church, Brady.
The Convert, or Leaves from My Experience, E. Dunigan.
Essays on Modern Popular Literature, H. F. Brownson of Detroit.
New Views on Christianity, Society, and the Church, J. Monroe of Boston.
Selected Essays, Regnery.
The Spirit-Rapper: An Autobiography, Little, Brown.

46. Matthias Joseph Scheeben

The Glories of Divine Grace, Benzinger; R. Washbourne.
Mariology (2 vols.), B. Herder.
The Mysteries of Christianity, B. Herder.
Nature and Grace, B. Herder.

47. William Bernard Ullathorne

The Catholic Mission in Australia, Rockliff and Duckworth; Keating and Brown.
Horrors of Transportation, R. Coyne of Dublin.

Reply to Judge Burton.

Sermons.

Remarks on the Proposed Education Bill, T. Jones of London.

Plea for Rights and Liberties of Religious Women, T. Richardson.

La Salette, T. Richardson; City Printing; also published as *The Holy Mountain of La Salette,* La Salette Press of New York.

The Immaculate Conception, Benzinger; J. Murphy; G. Quigley.

Pilgrimage to Subiaco.

Notes on Education Question, T. Richardson.

Speech on the Pontifical States.

Letter on the Rambler.

Methods of the Rambler.

Anglican Theory of Union.

Management of Criminals.

The Confessional.

Lectures on Conventual Life, Paulist Press; Burns and Oates.

Autobiography (with Selections from his Letters), Burns and Oates; Catholic Publications Society.

Address on Catholic Education.

The Council and Papal Infallibility.

History of the Restoration of the Hierarchy, Burns and Oates.

Dollingerites (Against Gladstone).

Mr. Gladstone's Expostulation Unravelled, Catholic Publications Society.

Doctrinal Letters, Burns and Oates; Catholic Truth Society.

Ecclesiastical Discourses, Burns and Oates.

Discourse on Church Music.

The Endowments of Man (3rd ed.), Burns and Oates; Benzinger.

The Groundwork of the Christian Virtues, Burns and Oates.

Christian Patience, Burns and Oates.

The Little Book of Humility and Patience, Newman Press.

From Cabin Boy to Archbishop: Autobiography, Burns and Oates.

Memoir of Bishop Willson, First Bishop of Hobart, Tasmania, Burns and Oates.

Characteristics from the Writings of Archbishop Ullathorne, Burns and Oates; Catholic Publication Society.

Letters of Archbishop Ullathorne, Burns and Oates; Benzinger.

48. John Henry Newman

The Collected Edition of the Works of Cardinal Newman, Longman, Green.

John Henry Newman, Autobiographical Writings, Sheed and Ward.

Meditations and Devotions, Longman, Green.

Letters and Correspondence of J. H. Newman, Longman, Green.

Letters and Diaries of John Henry Newman, Nelson; Oxford University Press.

Letters, Longman, Green; Newman Press; Oxford University Press.

Diaries, Oxford University Press; Nelson.

Meditations and Devotions, Longman, Green.

Newman Against the Liberals: Sermons, Arlington House.

Loss and Gain, Garland; Longman, Green.

Callista: A Sketch of the Third Century, Longman, Green; Garland Publications.
St. Bartholomew's Eve: A Tale of the Sixteenth Century.
Memorials of the Past, W. King.
Lyra Apostolica.
Verses on Religious Subjects.
The Dream of Gerontius, Catholic Truth Society; Schwartz, Kerwin, and Fauss; Longman, Green; Burns and Oates.
Verses on Various Occasions, Burns and Oates.
Echoes from the Oratory: Selections, A. D. F. Randolph.
The Life of Apollonius Tyanaeus, with a Comparison Between the Miracles of Scriptures and Those Elsewhere Related, Glasgow, Bell & Bain.
Suggestions to Certain Resident Clergymen of the University in Behalf of the Church Missionary Society, H. Cooke.
The Arians of the Fourth Century: Their Doctrine, Temper, and Conduct, B. M. Pickering; Longman, Green.
Parochial Sermons (6 vols.), J. G. & F. Rivington; Appleton.
The Restoration of Suffragan Bishops Recommended, J. G. & F. Rivington.
Elucidations of Dr. Hampden's Theological Statements, J. H. Parker; J. G. & F. Rivington.
Lectures on the Prophetical Office of the Church, J. H. Parker; J. G. & F. Rivington.
Letters on Justification.
The Church of the Fathers, Burns, Oates & Washbourne; J. Lane.
The Tamworth Reading Room: Letters on an Address by Sir Robert Peel, Georgetown University Press.
Sermons, Bearing on Subjects of the Day, Christian Classics; Longman, Green.
Sermons, Chiefly on the Theory of Religious Belief, J. G. & F. Rivington.
Plain Sermons by Contributors to Tracts for the Times, Vol. 5 of 6 vols. (published in 2 vols.).
An Essay on the Development of Christian Doctrine, Penguin; Image; Longman, Green.
Discourses Addressed to Mixed Congregations, Longman, Green.
Lectures on Certain Difficulties Felt by Anglicans in Submitting to the Catholic Church (2 vols.), Longman, Green.
Lectures on the Present Position of Catholics in England, Loyola University Press; Longman, Green.
Discourses on the Scope and Nature of University Education, Image Books; Oxford University Press.
Lectures on the History of the Turks in Its Relation to Christianity, J. Duffy; C. Dolman.
The Office and Work of Universities, Longman, Brown & Green.
Sermons Preached on Various Occasions, Christian Classics.
Lectures and Essays on University Subjects, Longman, Green.
Mr. Kingsley and Mr. Newman: A Correspondence on the Question Whether Dr. Newman Teaches That Truth Is No Virtue?, Longman, Green.
Apologia Pro Vita Sua, Being a Reply to a Pamphlet Entitled What, Then, Does Dr. Newman Mean?, W. W. Norton; Clarendon Press, Oxford; Houghton Mifflin-Riverside; Longman, Green; Sheed and Ward.
An Essay in Aid of a Grammar of Assent, Oxford University Press; University of Notre Dame Press.
Miscellanies from the Oxford Sermons and Other Writings, Shahan; W. H. Allen, Edinburgh.

Two Essays on Scripture Miracles and on Ecclesiastical, Essays Critical and Historical (2 vols.), Longman, Green.

Historical Sketches (3 vols.), Longman, Green.

Discussions and Arguments on Various Subjects, B. M. Pickering.

The Idea of a University Defined and Illustrated, Oxford University Press; Christian Classics; Holt, Rinehart & Winston.

Six Selections.

Tracts Theological and Ecclesiastical, B. M. Pickering; Longman, Green.

Characteristics from the Writings, Folcraft Library Editions.

The Via Media of the Anglican Church, Illustrated in Lectures, Letters, and Tracts Written Between 1830 and 1841.

Sayings, Catholic Publication Society.

Stray Essays and Controversial Points.

Meditations and Devotions, Longman, Green.

My Campaign in Ireland, A. King.

Sermon Notes 1849–1878, Longman, Green.

Letters and Poems from Malta 1832–1833.

Essays and Sketches, Greenwood Press.

Sermons and Discourses, Longman, Green.

Autobiographical Writings, Sheed and Ward.

Faith and Prejudice and Other Unpublished Sermons.

Catholic Sermons.

On Consulting the Faith on Matters of Doctrine, Sheed and Ward.

A Newman Companion to the Gospels: Sermons, Palm Publishers.

Newman, the Oratorian: Unpublished Oratory Papers.

The Philosophical Notebook. Nawvel Arts.

The Theological Papers on Faith and Certainty, Clarendon Press, Oxford.

Editor and contributor, *Tracts for the Times* (6 vols.), J. G. & F. Rivington.

Editor, *The Cistercian Saints of England*, Vols. 1 and 2, (part of *Lives of the English Saints)*, J. Toovey.

Editor, with John Keble, *Remains of Rev. R. H. Froude.*

Editor, *Thoughts on the Work of the Six Days of Creation.*

Editor and translator, *Auluaria.*

Editor and translator, *Phormio, Pincerna, and Andria.*

Editor, *Notes on a Visit to the Russian Church in the Years 1840, 1841.*

Translator, *The Devotions of Bishop Andrewes*, G. H. Richman.

Translator, *The Ecclesiastical History of M. Abbe Fleury, Tract 90, On Certain Passages in the 39 Articles, by J. H. Newman, 1841*, J. G. & F. Rivington.

49. Coventry Patmore

Poems of Coventry Patmore, G. Bell; Oxford University Press.

Selected Poems of Coventry Patmore, Chatto and Windus.

The Rod, the Root, and the Flower: Prose, G. Bell; Ayer.

The Memories and Correspondence of Coventry Patmore (2 vols.), G. Bell.

The Unknown Eros.

The Angel in the House: the Espousals, G. Bell; Ticknor & Fields.

The Angel in the House, Together with the Victories of Love, G. Rutledge; Arden Library.

Religio Poetae Etc.: Essays, G. Bell; Duckworth.
Principle in Art, G. Bell; Duckworth; Gregg International of England.
Courage in Politics and Other Essays, Oxford University Press; Ayer.
The Poetry of Pathos and Delight: Selected and Edited by Alice Meynell, W. Heinemann;
     G. P. Putnam.
Editor, *The Children's Garland From the Best Poets*, Macmillan; Ayer.
*Further Letters of Gerard Manley Hopkins, Including His Correspondence with Coventry
     Patmore*, Oxford University Press.
Mystical Poems of Nuptial Love: The Wedding Sermon, The Unknown Eros, and Other Odes,
     B. Humphries.
"The Toys," from *The Oxford Book of English Verse*, Clarendon Press, Oxford.

50. St. Thérèse of Lisieux

Autobiography of St. Thérèse, Collins; Harvill; P. J. Kenedy; Burns, Oates, and
     Washbourne; Institute of Carmelite Studies.
The Story of a Soul, Newman Press.
Selected Letters of St. Thérèse of Lisieux, Sheed and Ward; Stag Books.
The Little Way of Spiritual Childhood According to Bl. Thérèse, P. J. Kenedy.
Poems, Burns and Oates.
*A Compendious Critical Life of St. Thérèse (Containing the Prayers of St. Thérèse and the
     Poems of St. Thérèse)*, Keystone Printing of Milwaukee.
General Correspondence of St. Thérèse of Lisieux, Institute of Carmelite Studies.
St. Thérèse of Lisieux: Her Last Conversations, Institute of Carmelite Studies.
Collected Letters, Sheed and Ward.

51. Eugene Boylan

Difficulties in Mental Prayer, M. H. Gill; Newman Press.
The Mystical Body; The Foundation of the Spiritual Life, Newman Press.
The Priest's Way to God, Newman Press.
This Tremendous Lover, Mercier Press; Paulist Press; Newman Press.
A Mystic Under Arms, The Newman Bookshop.
The Spiritual Life of the Priest, Mercier Press; Newman Press.

52. Francis Thompson

Works (3 vols.), Burns and Oates; Scribner; A.M.S. Press; Ayer Co.
Poems, Burns and Oates; Greenwood Press; retitled as *Complete Poetical Works*,
     Modern Library.
Poems by Francis Thompson, Century; E. Matthews and J. Lane; Bruce.
The Man Has Wings: New Poems and Plays, Hanover House.
The Life and Labours of Saint John Baptist de la Salle, Burns, Oates & Washbourne.
Health and Holiness, B. Herder.
Shelley, Scribner.
Saint Ignatius Loyola, Burns and Oates; Benzinger.
A Renegade Poet and Other Essays, Ball Publishing; Ayer.

Essays of Yesterday and Today, Norwood Editions.
Sir Leslie Stephen as a Biographer.
Literary Criticisms Newly Discovered and Collected, Anderson and Ritchie.
Minor Poems Newly Discovered and Collected, Anderson and Ritchie.

53. Robert Hugh Benson

By What Authority?: Fiction, P. J. Kenedy; Burns and Oates; Benzinger.
Christ in the Church: A Volume of Religious Essays, B. Herder.
Come Rack! Come Rope!: Fiction, P. J. Kenedy; Dodd, Mead.
Confessions of a Convert, Longman, Green.
The Conventionalists: Fiction, B. Herder.
The Friendship of Christ, Longman, Green; Thomas More.
Lord of the World: Fiction, Dodd, Mead; The Newman Press; Ayer.
A Mirror of Shalott, Being a Collection of Tales Told at an Unprofessional Symposium, Benzinger.
The Mystical Body and Its Head, Sheed and Ward.
Non-Catholic Denominations, Longman, Green.
Papers of a Pariah, Longman, Green; Ayer.
Paradoxes of Catholicism, Longman, Green.
The Religion of the Plain Man, The Newman Press; Burns and Oates.
The History of Richard Raynal, Solitary, Regnery; B. Herder.
Spiritual Letters of Monsignor R. Hugh Benson to One of His Converts, Longman, Green.
A Winnowing, B. Herder.
An Average Man, Burns and Oates; Dodd, Mead.
The Cost of a Crown, Longman, Green. Drama.
The Coward: Fiction, B. Herder.
The Dawn of All, B. Herder; Hutchinson.
The King's Achievement, Newman Press; B. Herder; P. J. Kenedy; Burns and Oates.
The Necromancers, B. Herder; Hutchinson; Ayer.
None Other Gods, B. Herder; Hutchinson.
Oddsfish, P. J. Kenedy; Dodd, Mead; Hutchinson.
The Queen's Tragedy, B. Herder; Isaac Pitman and Sons.
The Sentimentalist, Benzinger.
A Child's Rule of Life, Newman Press; Longman, Green. Verse.
Old Testament Rhymes, Newman Press; Longman. Verse.
St. Thomas à Becket, Newman Press.
The Upper Room: A Drama of Christ's Passion, Longman, Green.
A Mystery Play in Honor of the Nativity of Our Lord, Longman, Green.
Vexilla Regis: A Book of Devotions and Intercessions, Longman, Green.
Initiation: Fiction, P. J. Kenedy; B. Herder; Pitman.
An Alphabet of Saints: Rhymed, Benzinger.
Loneliness: Fiction, Dodd, Mead.
A City Set in a Hill: Apologetics.
A Book of the Love of Jesus: Apologetics.
Lourdes, B. Herder; Manresa Press.
The Maid of Orleans: A Play, Longman, Green.
Maxims from the Writings of Msgr. Benson, R. and T. Washbourne.

Mysticism, Sands; B. Herder.
Sermon Notes (2 vols.), Longman, Green.
Book of Essays, Ayer.
Light Invisible, Benziger; Burns, Oates & Washbourne.

54. Henryk Sienkiewicz

Portrait of America: Letters-Travel Reports, Columbia University Press.
Without Dogma: A Novel of Modern Poland (1893), Little, Brown.
Children of the Soil, Little, Brown.
Charcoal Sketches: Short Stories.
Yanko the Musician (American title) or *A Country Artist* (English title), Little, Brown.
For Bread (or Her Tragic Fate), Hurst.
The Lighthouse Keeper.
Paul: Short Stories.
With Fire and Sword: An Historical Novel of Poland and Russia, F. M. Lupton; Little, Brown.
The Deluge (2 vols.), Little, Brown; Scholarly Press; A.M.S. Press.
Pan Michael, F. M. Lupton Co.; Little, Brown; Altemus of Philadelphia; Greenwood Press.
The Knights of the Cross (or *The Teutonic Knights)* (2 vols.), Little, Brown.
Let Us Follow Him, or Anthea.
Quo Vadis? A Narrative of the Time of Nero, Crosset; Dodd, Mead; E. P. Dutton; Everyman; J. M. Dent; F. M. Lupton; Little, Brown; River City Press-Amereon; Airmont.
In Vain, Little, Brown.
The Old Servant.
Sielanka: A Forest Picture.
Hania, Little, Brown.
Comedy of Errors.
Lillian Morris, Little, Brown.
Orso or A Circus Hercules, Book Club of California.
Western Septet: Seven Stories of the American West (new ed.), Alliance College.
Whose Fault?
Yamyol.
Tartar Captivity.
On a Single Card.
Is He the Dearest One?
Memories of Mariposa.
Bartek the Victor.
Sachem.
A Legend of the Sea.
That Third Woman, J. S. Ogilvie.
The Bull Fight.
The Decision of Zeus.
Light in the Darkness.
The Organist of Ponikla.

Be Thou Blessed or *Be Blessed.*
The Cranes.
On the Bright Shore (In Monte Carlo), Little, Brown.
The Judgement of Peter and Paul on Olympus.
On the Field of Glory: A Historical Novel of the Time of King John Sobreski, Little, Brown.
Life and Death: A Hindu Legend.
The Whirlpools, Little, Brown.
In Desert and Wilderness (Through the Desert): Juvenile Literature.
Tales, Everyman; J. M. Dent; E. P. Dutton.
Where Worlds Meet, F. Tennyson Neely.
Selected Tales, Piast Publishing Co.-American Institute of Polish Culture.
Peasants in Exile (For Daily Bread), Ave Maria Press.

55. Augustin Poulain

The Graces of Interior Prayer: A Treatise on Mystical Theology, Kegan Paul; B. Herder; Rutledge; Celtic Cross Books.
Editor, *Spiritual Journal of Lucie Christine (pseud.),* Kegan Paul; L. Schwan.

56. James Gibbons

The Faith of Our Fathers, J. Murphy; Ayer.
The Ambassador of Christ, J. Murphy.
Our Christian Heritage, J. Murphy.
Discourses and Sermons (For Every Sunday and the Principal Feasts of the Year), J. Murphy; R. and T. Washbourne.
A Retrospect of Fifty Years, J. Murphy; Ayer (2 vols. in one).
Words of Wisdom to the People, J. Murphy.

57. Alice Meynell

Poems: Complete Edition, Scribner; Oxford University Press; Burns and Oates; Hollis and Carter.
Prose and Poetry, Jonathan Cape.
Preludes, Henry S. King.
Poems, E. Matthews and J. Lane.
Other Poems, privately printed.
The Flower and the Mind: A Choice Among the Best Poems.
Later Poems, J. Lane; The Bodley Head.
Poems, Burns and Oates.
Ten Poems, Romney Stred Press.
A Father of Women and Other Poems, Burns and Oates.
Last Poems, Burns and Oates.
The Poor Sisters of Nazareth: An Illustrated Record of Life at Nazareth House, Hammersmith, Burns and Oates.
The Life and Work of Holman Hunt (with F. W. Farrar), Art Journal Office.
The Rhythm of Life and Other Essays, J. Lane.

The Colour of Life and Other Essays on Things Seen and Heard, J. Lane.
The Children, J. Lane; The Bodley Head.
London Impressions, Constable.
The Spirit of Place and Other Essays, J. Lane; The Bodley Head.
John Ruskin: A Biography, William Blackwood; Dodd, Mead.
Children of Old Masters, Duckworth.
Ceres' Runaway and Other Essays, Constable; Burns and Oates; J. Lane.
Mary, The Mother of Jesus: An Essay, The Medici Society.
Childhood, D. T. Batsford; E. P. Dutton.
Essays, Burns and Oates; Scribner; Newman Bookshop.
Hearts of Controversy, Scribner; Burns and Oates.
The Second Person Singular and Other Essays, Oxford University Press.
Wayfaring: Essays, Jonathan Cape.
Essays of To-day and Yesterday: Alice Meynell, Harrap.
The Wares of Autolycus: Selected Literary Essays.
Editor, *The Poems of T. G. Hake,* J. Lane.
Editor, *The Poetry of Pathos and Delight: Coventry Patmore* W. Heinemann; G. P.
  Putnam.
Editor, *A Selection of the Verses of John B. Tabb,* Burns and Oates; Small, Maynard.
Editor, *Poems by William Blake,* Blackie and Son.
Editor, with G. K. Chesterton, *Samuel Johnson,* Herbert and Daniel.
Editor, *The School of Poetry: An Anthology for Young Readers,* W. Collins; Scribner.
Translator, *Lourdes Yesterday, To-day, and To-morrow,* Burns and Oates.
Translator, *The Madonna,* Burns and Oates.
Translator, René Bazin's *The Nun,* Eveleigh Nash; Scribner.
The Flower of the Mind: A Choice Among the Best Poems Made By Alice Meynell, Grant
  Richards.
A Seventeenth-Century Anthology, Blackie and Son.
The Mystics, Seventeenth Century, Alexander Moring.

58. Adolphe Tanquerey

Doctrine and Devotion, Desclee.
A Manual of Dogmatic Theology (2 vols.), St. Thomas' Seminary, Denver, Colorado.
The Spiritual Life: A Treatise on Ascetical and Mystical Theology, Peter Reilly; Desclee.
Synopsis of Dogmatic Theology.
Synopsis of Moral and Pastoral Theology.
The Spiritual Life.

59. Joseph Columba Marmion

Christ, the Life of the Soul, Sands; B. Herder.
Christ in His Mysteries, Sands; B. Herder.
Christ the Ideal of the Monk, Sands; B. Herder.
Christ the Ideal of the Priest, Sands; B. Herder.
Sponsa Verbi; The Virgin Consecrated to Christ, Sands; B. Herder.
Union with God, Sands; B. Herder.
The English Letters of Abbot Marmion, Helicon Press.

Words of Life, Sands; B. Herder.
Suffering with Christ, Newman Press.
The Trinity in Our Spiritual Life, Newman Press.
The Way of the Cross, Sands.
The Mysteries of the Rosary, Marmion Abbey.
Our Way and Our Life (an abridged edition of *Christ in His Mysteries),* Sands.

60. Ottokár Prohászka

Meditations on the Gospels (three vols. in one), The Newman Press; Sheed and
  Ward.
God and the World.
Christian Repentance and Forgiveness.
Earth and Heaven.

61. Ludwig von Pastor

The History of the Popes, from the Close of the Middle Ages (40 vols.), B. Herder; Rutledge and Kegan Paul.

62. Jean-Baptiste Chautard

The True Apostolate, B. Herder.
The Soul of the Apostolate, Burns and Oates; J. P. Kenedy; Gethsemani Mission
  Press; Image; Tan Books.

63. G. K. Chesterton

Collected Works (Vols. 1, 2, 3 et seq.), Ignatius Press.
Greybeards at Play, R. Brimley Johnson.
The Wild Night, Grant Richards.
The Defendant, R. Brimley Johnson.
Twelve Types, Arthur L. Humphreys.
Englishmen of Letters: Robert Browning, Macmillan.
G. F. Watts, Duckworth.
The Napoleon of Notting Hill, J. Lane; The Bodley Head.
The Club of Queer Trades, Harper.
Heretics, J. Lane; The Bodley Head.
Charles Dickens, Methuen.
The Man Who Was Thursday, J. W. Arrowsmith.
All Things Considered, Methuen.
Orthodoxy, J. Lane; The Bodley Head; Doubleday-Image.
Varied Types, Dodd, Mead.
George Bernard Shaw, J. Lane.
Tremendous Trifles, Methuen.
The Ball and the Cross, Wells Gardner, Darton.
What's Wrong with the World, Cassell; Sheed and Ward.

Alarms and Discursions, Methuen.

William Blake, Duckworth, E. P. Dutton.

Appreciations and Criticisms of the Works of Charles Dickens, J. M. Dent, E. P. Dutton.

The Innocence of Father Brown, Cassell.

The Ballad of the White Horse, Methuen; Catholic Authors Press.

Manalive, Thomas Nelson.

A Miscellany of Men, Methuen.

The Victorian Age in Literature, Williams and Norgate.

Magic A Fantastic Comedy, Martin Secker.

The Flying Inn, Methuen.

The Wisdom of Father Brown, Cassell.

The Barbarism of Berlin, Cassell.

London, privately printed for Alvin Langdon Coburn and Edmund D. Brooks and their friends.

Letters to an Old Garibaldian, Methuen.

Poems, Burns and Oates.

Wine, Water and Song, Methuen.

The Crimes of England, Cecil Palmer & Hayward.

Divorce Versus Democracy, The Society of SS. Peter and Paul; Publishers to the Church of England.

A Short History of England, Chatto and Windus.

Utopia of Usurers and Other Essays, Boni and Liverright.

Irish Impressions, W. Collins.

The Superstition of Divorce, Chatto and Windus.

The Uses of Diversity: A Book of Essays, Methuen.

The New Jerusalem, Hodder and Stoughton.

Eugenics and Other Evils, Cassell.

What I Saw in America, Hodder and Stoughton.

The Ballad of St. Barbara and Other Verses, Cecil Palmer.

The Man Who Knew Too Much, Cassell.

Fancies Versus Fads, Methuen.

St. Francis of Assisi, Hodder and Stoughton; Image.

The End of the Roman Road: A Pageant of Wayfarers, Classic Press.

The Superstitions of the Sceptic, W. Heffer.

Tales of the Long Bow, Cassell.

The Everlasting Man, Hodder and Stoughton; Image.

William Cobbett, Hodder and Stoughton.

The Incredulity of Father Brown, Cassell.

The Outline of Sanity, Methuen.

The Queen of Seven Swords, Sheed and Ward.

The Catholic Church and Conversion, Burns, Oates & Washbourne; Macmillan.

The Return of Don Quixote, Chatto and Windus.

The Collected Poems of G. K. Chesterton, Cecil Palmer; Dodd, Mead.

The Secret of Father Brown, Cassell.

The Judgement of Dr. Johnson: A Comedy in Three Acts, Sheed and Ward.

Robert Louis Stevenson, Hodder and Stoughton.

Generally Speaking: A Book of Essays, Methuen.

The Poet and the Lunatics: Episodes in the Life of Gabriel Gale, Cassell.

The Thing: Why I Am a Catholic, Sheed and Ward.
G. K. C. as M. C.: Being a Collection of Thirty-Seven Introductions, Methuen.
Four Faultless Felons, Cassell.
The Resurrection of Rome, Hodder and Stoughton.
Come to Think of It . . . A Book of Essays, Methuen.
The Turkey and the Turk, St. Dominic's Press.
All is Grist: A Book of Essays, Methuen.
Chaucer, Faber & Faber.
Sidelights: On New London and Newer York and Other Essays, Sheed and Ward.
Christendom in Dublin, Sheed and Ward.
"All I Survey": A Book of Essays, Methuen.
St. Thomas Aquinas, Hodder and Stoughton; Image.
Avowals and Denials: A Book of Essays, Methuen.
The Scandal of Father Brown, Cassell.
The Well and the Shadows, Sheed and Ward.
As I Was Saying: A Book of Sayings, Methuen.
Autobiography, Hutchinson.
The Paradoxes of Mr. Pond, Cassell.
The Colored Lands, Sheed and Ward.
The End of the Armistice, Sheed and Ward.
The Common Man, Sheed and Ward.
The Surprise, Sheed and Ward.
A Handful of Authors, Sheed and Ward.
The Glass Walking-Stick and Other Essays, Methuen.

64. Fernand Cabrol

Liturgical Prayer: Its History and Spirit, Burns and Oates; Newman Press.
The Prayer of the Early Christians, Burns and Oates.
Books of the Latin Liturgy, Sheed and Ward; Sands; Herder.
Holy Sacrifice: A Simple Explanation of the Mass, Burns and Oates.
Holy Week: The Complete Office in Latin and English; A New Explanatory Edition, P. J.
  Kenedy.
Lay Folks Ritual.
Liturgical Prayerbook.
Mass of the Western Rites, B. Herder; Sands.
My Missal.
St. Benedict, Burns and Oates.
The Year's Liturgy.
The Holy Eucharist and the Roman Missal, Paulist Press.
The Holy Eucharist in the Liturgy, Paulist Press.
The Mass: Its Doctrine, Its History, P. J. Kenedy.

65. Ferdinand Prat

Theology of St. Paul (2 vols.), Burns and Oates; Newman Bookshop; B. Herder.
Jesus Christ: His Life, His Teaching, and His Work (2 vols.), Bruce.
Saint Paul, Burns and Oates.

66. Marie Joseph Lagrange

Historical Criticism of the Old Testament, E. Myers; London Catholic Truth Society.
Notes on the Orpheus of M. Solomon Reinach, Oxford.
The Gospel According to St. Mark, Benzinger.
The Meaning of Christianity According to Luther and his Followers in Germany, Longman.
Luther on the Eve of His Revolt: A Criticism of Luther's Lectures on the Epistles to the Romans,
   New York Catholic Library Association.
The Gospel According to St. Mark, Benzinger.
Christ and Renan—A Commentary on Ernest Renan's "Life of Jesus", Benzinger.
A Catholic Harmony of the Four Gospels, Being an Adaptation of the "Synopsis Evangelica",
   Burns, Oates & Washbourne.
The Gospel of Jesus Christ (2 vols.), Burns, Oates & Washbourne; Newman Press.
Pere Lagrange: Personal Reflections and Memoirs, Paulist Press.
Studies in Semitic Religions.
The Historic Method.
Messianism Among the Jews.
Judaism Before Jesus Christ.

67. Alban Goodier

An Introduction to the Study of Ascetical and Mystical Theology, Bruce.
The Jesuits, Sheed and Ward.
The Meaning of Life and Other Essays, St. Meinrad's Abbey.
The Passion and Death of Our Lord Jesus Christ, P. J. Kenedy; St. Paul Books and
   Media.
The Public Life of Our Lord Jesus Christ (2 vols.), Burns and Oates; St. Paul Books
   and Media.
The Risen Jesus: Meditations, P. J. Kenedy; Burns and Oates; St. Paul Books and
   Media.
St. Ignatius Loyola and Prayer As Seen in the Book of the Spiritual Exercises, Benzinger.
Saints for Sinners, Longman, Green; Ayer.
The School of Love and Other Essays, Benzinger.
Witnesses to Christ: A Harmony of the Gospels, Burns and Oates, P. J. Kenedy.
The Life That Is Light, Burns and Oates.
Inner Life of a Catholic, Longman, Green.
Jesus Christ, the Son of God, Burns and Oates.
About the Old Testament, Benzinger.
The Bible for Every Day, Burns and Oates.
The Crown of Sorrow, Burns and Oates; St. Paul Books and Media.
The Prince of Peace, St. Meinrad Grail Publications; St. Paul Books and Media.
History and Religion, Burns and Oates.
St. Ignatius and Prayer.

68. St. Maximilian Kolbe

Complete Works:
  Vol. I: *Personal Letters,*
  Vol. II: *Spiritual Writings,*
  Vol. III: *Theological Writings,* Ignatius Press (forthcoming).
Last Days of Maximilian Kolbe, New City Press.

69. Bl. Edith Stein

The Science of the Cross, Regnery; Burns and Oates.
On the Problem of Empathy, M. Nijhoff.
Ways to Know God.
The Writings of Edith Stein: Selected, Newman Press.
Life in a Jewish Family: Her Unfinished Autobiography, Institute of Carmelite Studies.
Essays on Woman, Institute of Carmelite Studies.
The Mysteries of Christmas, Paul VI Institute of the Arts.
On Truth.
Finite and Eternal Being.
Edith Stein. Thoughts on Her Life and Times, Bruce.

70. Henri Ghéon

Three Plays, Sheed and Ward.
The Comedian, Sheed and Ward.
The Marriage of St. Francis, Sheed and Ward.
Marvelous History of St. Bernard: A Play, Sheed and Ward.
The Mystery of the Finding of the Cross: A Play in Three Acts, Dacre Press.
The Way of the Cross, Pax House of London.
St. Anne and the Gouty Rector, and Other Plays, Longman, Green.
Parade at the Devil's Bridge. Play.
Christmas in the Village Square, translated by Sister Marie Thomas O.P., Rosary
  College.
Secret of St. John Bosco, Sheed and Ward.
The Secret of the Cure d'Ars, Sheed and Ward.
The Secret of the Little Flower, Sheed and Ward; Longman, Green.
St. Germain of the Wolf Country, Sheed and Ward; Longman.
St. Vincent Ferrar, Sheed and Ward.
The Secret of St. Margaret Mary, Sheed and Ward.
The Secret of Saint Martin of Tours, Sheed and Ward.
The Art of the Theatre, Hill and Wang.
In Search of Mozart, Sheed and Ward.
Secrets of the Saints: Cure d'Ars; The Little Flower; Margaret Mary; John Bosco (in one
  vol.), Sheed and Ward.
Christmas in the Market Place, Muller.

71. Edward Leen

The Church Before Pilate, Preservation Press.
The Holy Ghost and His Work in Souls, Sheed and Ward.
In the Likeness of Christ, Sheed and Ward.
Our Blessed Mother: Talks on Our Lady.
Progress Through Mental Prayer, Sheed and Ward; Arena Letters.
Retreat Notes for Religious.
The True Vine and Its Branches, Sheed and Ward.
The Voice of a Priest, Sheed and Ward.
What is Education?, Sheed and Ward.
Why the Cross?, Sheed and Ward.

72. Alexis Carrel

Man the Unknown, Harper.
The Prayer, Morehouse, Gordham.
Reflections on Life, Hawthorn.
The Voyage to Lourdes, Harper.
Selections From His Writings in J. T. Durkin's *Hope for Our Time: Alexis Carrel on Man and Society*, Harper & Row.

73. Sigrid Undset

Kristin Lavransdatter. Trilogy of Historical Novels of Medieval Catholic Norway.
  1. *The Bridal Wreath*, Knopf.
  2. *The Mistress of Husaby*, Knopf.
  3. *The Cross*, Knopf.
The Master of Hestviken. Tetrology of Historical Novels of Medieval Norway:
  1. *The Axe*, Knopf.
  2. *The Snake Pit*, Knopf.
  3. *In the Wilderness*, Knopf.
  4. *The Son Avenger*, Knopf.
The Burning Bush, Knopf.
Catherine of Siena, Sheed and Ward.
Christmas and Twelfth Night, Longman.
The Faithful Wife, Knopf.
Four Stories, Knopf.
Gunnar's Daughter, Knopf.
Ida Elizabeth, Knopf.
The Longest Years, Knopf.
Madame Dorothea, Knopf.
Return to the Future, Knopf.
Saga of the Saints, Longman.
Stages on the Road, Knopf.
The Wild Orchid, Knopf.

74. William Thomas Walsh

Isabella of Spain, the Last Crusader, Sheed and Ward; R. M. McBride; Tudor.
Philip II, Sheed and Ward; Farrar.
Saint Peter the Apostle, Image; Macmillan.
St. Teresa of Avila, Bruce.
Mother of Carmel.
Characters of the Inquisition, P. J. Kenedy; Tan Books.
Editor, *Hispanic Anthology.*
Out of the Whirlwind: A Novel, R. M. McBride.
Shekels: A Blank-Verse Play.
Lyric Poems, P. J. Kenedy.
Our Lady of Fatima, Sheed and Ward; Image; Newman Press; Macmillan.
Saints in Action: The Lives of Eight Great Saints of the Early Church, Doubleday (Hanover House).
The Mirage of the Many, Holt.
Thirty Pieces of Silver.
The Carmelites of Compiègne: A Play in Verse.

75. Owen Francis Dudley

Pageant of Life: A Human Drama, Longman.
Will Men Be Like Gods? Humanitarianism or Human Happiness, Longman.
The Shadow on the Earth: A Tale of Tragedy and Triumph, Longman.
The Masterful Monk (also known as *Michael, a Tale of the Masterful Monk*), Longman.
The Coming of the Monster: A Tale of the Masterful Monk, Longman, Green.
The Tremaynes and the Masterful Monk: a Most Hateful and Lovable Tale, Longman.
You, and Thousands Like You: For Such as Can Take It, Longman.

76. Hilaire Belloc

Verses and Sonnets, Ward and Downey.
The Bad Child's Book of Beasts, Alden; Bocardo Press; Simpkin; Marshall, Hamilton, Kent.
More Beasts for Worse Children, Edward Arnold.
The Modern Traveller, Edward Arnold.
Danton, a Study, James Nisbit.
A Moral Alphabet, Edward Arnold.
Lambkin's Remains, The Proprietors of the J.C.R. at J. Vincent's.
Paris, Edward Arnold.
Robespierre, James Nisbit.
The Path to Rome, George Allen; Penguin.
Caliban's Guide to Letters: The Aftermath or Gleanings from a Busy Life, Duckworth.
Translator, *The Romance of Tristan and Iseult,* George Allen.
Avril: Being Essays on the Poetry of the French Renaissance, Duckworth.
Emmanuel Burden, Methuen.

The Old Road, Constable.
Esto Perpetua: Algerian Studies and Impressions, Duckworth.
Sussex, Adam and Charles Black.
Hills and the Sea, Methuen; Scribner.
The Historic Thames, J. M. Dent.
Cautionary Tales for Children, Eveleigh Nash.
On Nothing and Kindred Subjects, Methuen.
Mr. Clutterbuck's Election, Eveleigh Nash.
The Eye-Witness, Eveleigh Nash.
The Pyrenees, Methuen.
A Change in the Cabinet, Methuen.
Marie Antoinette, Methuen.
On Everything, Methuen.
On Anything, Constable.
Pongo and the Bull, Constable.
On Something, Methuen.
Verses, Duckworth.
The Party System (with Cecil Chesterton), Stephen Swift.
The French Revolution, Williams and Norgate.
The Girondin, Nelson and Sons (U.K.).
More Peers: Verses, Stephen Swift.
First and Last, Methuen.
The Battle of Blenheim, Stephen Swift.
Malplaquet, Stephen Swift.
Waterloo, Stephen Swift.
The Four Men, Nelson and Sons (U.K.); Oxford University Press.
The Green Overcoat, J. W. Arrowsmith.
Turcoing, Stephen Swift.
Warfare in England, Williams and Norgate.
This and That: Essays, Methuen.
The Servile State, T. N. Foulis; Liberty Classics.
The River of London, T. N. Foulis.
Crecy, Stephen Swift.
The Stane Street, Constable.
Poitiers, Hugh Rees.
Anti-Catholic History: How It Is Written, Catholic Truth Society.
The Book of the Bayeux Tapestry, Chatto and Windus.
Land and Water Map of the War, Land and Water Central House.
The History of England (Vol. 2), The Catholic Publication Society of America;
    Sands; Methuen.
A General Sketch of the European War, Nelson and Sons (U.K.).
The Two Maps of Europe, C. Arthur Pearson.
The Last Days of the French Monarchy, Chapman & Hall.
A General Sketch of the European War: The Second Phase, Nelson and Sons (U.K.).
The Second Year of the War, Burrup, Mathieson & Sprague.
The Free Press, George Allen & Unwin.
The Principles of War, Chapman and Hall.
Precepts and Judgements, Chapman and Hall.

The Catholic Church and the Principle of Private Property, Catholic Truth Society.

Europe and the Faith, Constable.

The House of Commons and Monarchy, George Allen & Unwin.

Pascal's "Provincial Letters", Catholic Truth Society.

Catholic Social Reform Versus Socialism, Catholic Truth Society.

The Jews, Constable.

The Mercy of Allah, Chatto and Windus.

The Road, Charles W. Hobson.

Sonnets and Verse, Duckworth.

The Contrast, J. W. Arrowsmith.

Economics for Helen, J. W. Arrowsmith.

The Campaign of 1812 or Napoleon's Campaign of 1812 and the Retreat from Moscow, Nelson and Sons (U.K.).

The Cruise of the "Nona", Methuen; Century Publishing; Hippocrene Books; Penguin; Houghton Mifflin; Newman Press.

Mr. Petre, Arrowsmith.

Miniatures of French History, Nelson and Sons (U.K.).

The Highway and Its Vehicles, Studio Limited.

Short Talks with the Dead and Others, Cayme Press.

Mrs. Markham's New History of England, Cayme Press.

The Emerald of Catherine the Great, Sheed and Ward.

Mr. Belloc Still Objects, Sheed and Ward.

The Catholic Church and History, Burns, Oates & Washbourne.

The Haunted House, Arrowsmith.

Oliver Cromwell, Ernest Benn Limited.

Many Cities, Constable.

James the Second, Faber & Gwyer.

How the Reformation Happened, Jonathan Cape; Peter Smith.

But Soft—We Are Observed!, Arrowsmith.

A Conversation with an Angel, Jonathan Cape.

Belinda: A Tale of Affection in Youth and Age, Constable.

Survivals and New Arrivals, Sheed and Ward.

Joan of Arc, Cassell.

The Missing Masterpiece: A Novel, Arrowsmith.

Richelieu, Ernest Benn Limited.

Wolsey, Cassell.

The Man Who Made Gold, Arrowsmith.

New Cautionary Tales, Duckworth.

A Conversation with a Cat, Cassell.

On Translation, Clarendon Press, Oxford.

Essays of a Catholic Layman in England: "Truth Comes by Conflict", Sheed and Ward.

Cranmer, Cassell.

The Postmaster-General, Arrowsmith.

Ladies and Gentlemen, Duckworth.

Napoleon, Cassell.

The Tactics and Strategy of the Great Duke of Marlborough, Arrowsmith.

William the Conqueror, Peter Davies.

Becket, Catholic Truth Society.

Charles the First, King of England, Cassell.
Cromwell, Cassell.
A Shorter History of England, Harrap.
Milton, Cassell; Greenwood Press.
The Battle Ground, Cassell.
The County of Sussex, Cassell.
An Essay on the Restoration of Property, The Distributist League.
Characters of the Reformation, Sheed and Ward; Doubleday-Image.
The Hedge and the Horse, Cassell.
An Essay on the Nature of Contemporary England, Constable.
The Crusade, Cassell.
The Crisis of Our Civilization, Cassell.
Sonnets and Verse, Duckworth.
The Great Heresies, Sheed and Ward; Trinity Communications.
Return to the Baltic, Constable.
The Question and the Answer, Longman, Green.
Monarchy, Cassell.
The Last Rally: A Story of Charles II, Cassell.
The Catholic and the War, Burns and Oates.
On the Place of Gilbert Chesterton in English Letters, Sheed and Ward; Patmos Press.
The Silence of the Sea, Cassell; The Catholic Book Club.
Elizabethan Commentary, Cassell.
Places, Cassell; Sheed and Ward.
Cautionary Verses Illustrated Album Edition, Duckworth.
Complete Verse, Duckworth.
Selected Essays, Penguin; Lippincott.

77. Paul Claudel

Two Dramas: Break of Noon; The Tidings Brought to Mary, Regnery.
The Satin Slipper: or the Worst Is Not the Surest, Sheed and Ward.
Three Plays: The Hostage; Crusts; The Humiliation of the Father, John W. Luce.
The Tidings Brought to Mary. Yale University Press; Chatto and Windus; Regnery.
  A drama.
The Hostage, Yale University Press. A drama.
Tête d'Or, Yale University Press. Play in three acts.
The City, Yale University Press. A play.
The Book of Christopher Columbus: A Lyrical Drama, Yale University Press; Oxford
  University Press; Elliot Books.
Three Poems of the War, Yale University Press.
Letters to a Doubter (Jacques Riviere), A. & C. Boni.
Ways and Crossways: Essays (also called, Bitter Leaven), Sheed and Ward; Ayer.
Break of Noon: A Drama, Regnery.
Coronal: Corona Benignitatis Anni Dei, Pantheon.
The Correspondence, 1899–1926, Between Paul Claudel and Andre Gide, Pantheon.
The East I Know, Yale University Press.
Claudel on the Theatre, University of Miami Press.
The Essence of the Bible, Philosophical Library.

The Eye Listens, Philosophical Library.
I Believe in God: A Meditation on the Apostles' Creed, Holt, Rinehart & Winston.
Lord Teach Us to Pray, Longman, Green.
A Poet Before the Cross, Regnery.
Five Great Odes, Dufour Editions; Rapp and Carroll.
Poetic Art, Philosophical Library.
Stations of the Cross.
Letters from Paul Claudel, My Godfather, Newman Press.

78. Johannes Jørgensen

Jørgensen: An Autobiography (2 vols.), Longman, Green.
Saint Bridget of Sweden (2 vols.), Longman, Green.
Saint Catherine of Siena, Longman, Green.
St. Francis of Assisi, Longman, Green; Doubleday-Image.
War Pilgrim, Burns and Oates.
Don Bosco, Burns and Oates.
Truth and Falsehood.
The Book of the Journey.
Pilgrim Walks in Franciscan Italy, Sands.
False Witness, Hodder and Stoughton.
Foes of Hell.
The Last Day, A Story.
The Book About Rome: Catholic Apologetics (2 vols.).
Roman Mosaics.
Pictures of Roman Saints.
Our Lady of Denmark. A novel.
Lourdes, Longman, Green.
Legends of Spring.
Tree of Life.
The Pilgrim Book.
Bekendelse.

79. Pierre Pourrat

Christian Spirituality (4 vols.), Burns and Oates; Newman Press.
Theology of the Sacraments, B. Herder.
Father Olier: Founder of St. Sulpice, Voice Publishing.

80. Ronald A. Knox

A Still More Sporting Adventure.
Some Loose Stones, Longman.
Naboth's Vineyard in Pawn, Society of SS. Peter and Paul.
A Spiritual Aeneid, Longman.
Translator, *The Holy Bible,* Sheed and Ward.
A Commentary on the Gospels (2 vols.), Sheed and Ward; Burns and Oates.

The Essentials of Spiritual Unity, Catholic Truth Society.
Meditations on the Psalms, Longman.
Patrick Shaw-Stewart, W. Collins.
Memories of the Future, Methuen.
Editor, *Aeneid.*
A Book of Acrostics, Methuen.
Sanctions: a Frivolity, Methuen; Sheed and Ward.
The Viaduct Murder, Methuen.
Other Eyes than Ours, Methuen.
An Open Air Pulpit, Constable.
The Three Taps, Methuen; Simon & Shuster.
The Belief of Catholics, Ernest Benn; Harper; Sheed and Ward.
Essays in Satire, Sheed and Ward.
Anglican Cobwebs, Sheed and Ward.
The Footsteps at the Lock, Methuen; Dover.
The Trials of a Translator, Sheed and Ward.
The Rich Young Man, Sheed and Ward.
The Mystery of the Kingdom and Other Sermons, Sheed and Ward.
The Church on Earth, Burns, Oates.
On Getting There, Methuen.
Caliban in Grub Street, Sheed and Ward.
Broadcast Minds, Sheed and Ward.
Difficulties, Eyre & Spottiswoode.
The Body in the Silo, Hodder and Stoughton.
Still Dead, Hodder and Stoughton.
Heaven and the Charing Cross, Burns, Oates.
Barchester Pilgrimage, Sheed and Ward.
Double Cross Purposes, Hodder and Stoughton; Dover.
Let Dons Delight, Sheed and Ward.
Captive Flames, Burns, Oates.
In Soft Garments, Burns, Oates.
God and the Atom, Sheed and Ward.
A Retreat for Priests, Sheed and Ward.
The Mass in Slow Motion, Sheed and Ward.
The Creed in Slow Motion, Sheed and Ward.
On Englishing the Bible, Burns and Oates.
A Selection from the Occasional Sermons of the Right Reverend Monsignor R. A. Knox, Dropmore Press.
The Gospel in Slow Motion, Sheed and Ward.
St. Paul's Gospel, Catholic Truth Society.
Enthusiasm, Clarendon Press, Oxford; Oxford University Press; Christian Classics.
Stimuli, Sheed and Ward.
Off the Record, Sheed and Ward.
A Retreat for Lay People, Sheed and Ward.
Commentary on the New Testament, Burns and Oates.
The Window in the Wall and Other Sermons on the Holy Eucharist, Burns and Oates.
Bridegroom and Bride, Sheed and Ward.

Literary Distractions, Sheed and Ward; Greenwood Press.
Translator, *Autobiography of a Saint* (translation of St. Thérèse's *Autobiography*),
   Harvill Press.
In Three Tongues, Chapman & Hall.
The Priestly Life, Sheed and Ward.
Retreat for Beginners, Sheed and Ward.

81. Paul de Jaegher

One with Jesus: or, the Life of Identification with Christ, Newman Press; Burns and
   Oates.
The Virtue of Trust, P. J. Kenedy; Burns and Oates.
The Virtue of Love: Meditations, P. J. Kenedy.
The Lord is My Joy, Newman Press.
Editor, *Anthology of Mysticism,* Newman Press.

82. Francis Trochu

St. Bernadette Soubirous, 1844–1879, Pantheon; Longman.
Bernadette of Lourdes, Universe Books.
The Curé d'Ars: St. Jean Marie Baptiste Vianney, Newman Press; P. J. Kenedy; Burns
   and Oates. Full biography.
The Curé d'Ars: A Shorter Biography, Newman Press.
St. Bernadette: A Pictorial Biography, Regnery.
Jean Jugan: Foundress of the Institute of the Little Sisters of the Poor, Burns and Oates.

83. John Peter Arendzen

Reason and Revelation, Burns, Oates & Washbourne.
Faith and Common Sense, Burns, Oates & Washbourne.
Men and Manners in the Day of Christ, Sheed and Ward; B. Herder.
The Gospel, Fact, Myth, or Legend, B. Herder; Sands.
*The New Testament of Our Lord Jesus Christ According to the Douay Version: With Introduc-
tion and Notes by J. P. Arendzen,* Sheed and Ward.
The Holy Trinity: A Theological Treatise for Modern Laymen, Sheed and Ward.
Prophets, Priests, and Publicans: Character Sketches and Problems from the Gospels, Sands.
What Becomes of the Dead? A Study of Eschatology (2nd ed.), Sheed and Ward.
Whom Do You Say—? A Study in the Doctrine of the Incarnation, Sands.
Purgatory and Heaven, Tan Books.

84. Giuseppe Ricciotti

The Acts of the Apostles: Text and Commentary, Bruce.
The Age of Martyrs: Christianity from Diocletian to Constantine, Bruce.
The History of Israel (2nd ed.), Bruce.
Julian the Apostate, Bruce.

The Life of Jesus Christ, Bruce.
Paul the Apostle, Bruce.

85. Gerald Vann

The Paradise Tree: On Living the Symbols of the Church, Sheed and Ward.
The Wisdom of Boethius, Blackfriars.
The Seven Swords, Sheed and Ward; Collins.
Saint Thomas Aquinas, Benzinger; J. M. Dent.
The Pains of Christ and the Sorrow of God, Blackfriars.
Of His Fulness: A Christian Review, P. J. Kenedy.
Morals and Man (rev. ed.), Sheed and Ward.
The Heart of Man, Longman, Green; Image.
On Being Human, Sheed and Ward.
Morals Makyth Man.
Morality and War, Burns and Oates.
The Divine Pity: A Study in the Social Implications of the Beatitudes, Sheed and Ward;
    Doubleday-Image; Christian Classics.
Eve and the Gryphon: A Study of the Vocation of Women, Oxford-Blackfriars.
His Will Is Our Peace, Sheed and Ward.
*The Eagle's Word: a Presentation of the Gospel According to St. John with an Introductory
    Essay,* Harcourt, Brace.
The High Green Hill, Sheed and Ward.
The Son's Course.
The Water and the Fire, Collins; The Catholic Book Club.
To Heaven with Diana, Pantheon Books.
Awake in Heaven, Longman, Green.
The Two Trees, Collins.
Moral Dilemmas, Collins.
Stones or Bread, Collins.
The Temptations of Christ, Sheed and Ward.

86. Réginald Garrigou-Lagrange

Beatitude, B. Herder.
Christ the Savior, B. Herder.
*Christian Perfection and Contemplation According to St. Thomas Aquinas and St. John of the
    Cross,* B. Herder.
God: His Existence and Nature, B. Herder.
Grace, B. Herder.
Life Everlasting, B. Herder.
The Love of God and the Cross of Jesus, B. Herder.
The Mother of Our Savior and Our Interior Life, Golden Eagle Books.
The One God, B. Herder.
Our Savior and His Love for Us, B. Herder.
Predestination, B. Herder.
The Priest in Union with Christ, Newman Press.
The Priesthood and Perfection, Newman Press.

Providence, B. Herder.
Reality: A Synthesis of Thomistic Thought, B. Herder.
The Theological Virtues, Vol. 1, *On Faith*, B. Herder.
The Three Ages of the Interior Life: Prelude of Eternal Life, B. Herder.
The Three Ways of the Spiritual Life, Newman Press.
The Trinity, and God the Creator, B. Herder.
The Last Writings of Réginald Garrigou-Lagrange, New City.
Commentary on the Summa Theologica (7 vols.).

87. Henri Daniel-Rops

The Book of Mary, Hawthorn; Image.
The Church of the Apostles and Martyrs, J. M. Dent; E. P. Dutton.
The Church in the Dark Ages, J. M. Dent.
Cathedral and Crusade: Studies in the Medieval Age, J. M. Dent.
The Protestant Reformation, J. M. Dent; E. P. Dutton.
The Catholic Reformation, J. M. Dent; E. P. Dutton.
The Church in the Seventeenth Century, J. M. Dent; E. P. Dutton.
The Church in the Eighteenth Century, J. M. Dent; E. P. Dutton.
The Church in an Age of Revolution, J. M. Dent.
A Fight for God, J. M. Dent; E. P. Dutton.
Our Brothers in Christ, J. M. Dent; E. P. Dutton.
History of the Church of Christ, E. P. Dutton.
Daily Life in the Time of Jesus, Hawthorn; Servant.
The Heroes of God, Hawthorn.
Israel and the Ancient World: A History of the Israelites from the Time of Abraham to the Birth of Christ, Image.
Jesus and His Times (rev. ed.), E. P. Dutton.
The Life of Our Lord, Hawthorn.
Monsieur Vincent: The Story of St. Vincent de Paul, Hawthorn.
Saint Paul: Apostle of Nations, Fides.
The Second Vatican Council: the Story Behind the Ecumenical Council of Pope John XXIII, Hawthorn.
This Is the Mass, Hawthorn.
What Is the Bible? Hawthorn.
Two Men in Me, Ayer.
Death, Where Is Thy Victory? Cassell.
The Poor and Ourselves, Burns, Oates, & Washbourne.
Where Angels Pass, Cassell.
The Book of Books: The Story of the Old Testament.
The Book of Life: The Story of the New Testament.
The Miracle of Ireland, Helicon Press.
A Catholic Child's Book About St. Paul.
Golden Legend of Young Saints.
The Misted Mirror. A novel.
Sacred History, Longman, Green.
Bernard of Clairvaux, Hawthorn.

People of the Bible.
Scriptural and Ecclesiastical History.

88. Karl Adam

The Christ of Faith: the Christology of the Church, Pantheon.
Christ Our Brother, Macmillan; Sheed and Ward.
One and Holy, Sheed and Ward.
The Roots of the Reformation, Sheed and Ward.
Saint Augustine: the Odyssey of His Soul, Macmillan; Sheed and Ward.
The Son of God, Sheed and Ward; Doubleday-Image.
The Spirit of Catholicism, Macmillan; Doubleday-Image; Darby.
Two Essays: Christ and the Western Mind; Love and Belief, Macmillan; Sheed and Ward.
Holy Marriage, Liturgical Press.
Tertullian's Conception of the Church.
Eucharistic Teaching of St. Augustine.
German's New Religion: The German Faith Movement (with W. Hauer and K. Heim), Abingdon Press.

89. Evelyn Waugh

An Essay on the Pre-Raphaelite Brotherhood: 1847–1854, Alastair Graham.
Rossetti: His Life and Works, Duckworth; Dodd, Mead; Folcroft.
Decline and Fall, Chapman and Hall; Little, Brown.
Vile Bodies, Chapman and Hall.
Labels: A Mediterranean Journal, Duckworth; also known as *A Bachelor Abroad,* J. Cape and H. Smith.
Remote People, Duckworth.
Black Mischief, Chapman and Hall.
Ninety-Two Days: The Account of a Tropical Journey Through British Guiana and Parts of Brazil, Duckworth; Farrar & Rinehart; Longwood Publishing Group (2nd. ed.).
A Handful of Dust, Duckworth.
Edmund Campion, Doubleday; Sheed and Ward; Oxford University Press.
Waugh in Abyssinia, Longman, Green.
Mr. Loveday's Little Outing and Other Sad Stories, Little, Brown.
Scoop, Chapman and Hall; Little, Brown.
Robbery Under Law: The Mexican Object Lesson, Chapman and Hall.
Put Out More Flags, Chapman and Hall.
Work Suspended: Two Chapters of an Unfinished Novel, Chapman and Hall.
Brideshead Revisited: The Sacred and Profane Memories of Captain Charles Ryder, Chapman and Hall; Little, Brown.
When the Going Was Good, Little, Brown; Greenwood Press.
Scott-King's Modern Europe, Little, Brown.
Wine in Peace and War, Saccone and Speed.
The Loved One: An Anglo-American Tragedy, Chapman and Hall.
Helena, Doubleday.
Men at Arms, Little, Brown.

The Holy Places, Queen Anne Press.

Love Among the Ruins: a Romance of the Near Future, Chapman and Hall.

Tactical Exercise, Little, Brown; Ayer.

Officers and Gentlemen, Little, Brown.

The Ordeal of Gilbert Pinfold: A Conversation Piece, Little, Brown.

Monsignor Ronald Knox, Little, Brown; Chapman and Hall.

Brideshead Revisited: The Sacred and Profane Memories of Captain Charles Ryder (rev. ed.),
   Chapman and Hall; Penguin.

Tourist in Africa, Little, Brown.

Unconditional Surrender (The End of the Battle), Chapman and Hall.

Basil Seal Rides Again: The Rake's Regress, Little, Brown.

A Little Learning, An Autobiography: The Early Years, Little, Brown.

*Sword of Honor: The Final Versions of the Novels: "Men at Arms," "Officers and Gentlemen,"
   and "Unconditional Surrender,"* Chapman and Hall.

The Private Diaries, London Observer Magazine.

The Diaries of Evelyn Waugh, Little, Brown.

The Essays, Articles and Reviews of Evelyn Waugh, Little, Brown.

The Letters of Evelyn Waugh, Ticknor & Fields.

The World of Evelyn Waugh, Little, Brown.

Charles Ryder's Schooldays, and Other Stories, Little, Brown.

A Little Order: A Selection from Waugh's Journalism, Little, Brown.

90. Romano Guardini

Conscience, Benzinger; Sheed and Ward.

Europe: Reality and Mission.

The Faith and Modern Man, Pantheon; Regnery-Logos; Burns and Oates.

Freedom, Grace, Destiny: Three Chapters in the Interpretation of Existence, Pantheon;
   Greenwood Press; J. Murray.

In Praise of the Book.

Jesus Christus: Meditations, Regnery.

Kneeling and Standing.

Meditations Before Mass, Newman Press.

Myth and the Truth of Revelation.

Pascal for Our Time, Herder and Herder.

Power and Responsibility. A Course of Action for the New Age, Regnery.

Prayer in Practice, Pantheon; Burns and Oates; Images.

Prayers from Theology, Herder and Herder.

Rilke's Duino Elegies: An Interpretation, Regnery.

Sacred Images and the Invisible God.

Sacred Signs, Sheed and Ward; Pio Decimo Press; Michael Glazier.

Some Reflections on . . . Freudian . . . Psychology.

The Absolute and the Christian Religion.

The Church and the Catholic, and the Spirit of the Liturgy, Sheed and Ward.

The Church: Encounter with Christ.

The Church of the Lord: On the Nature and Mission of the Church, Regnery.

The Conversion of Augustine, Newman Press; Sands.

The Death of Socrates: An Interpretation of the Platonic Dialogues Euthyphro, Apology, Crito, and Phaedo, Sheed and Ward; Meridian Books.

The End of the Modern World: A Search for Orientation, Sheed and Ward.

The Focus of Freedom, Helicon.

The Humanity of Christ: Contributions to a Psychology of Jesus, Pantheon.

The Last Things. Concerning Death, Purification after Death, Resurrection, Judgment and Eternity, Pantheon.

The Legend of Grand Inquisitor.

The Life of Faith, Newman Press.

The Living God, Pantheon.

The Lord, Regnery.

The Lord's Prayer, Pantheon.

The "Memorial" of Pascal.

The Phenomenology of Religious Experience.

The Rosary of Our Lady, P. J. Kenedy.

The Saints in Daily Christian Life, Chilton Books; Dimension Books.

The Spirit of the Liturgy, Sheed and Ward.

The Stages of Life and Philosophy.

The Virtues: On Forms of Moral Life, Regnery.

The Way of the Cross of Our Lord and Our Savior Jesus Christ, Scepter; Sheed and Ward.

The Wisdom of the Psalms, Regnery.

The Word of God: On Faith, Hope and Charity, Regnery.

The World and the Person, Regnery.

91. Katherine Burton

Celestial Homespun: The Life of Isaac Thomas Hecker, Longman, Green.

Difficult Star: The Life of Pauline Jarricot, Longman, Green.

The Dream Lives Forever: The Story of St. Patrick's Cathedral, Longman, Green.

The Great Mantle: The Life of Guiseppe Melchiore Sarto, Pope Pius X, Longman, Green; Clonmore.

In Heaven We Shall Rest: The Life of Vincenzo Palloto, Founder of the Congregation of the Catholic Apostolate, Benzinger.

Leo the Thirteenth, the First Modern Pope, David McKay.

Make the Way Known: The History of the Dominican Congregation of St. Mary of the Springs, 1822 to 1957, Farrar, Straus, and Cudahy.

Sorrow Built a Bridge: The Life of Mother Alphonsa, Daughter of Nathaniel Hawthorne, Longman; Image.

Where There Is Love: The Life of Mother Mary Frances Siedliska of Jesus the Good Shepherd, P. J. Kenedy.

Faith Is the Substance: Life of Mother Theodore Guerin, Founders of the Sisters of Providence of Saint Mary-of-the-Woods, Indiana, B. Herder.

Witness of the Light: The Life of Eugenio Pacelli, Pope Pius XII, Longman, Green.

His Dear Persuasion: A Life of Elizabeth Ann Seton, Longman, Green.

Paradise Planters: The Story of Brook Farm, A.M.S. Press; Longman, Green.

In No Strange Land (Sketches of Some American Catholic Converts), Ayer Co.; Longman, Green.

No Shadow of Turning: A Life of James Kent Stone (Father Fidelis of the Cross, Passionist), Longman, Green.

Brother Andre of Mount Royal, Ave Maria Press.

Golden Door: The Life of Mother Katherine Drexel, P. J. Kenedy.

The Circus Lady: A Biography of Josephine De Mott, the Seventy-Year-Old Rider.

Mother Butler of Marymount, Longman, Green.

His Mercy Endureth Forever: A History of the Apostolate of the Sisters of Mercy, Sisters of Mercy.

Chaminade, Apostle of Mary, Founder of the Society of Mary, Bruce.

Children's Shepherd: The Story of John Christopher Drumgoole, P. J. Kenedy.

The Next Thing: Autobiography and Reminiscences, Longman, Green.

The Stars Beyond the Storms: Father Étienne Pernet, Benzinger.

Three Generations, Longman, Green.

Whom Love Impels, P. J. Kenedy.

The Life of Pauline von Mallinckrodt, P. J. Kenedy.

92. Christopher Dawson

The Age of the Gods, J. Murray; Sheed and Ward; Fertig.

Progress and Religion, Sheed and Ward; Doubleday-Image; Greenwood Press.

Christianity and Sex, Faber & Faber.

A Monument to St. Augustine, Dial Press.

Essays in Order, Sheed and Ward.

Christianity and the New Age, MacMillan; Sheed and Ward; Sophia Institute Press.

The Making of Europe, Sheed and Ward; Meridian Books.

The Modern Dilemma: The Problem of European Unity, Sheed and Ward.

Enquiries into Religion and Culture, Books for Libraries Press; Ayer.

The Spirit of the Oxford Movement, Sheed and Ward; A.M.S. Press.

Medieval Religion and Other Essays, Sheed and Ward; Ayer.

Medieval Christianity, Catholic Truth Society.

Religion and the Modern State, Sheed and Ward; Norwood Editions.

Twelve Selections from Christopher Dawson, Sheed and Ward.

Beyond Politics, Sheed and Ward; Ayer.

The Judgement of the Nations, Sheed and Ward; Norwood Editions.

Religion and Culture, Sheed & Ward; Meridian Books; A.M.S. Press.

Religion and the Rise of Western Culture, Sheed and Ward; Doubleday-Image.

Understanding Europe, Sheed and Ward; Doubleday-Image.

Medieval Essays, Sheed and Ward; Doubleday-Image; Telegraph Books.

Dynamics of World History, Sheed and Ward; New American Library (Mentor); Sherwood Sugden.

The Revolt of Asia, Sheed and Ward.

The Movement of World Revolution, Sheed and Ward.

The Historic Reality of Christian Culture, Routledge and Keegan Paul; Harper Torchbooks; The Cathedral Library.

America and the Secularization of Modern Culture, University of St. Thomas.

The Crisis of Western Education, Sheed and Ward; Doubleday-Image.

The Dividing of Christendom, Sheed and Ward; Doubleday-Image.

Mission to Asia, Harper & Row; University of Toronto Press; or *The Mongol Mission: The Crusades and Military Orders*, Second Series, A.M.S. Press.
The Formation of Christendom, Sheed and Ward.
Religion and World History, Doubleday-Image.
The Gifford Lectures: I. Religion and Culture, II. Religion and the Rise of Western Culture, A.M.S. Press.
Christianity in East and West, Sherwood Sugden.
An Introduction to the History of European Unity.

93. François Mauriac

Anguish and Joy of the Christian Life, Dimension Books; University of Notre Dame Press.
De Gaulle, Doubleday; The Bodley Head.
The Desert of Love, Covici; Eyre and Spottiswoode; Pellegrini & Cudahy.
The Eucharist: The Mystery of Holy Thursday, Longman, Green; Burns and Oates; David McKay.
Genitrix; and A Kiss for the Leper (two works in one vol.), Farrar, Straus; Eyre & Spottiswoode.
God and Mammon, Sheed and Ward.
Letters on Art and Literature, Philosophical Library; Kennikat Press.
Lines of Life (also called *Destinies*), Farrar, Straus.
The Loved and the Unloved, Farrar, Straus; Pellegrini & Cudahy.
Memoires Intérieurs, Farrar, Straus.
Men I Hold Great, Philosophical Library; Salisbury Square; Rockliff.
Questions of Precedence, Farrar, Straus/Noonday Press; Eyre & Spottiswoode.
Saint Margaret of Cortona, Philosophical Library; Burns and Oates; Clonmore & Reynolds.
Second Thoughts: Reflections on Literature and on Life, Philosophical Library; World Publishing; D. Finlayson.
The Son of Man, World Publishing; Burns and Oates.
The Stumbling Block, Philosophical Library.
Thérèse, Farrar, Straus; Doubleday-Anchor; Henry Holt.
The Unknown Sea, Farrar, Straus; Henry Holt.
Vipers' Tangle, Farrar, Straus; Image; Sheed and Ward.
What I Believe, Farrar, Straus.
Woman of the Pharisees, Farrar, Straus; Henry Holt; Image.
Words of Faith, Philosophical Library.
Young Man in Chains, Eyre & Spottiswoode; Farrar, Straus.
The Stuff of Youth, Eyre & Spottiswoode.
The Weakling and the Enemy, Farrar, Straus; Pelligrini & Cudahy.
The Mask of Innocence, Farrar, Straus.
Life of Jesus, Longman, Green; Avon Books; Hodder and Stoughton; David McKay.
The Holy Terror, J. Cape; Funk & Wagnalls.
The Egoists.
Proust's Way, Philosophical Library.

Desert of Love, and The Enemy (two works in one volume), Farrar, Straus; Eyre &
    Spottiswoode.
Flesh and Blood, Farrar, Straus; Eyre & Spottiswoode.
The Frontenac Mystery, Farrar, Straus; Eyre & Spottiswoode.
Kiss for the Leper; and Genitrix (two works in one vol.), Eyre & Spottiswoode.
The Lamb, Farrar, Straus.
River of Fire, Farrar, Straus; Eyre & Spottiswoode.
The Family, Covici, Friede.
Assmodée, the Intruder: A Comic Drama, Samuel French; Secker & Warburg.
The Little Misery, Farrar, Straus; Eyre & Spottiswoode.
That Which Was Lost; and the Dark Angels (two works in one vol.), Farrar, Straus;
    Eyre & Spottiswoode.
A Mauriac Reader (or Five Novels): A Kiss for the Leper; Genitrix; The Desert of Love; The
    Knot of Vipers; Woman of the Pharisees (five works in one vol.), Farrar, Straus; Eyre
    & Spottiswoode.
The Inner Presence: Recollections of My Spiritual Life, Bobbs-Merrill.
Cain, Where Is Your Brother?, Coward-McCann.
The Living Thoughts of Pascal, Presented by François Mauriac, Longman, Green; David
    McKay; Cassell.
Proust: Portrait of a Genius, Harper.

94. James Alberione

Call to Total Consecration, St. Paul Books and Media.
Christ, Model and Reward of Religious, St. Paul Books and Media.
Daily Meditations: The Great Prayers, St. Paul Books and Media.
Daily Meditations: The Great Truths, St. Paul Books and Media.
Daily Meditations: The Great Virtues, St. Paul Books and Media.
Designs for a Just Society, St. Paul Books and Media.
Insights into Religious Life, St. Paul Books and Media.
Last Things, St. Paul Books and Media.
Living Our Commitment, St. Paul Books and Media.
Lord, Teach Us to Pray, St. Paul Books and Media.
Month with Saint Paul, St. Paul Books and Media.
Paschal Mystery in Christian Living, St. Paul Books and Media.
Pray Always, St. Paul Books and Media.
Queen of Apostles Prayerbook, St. Paul Books and Media.
Saint and Thought for Every Day, St. Paul Books and Media.
The Spirit in My Life, St. Paul Books and Media.
That Christ May Live in Me, St. Paul Books and Media.
Thoughts, St. Paul Books and Media.
A Time for Faith, St. Paul Books and Media.
Personality and Configuration with Christ, St. Paul Books and Media.
Glories and Virtues of Mary, St. Paul Books and Media.
Growing in Perfect Union, St. Paul Books and Media.

95. Jacques Maritain

Bergsonian Philosophy and Thomism, Philosophical Library.
The Philosophy of Art, St. Dominic's Press.
Art and Scholasticism, Sheed and Ward.
An Introduction to Philosophy, Sheed and Ward.
Théonas: Conversations of a Sage, Sheed and Ward.
Freedom of the Intellect and Other Conversations with Théonas, Sheed and Ward.
Prayer and Intelligence, Sheed and Ward.
An Introduction to Logic, Sheed and Ward.
Three Reformers: Luther, Descartes, Rousseau, Scribner.
Georges Rouault, Harry N. Abrams.
Art and Faith: Letters Between Jacques Maritain and Jean Cocteau, Philosophical Library.
The Things That Are Not Caesar's, Sheed and Ward.
The Angelic Doctor: The Life and Thought of Saint Thomas Aquinas, Sheed and Ward.
St. Thomas Aquinas: Angel of the Schools, Sheed and Ward.
St. Thomas Aquinas, Meridian Books.
Religion and Culture, Sheed and Ward.
The Degrees of Knowledge, Scribner.
Distinguish to Unite: or, the Degrees of Knowledge, Scribner.
The Dream of Descartes, Together with Some Other Essays, Philosophical Library.
An Essay on Christian Philosophy, Philosophical Library.
Freedom in the Modern World, Sheed and Ward.
Some Reflections on Culture and Liberty, University of Chicago Press.
A Preface to Metaphysics: Seven Lectures on Being, Sheed and Ward.
Art and Poetry, Philosophical Library.
Philosophy of Nature, Philosophical Library.
Science and Wisdom, Scribner; Centenary Press.
True Humanism, G. Bles; Centenary Press; Scribner.
A Christian Looks at the Jewish Question, Longman, Green.
Antisemitism, G. Bles; Centenary Press.
The Situation of Poetry, Philosophical Library.
The Twilight of Civilization, Sheed and Ward.
Scholasticism and Politics, Macmillan; G. Bles; Centenary Press; Doubleday-Image.
France, My Country, Through the Disaster, Longman, Green.
The Living Thoughts of St. Paul, Longman, Green; David McKay.
Ransoming the Time, Scribner.
The Rights of Man and Natural Law, Scribner; G. Bles; Centenary Press.
The Rights of Man, Hilary House.
Saint Thomas and the Problem of Evil—The Aquinas Lecture, Marquette University
   Press.
Christianity and Democracy, Scribner; G. Bles; Centenary Press; Ignatius Press.
Education at the Crossroads, Yale University Press; Oxford University Press.
Existence and the Existent, Pantheon Books; Doubleday-Image.
The Person and the Common Good, Scribner; G. Bles; Centenary Press.
The Range of Reason, Scribner; G. Bles; Centenary Press.
Man and the State, University of Chicago Press; Hollis and Carter.

Approaches to God, Allen & Unwin.

Creative Intuition in Art and Poetry, Pantheon; Harvill Press; Meridian Books; Longman, Green.

On the Philosophy of History, Scribner.

Truth and Human Fellowship, Princeton University Press.

Reflections on America, Scribner.

The Sin of the Angel, Newman Press.

Liturgy and Contemplation, P. J. Kenedy.

The Responsibility of the Artist, Scribner.

Man's Approach to God, Archabbey Press.

On the Use of Philosophy, Princeton University Press.

Sheed and Ward Sampler: Jacques Maritain, Sheed and Ward.

The Social and Political Philosophy of Jacques Maritain, Scribner.

The Education of Man: The Educational Philosophy of Jacques Maritain, Doubleday.

96. Arnold Lunn

Christian Counter-Attack, Arlington House.

Now I See: Autobiography, Sheed and Ward.

Within That City: An Autobiography, Sheed and Ward.

Come What May: An Autobiography, Little, Brown.

The Revolt Against Reason, Sheed and Ward; Greenwood Press.

Roman Converts, Irvington; Ayer.

A Saint in the Slave Trade: Peter Claver, 1581–1654, Sheed and Ward.

The Third Day, Burns and Oates; Newman Bookshop.

Whither Europe, Sheed and Ward.

And the Floods Came, Eyre & Spottiswoode.

The Good Gorilla, Hollis & Carter.

Alpine Skiing at All Heights and Seasons, E. P. Dutton; Metheson.

The Harrovians, Metheson. A novel.

History of Skiing, Oxford University Press; H. Milford.

The Mountains of Youth, Oxford University Press; H. Milford.

Difficulties: Controversy Through an Exchange of Letters with Ronald H. Knox, Eyre and Spottiswoode.

Is Christianity True?: A Correspondence Between Arnold Lunn and C. E. M. Joad, Eyre and Spottiswoode.

Science and the Supernatural: A Correspondence Between Arnold Lunn and J. B. S. Haldane, Sheed and Ward.

The Cult of Softness, Blandford Press.

Guide to Montana.

Editor, *Oxford Mountaineering Essays,* E. Arnold.

Was Switzerland Pro-German?, London, Hazell, Watson & Viney.

Loose Ends, Hutchinson.

Cross Country Skiing.

The Alpine Ski Guides.

Auction Piquet, Methuen.

Skiing for Beginners.

Switzerland, Its Literary, Historical and Topographical Landmarks, Harrap; Doubleday, Doran.

Things That Have Puzzled Me.

John Wesley, Dial Press; Longman, Green.

The Flight from Reason, Dial Press; Longman, Green.

Family Name, Methuen.

Within the Precincts of the Prison, Hutchinson.

The Italian Lakes and Lakeland Cities, Harrap.

Venice, Its Story, Architecture, and Art, Farrar and Rinehart.

Spanish Rehearsal, Sheed and Ward.

Communism and Socialism, Eyre & Spottiswoode.

The Science of World Revolution, Sheed and Ward.

Mountain Jubilee, Eyre & Spottiswoode.

And Yet So New, Sheed and Ward.

Is the Catholic Church Anti-Social? A Debate Between G. G. Coulton and Arnold Lunn, Burns and Oates.

Mountains of Memory, Hollis and Carter.

The New Morality, Blandford.

The Swiss and Their Mountains: A Study on the Influence of Mountains on Man, Rand McNally.

Switzerland in English Prose and Poetry, Eyre and Spottiswoode; Gordon Press.

97. Charles Journet

The Church of the Word Incarnate: An Essay in Speculative Theology—Vol. I: The Apostolic Hierarchy, Sheed and Ward.

The Primacy of Peter: From the Protestant and the Catholic Point of View, Sheed and Ward; Burns and Oates.

The Dark Knowledge of God, Sheed and Ward.

The Meaning of Evil, P. J. Kenedy.

The Meaning of Grace, P. J. Kenedy.

Our Lady of Sorrows, Sheed and Ward.

What Is Dogma? Hawthorn.

The Wisdom of Faith: An Introduction to Theology, Newman Press.

98. Dietrich von Hildebrand

The Art of Living, Franciscan Herald.

Celibacy and the Crisis of Faith, Franciscan Herald.

The Devastated Vineyard, Franciscan Herald.

Ethics, Franciscan Herald.

In Defense of Purity: An Analysis of the Catholic Ideals of Purity and Virginity, Franciscan Herald; Longman; Sheed and Ward.

Liturgy and Personality, Helicon; Sophia Institute Press; Longman, Green.

Man and Woman, Regnery; Franciscan Herald.

Marriage: the Mystery of Faithful Love, Longman, Green.

Morality and Situational Ethics, Franciscan Herald.

The New Tower of Babel: Essays, P. J. Kenedy.

Fundamental Moral Attitudes, Ayer.
Not as the World Gives: St. Francis' Message to Laymen Today, Franciscan Herald.
Teilhard de Chardin: A False Prophet, Franciscan Herald.
The Role of Human Love, Franciscan Herald.
Transformation in Christ: On the Christian Attitude of Mind, 2nd. ed. Image; Helicon;
    Longman, Green.
Trojan Horse in the City of God, Franciscan Herald.
True Morality and Its Counterfeits, David McKay.
What Is Philosophy?, Franciscan Herald.
Encyclical Humane Vitae: A Sign of Contradiction, Franciscan Herald.
What Is the Liturgical Movement?, Liturgical Press.
Christian Ethics, David McKay.
Graven Images: Substitutes for True Morality, David McKay.
The Sacred Heart: An Analysis of Human and Divine Affection, Helicon Press.

99. Étienne Gilson

Being and Some Philosophers, Pontifical Institute of Medieval Studies.
Christianity and Philosophy, Published for the Institute of Medieval Studies by
    Sheed and Ward.
Dante the Philosopher, Sheed and Ward; retitled *Dante and Philosophy*, Harper & Row.
Choir of Muses, Sheed and Ward.
Elements of Christian Philosophy, Doubleday; Greenwood Press.
Elements of Christian Philosophy, New American Library (Mentor-Omega).
The Spirit of Medieval Philosophy, Sheed and Ward; Scribner.
God and Philosophy, Yale University Press; Oxford University Press.
Heloïse and Abelard, Hollis and Carter; Regnery.
History of Christian Philosophy in the Middle Ages, Random House; Sheed and Ward.
History of Philosophy and Philosophical Education, Marquette University Press.
The Arts of the Beautiful, Scribner.
Modern Philosophy: Descartes to Kant, Random House.
Painting and Reality, Pantheon; Routledge and Kegan Paul.
The A. W. Mellon Lectures in the Fine Arts, Meridian; World Publishing.
The Philosopher and Theology, Random House.
The Philosophy of St. Bonaventure, Sheed and Ward; St. Anthony's Guild Press.
For the Establishment of a Catholic Order, Pontifical Institute of Medieval Studies.
Thomistic Realism and the Critique of Knowledge, Pontifical Institute of Medieval Stud-
    ies.
Reason and Revelation in the Middle Ages, Scribner.
Recent Philosophy: Hegel to the Present, Random House.
Saint Thomas Aquinas, Oxford University Press.
Moral Values and the Moral Life: the System of St. Thomas Aquinas, B. Herder; Shoe
    String Press.
The Spirit of Thomism, P. J. Kenedy; Harper & Row.
The Mystical Theology of Saint Bernard, Sheed and Ward.
Thomas Aquinas and our Colleagues, Princeton University Press.
The Philosophy of St. Thomas Aquinas, Heffer.

The Philosophy of St. Thomas Aquinas (second edition revised and enlarged), Heffer; B. Herder; Books for Libraries Press.
The Christian Philosophy of St. Thomas Aquinas, Random House; V. Gollancz.
Thomist Realism and the Critique of Knowledge, Ignatius Press.
The Unity of Philosophical Experiences, Scribner; Sheed and Ward.
Wisdom and Love in St. Thomas Aquinas, Marquette University Press.
Editor, *The Church Speaks to the Modern World: the Social Teachings of Leo XIII,* Doubleday-Image.
A Gilson Reader: Selected Writings, Hanover House; Image.
From Aristotle to Darwin and Back Again: A Journey in Final Causality, Species, and Evolution, University of Notre Dame Press.
Linguistics and Philosophy, University of Notre Dame Press.

100. Fulton J. Sheen

A Fulton Sheen Reader, Garden City Books.
God and Intelligence in Modern Philosophy: A Critical Study in the Light of the Philosophy of St. Thomas, Garden City Books; Longman, Green.
Religion Without God, Garden City Books; Garder; Longman, Green.
The Life of All Living, Doubleday-Image; Century.
The Divine Romance, Garden City Books; Century.
Old Errors and New Labels, Garden City Books; Century.
Moods and Truths, Garden City Books; Century.
The Way of the Cross, Garden City Books; Our Sunday Visitor.
The Last Seven Words, or *The Rainbow of Sorrow.* P. J. Kenedy; Garden City Books; Alba.
The Eternal Galilean, Garden City Books; Appleton-Century.
The Power of Love, Simon & Shuster; Doubleday-Image.
Seven Words of Jesus and Mary, P. J. Kenedy.
The Philosophy of Science, Garden City Books; Bruce.
The Mystical Body of Christ, Garden City Books; Sheed and Ward.
Calvary and the Mass, A Missal Companion, Garden City Books; P. J. Kenedy.
The Moral Universe: A Preface to Christian Living, Ayer; Garden City Books.
The Cross and the Beatitudes, Garden City Books; P. J. Kenedy.
The Cross and the Crisis, Garden City Books; Bruce; Ayer.
Liberty, Equality and Fraternity, Garden City Books; Macmillan.
Victory Over Vice, Garden City Books; P. J. Kenedy.
Whence Come Wars, Garden City Books; Sheed and Ward.
The Seven Virtues, Garden City Books; retitled *Our Sunday Visitor,* P. J. Kenedy.
For God and Country, Garden City Books; P. J. Kenedy.
A Declaration of Dependence, Garden City Books; Bruce.
God and War, Garden City Books.
The Divine Verdict, Garden City Books; P. J. Kenedy.
The Armour of God, Garden City Books.
Philosophies at War, Garden City Books; Scribner.
Seven Words to the Cross, Garden City Books.
Seven Pillars of Peace, Garden City Books; Scribner.
Love One Another, Garden City Books; P. J. Kenedy.

Communism and the Conscience of the West, Garden City Books; Brown and Nolan; Bobbs-Merrill.

The Philosophy of Religion, Garden City Books; Appleton, Century, Crofts.

Peace of Soul, Garden City Books; Whittlesey House; Doubleday-Image.

Lift Up Your Heart, Doubleday-Image; McGraw-Hill.

Three to Get Married, Garden City Books; Appleton-Century-Crofts.

The World's First Love, Doubleday; McGraw-Hill.

Life Is Worth Living, Doubleday; McGraw-Hill.

Way to Happiness, Garden City Books; Fawcett.

Life Is Worth Living: Series Two, Garden City Books; McGraw-Hill.

Way to Inner Peace, Garden City Books.

God Love You, Garden City Books; Doubleday-Image.

Thoughts for Daily Living, Garden City Books.

Thinking Life Through, McGraw-Hill.

Guide to Contentment, Doubleday.

Children and Parents, Simon & Schuster.

Footprints in a Darkened Forest, Meredith Press.

Go to Heaven, McGraw-Hill.

Characters of the Passion, Garden City Books.

Freedom Under God, Bruce.

Justice and Charity: Part I, The Social Problem and the Church, National Council of Catholic Men.

Justice and Charity: Part II, The Individual Problem and the Cross, National Council of Catholic Men.

Lenten and Easter Inspirations, Maco Publishing.

On Being Human: Reflections on Life and Living, Doubleday.

Peace, National Council of Catholic Men.

Peace, the Fruit of Justice, National Council of Catholic Men.

Preface to Religion, Appleton, Century, Crofts; P. J. Kenedy.

The Prodigal World, National Council of Catholic Men.

Manifestations of Christ, National Council of Catholic Men.

The Quotable Fulton Sheen, Droke House.

Compiler, *That Tremendous Love: An Anthology of Inspirational Quotations, Poems, Prayers, and Philosophical Comments,* Harper & Row.

These Are the Sacraments, Hawthorn.

This Is Rome: A Pilgrimage in Words and Pictures, Image.

This Is the Holy Land: A Pilgrimage in Words and Pictures, Hawthorn.

This Is the Mass, Hawthorn.

Those Mysterious Priests, Doubleday; Lumen Christi.

Treasure in Clay: the Autobiography of Fulton J. Sheen, Doubleday.

War and Guilt, National Council of Catholic Men.

Life of Christ, McGraw-Hill; Doubleday-Image.

The Wit and Wisdom of Bishop Fulton J. Sheen, Prentice-Hall.

The Priest Is Not His Own, McGraw-Hill.

Our Wounded World, National Council of Catholic Men.

Light Your Lamps, National Council of Catholic Men.

Jesus, Son of Mary: A Book for Children, D. X. McMullen; Harper & Row.

The Hymn of the Conquered, National Council of Catholic Men.

Freedom and Peace, Our Sunday Visitor Press.
Through the Year with Fulton Sheen: Selections, Servant.
Cross-Ways: A Book of Inspiration, Doubleday-Image.
Rejoice, Doubleday-Image.
The World's Great Love: The Prayer of the Rosary, Harper & Row.

101. Igino Giordani

Mary of Nazareth, St. Paul Editions; Macmillan; St. Paul Books and Media.
Pius X, a Country Priest, Bruce.
Saint Catherine of Siena, Doctor of the Church: Fire and Blood, Bruce.
Saint Paul, Apostle and Martyr, Macmillan; St. Paul Books and Media.
Saint Vincent De Paul, Servant of the Poor, Bruce.
The Social Message of Jesus, St. Anthony Guild Press; St. Paul Books and Media.
The Social Message of the Early Church Fathers, St. Anthony Guild Press; St. Paul
   Books and Media; Tan Books.
The Social Message of the Apostles.

102. Frank Sheed

Compiler, *The Book of the Savior,* Sheed and Ward.
Compiler, *The Book of Mary,* Sheed and Ward.
Compiler, *Born Catholics,* Sheed and Ward.
Catholic Evidence Training Outlines, Sheed and Ward.
The Church and I, Doubleday. Autobiography.
Translator, *Collected Letters of Saint Thérèse of Lisieux,* Sheed and Ward.
Communism and Man, Sheed and Ward.
Translator, *The Confessions of St. Augustine,* Sheed and Ward.
Genesis Regained, Sheed and Ward.
God and the Human Condition, Sheed and Ward.
The Holy Spirit in Action: Why Christians Call Him "the Lord and Giver of Life," Servant
   Books.
The Instructed Heart: Sounding at Four Depths, Our Sunday Visitor.
Is It the Same Church? Pflaum Press.
A Map of Life, Sheed and Ward; Arena Letters.
The New Guest-Room Book, Sheed and Ward; Arden Library.
Nullity of Marriage, Sheed and Ward.
Compiler, *Poetry and Life: An Anthology of English Catholic Poetry,* Sheed and Ward.
Saints Are Not Sad: Forty Biographical Portraits, Sheed and Ward.
Sidelights on the Catholic Revival, Sheed and Ward; Ayer.
Death into Life: A Conversation, Arena Letters.
Christ in the Classroom, Sheed and Ward.
Society and Sanity, Sheed and Ward.
Theology and Sanity, Sheed and Ward; Our Sunday Visitor.
Theology for Beginners, Sheed and Ward; Servant.
To Know Jesus Christ, Sheed and Ward; Servant.
What Difference Does Jesus Make? Sheed and Ward; Our Sunday Visitor.
Editor, *The Irish Way,* Sheed and Ward.

Ground Plan for Catholic Reading, Sheed and Ward.
Christ in Eclipse, Sheed, Andrews, and McMeel.
Our Hearts Are Restless: the Prayer of St. Augustine, Seabury Press; Harper & Row.
Marriage and the Family, Sheed and Ward.

103. Hubert van Zeller

Prophets and Princes, Burns, Oates & Washbourne.
Watch and Pray, Burns, Oates & Washbourne. Later issued as *The Outspoken Ones: Twelve Prophets of Israel,* Sheed and Ward.
Sackcloth and Ashes.
From Creation to Christmas, Burns, Oates, and Washbourne; Newman. (Later issued as *Old Testament Stories,* Newman Press.)
Isaias: Man of Ideas, Burns and Oates; Newman Press.
Jeremias: Man of Tears, Sands.
Ezechiel: Man of Signs, Sands.
Daniel: Man of Desires, Burns and Oates; Newman Press.
Moments of Light: Notes on the Spiritual Life, Burns and Oates; Templegate.
Famine of the Spirit: Fragmentary Comments on the Interior Life, Burns and Oates; Templegate.
The Yoke of Divine Love: A Study of Conventual Perfection, Burns and Oates; Templegate.
The Inner Search, Sheed and Ward.
The Choice of God, Burns and Oates; Templegate.
The Gospel Priesthood, Burns and Oates; Sheed and Ward.
We Die Standing Up, Sheed and Ward.
We Live with Our Eyes Open, Sheed and Ward.
We Work While the Light Lasts, Sheed and Ward.
We Sing While There's Voice Left, Sheed and Ward.
Approach to Penance, Sheed and Ward.
Approach to Prayer, Sheed and Ward.
Approach to Calvary, Sheed and Ward.
Sanctity in Other Words, Templegate.
Our Lady in Other Words, Templegate.
Prayer in Other Words, Templegate.
The Mass in Other Words, Templegate.
Church History in Other Words, Templegate.
Death in Other Words, Templegate.
The Old Testament in Other Words, Templegate.
The New Testament in Other Words, Templegate.
The Catechism in Other Words, Templegate.
Suffering in Other Words, Templegate.
Holy Communion in Other Words, Templegate.
The Saints in Other Words, Templegate.
The Holy Rule: Notes on St. Benedict's Legislation for Monks, Sheed and Ward.
The Benedictine Idea, Burns and Oates; Templegate.
Approach to Monasticism, Sheed and Ward.
The Benedictine Nun, Helicon.

Liturgical Asides: A Book of Prayers for Sundays and Various Feasts, Burns and Oates.
A Book of Private Prayer, Templegate.
The Way of the Cross, Templegate.
Lord God: A Prayer Book for Boys and Young Men, Burns and Oates.
Come Lord: A Prayer Book for Girls and Young Women, Templegate.
Giving to God: A Year's Prayers for Young People, Burns and Oates; Templegate.
Praying While You Work: Devotions for the Use of Martha Rather Than Mary, Burns and Oates; Templegate.
The End: A Projection Not a Prophecy, as by Hugh Venning (pseud.), Desmond and Stapleton.
Portmanteau. A play.
Kaleidoscope: A Collection of Essays, Stories and Plays, Sands.
Family Case-Book, Collins.
Willingly to School: A Study in Unceremonial Portraiture, Sheed and Ward.
Downside By and Large: A Double Fugue in Praise of Things Lasting and Gregorian, Sheed and Ward.
Approach to Christian Sculpture, Sheed and Ward.
Up the Garden Path. A one-act play.
The King with Half a Crown. A play.
A Quiet Afternoon: A Short Story About Plato.
The Crescent Which Lost Its Star.
Private View.
Ideas for Prayers: 200 Suggestions, Templegate.
More Ideas for Prayer: 200 Suggestions, Templegate.
One Foot in the Cradle: An Autobiography.
Cracks in the Cloister, as by Brother Choleric (pseud.), Sheed and Ward.
Further Cracks in Fabulous Cloisters, as by Brother Choleric (pseud.), Sheed and Ward.
Prophets and Princes; a Retreat with Our Books of Kings, Burns and Oates.
Approach to Spirituality, Sheed and Ward.
Benedictine Life at Minster Abbey, Catholic Records Press.
The Benedictine Nun: Her Story and Aim, Helicon.
The Book of Beginnings, Templegate.
Considerations, Templegate.
Cracks in the Curia, or, Brother Choleric Rides Again, as by Brother Choleric (pseud.), Sheed and Ward.
The Current of Spirituality, Templegate.
Death in Other Words: A Presentation for Beginners, Templegate.
Famine of the Spirit, Templegate.
First Person Singular, J. Murray.
The Gospel in Other Words: A Presentation for Beginners, Templegate.
Last Cracks in Legendary Cloisters, as by Brother Choleric (pseud.), Sheed and Ward.
Leave Your Life Alone, Sheed and Ward.
Letters to a Soul, Sheed and Ward.
The Other Kingdom: A Book of Comfort, Templegate.
Posthumous Cracks in the Cloisters, as by Brother Choleric (pseud.), Sheed and Ward.
The Psalms in Other Words, Templegate.
The Will of God in Other Words, Templegate.

Logic for Lunatics: A Fabulous Primer with Illustrations, as by Brother Choleric (pseud.), Sheed and Ward.

104. John Ching-Hsiung Wu

The Science of Love: A Study in the Teachings of Thérèse of Lisieux, Our Sunday Visitor Press.

The Art of Law, and Other Essays, Juridical and Literary.

Essays in Jurisprudence and Legal Philosophy, with M. C. Laing.

Beyond East and West, Sheed and Ward; Mei Ya China, Intl. Spec. Bks.

Fountain of Justice: A Study in the Natural Law, Sheed and Ward; Intl. Spec. Bks. .

The Interior Carmel: The Threefold Way of Love, Sheed and Ward.

Cases and Materials on Jurisprudence, West Publishing Co.

Indexes

SOURCES

AUTHORS

WRITINGS

John A. Hardon, S.J., holds a master's degree in philosophy from Loyola University and a doctorate in theology from the Gregorian University in Rome. He has taught at the Jesuit School of Theology in Chicago and is an author-in-residence at the University of Detroit. He is the author of *The Catholic Catechism, Modern Catholic Dictionary, Pocket Catholic Dictionary, Question and Answer Catholic Catechism,* and *The Treasury of Catholic Wisdom.* Father Hardon is also the founder of the Catholic Home Study Institute, a correspondence school which operates under pontifical approval.